S0-CPQ-362

COMPLETE PLAYS

AND

SELECTED POEMS

OF

CHARLES DICKENS

COMPLETE PLAYS

AND

SELECTED POEMS

OF

CHARLES DICKENS

VISION

Vision Press Limited
157 Knightsbridge
London, S.W.1

SBN 85478 122 6

Printed in Great Britain
by Clarke, Doble & Brendon Ltd., Plymouth

MCMLXX

CONTENTS

FOREWORD

Although it is known that Charles Dickens wrote his first play, *Misnar, The Sultan of India*, when he was no more than ten years old and that a burlesque, *O'Thello, (Part of the Great Unpaid)*, was performed by amateurs, including his father, John Dickens, in 1833, neither play has survived. The first play performed publicly was *The Strange Gentleman*, which was staged at the St. James's Theatre, London, in September 1836. Founded on one of the *Sketches of Boz, The Great Winglebury Duel*, the play is a light comedy which owes much to Oliver Goldsmith. An instant success, it ran for fifty performances and was revived more than once in 1837. At this time the St. James's Theatre was under the management of the famous singer, John Braham, who was sufficiently impressed by the young dramatist to sponsor two more of his works, the first of which, *The Village Coquettes*, a comic opera with music by John Hullah, was first performed in December 1836 and was well received. Richard Herne Shepherd, the first editor of Dickens's plays, wrote that no English musical piece equal to *The Village Coquettes* had appeared since Sheridan's *The Duenna*, and, even if this praise was excessive, it is true that the workmanlike unfolding of the action and the charm of the dialogue were exceptional in an English libretto of the early nineteenth century.

The third and probably the best of the Dickens plays to be performed at the St. James's Theatre was *Is She his Wife? or, Something Singular!*, which was first staged in March 1837 and, like its predecessors, was a success, although it is barely mentioned in Forster's *Life of Dickens. Is She his Wife?*, a Comic Burletta or farce, is the last publicly performed and published dramatic work of which Dickens was the sole author. *The Lamplighter*, a farce written in 1838 for Macready, was withdrawn during rehearsal but reached the public in narrative form as one of the stories in the *Pic Nic Papers*. Thenceforth, Dickens's dramatic efforts were to be in collaboration with others.

Mr. Nightingale's Diary was written by Dickens and Mark Lemon for the Guild of Literature and Art and was first performed at Devonshire House in May 1851 in the presence of Queen Victoria and Prince Albert. Slight but amusing, this farce was well adapted to the histrionic abilities of the joint authors. Mark Lemon appeared as Slap, Dickens as Gabblewig, changing his voice and manner with a skill that earned him much praise.

A Message From the Sea, a dramatisation by Dickens and Wilkie Collins of their short story, was neither published nor publicly performed, and no text of the play is known to the present editor, but an eight-page pamphlet containing a list of characters and an outline of the plot was published in 1861 for copyright purposes.

The last and most important of the plays, *No Thoroughfare*, was also the fruit of collaboration with Wilkie Collins. First performed at the Adelphi Theatre, London, in December 1867 and based on the Christmas Number of *All the Year Round* for that year, the dramatised version owes more to Collins than to Dickens, although the Prologue is wholly Dickens's work. The play was a success in Britain, France and the United States of America and received the unwelcome tribute of frequent plagiarisation.

Dickens the poet is perhaps as unfamiliar as Dickens the playwright, but some of his verses, notably *The Ivy Green*, are known to many unaware of their authorship. *A Child's Hymn* from *The Wreck of the Golden Mary* appeared in the Christmas number of Household Words for 1856 and is one of Dickens's rare expressions of Christian sentiment.

The first collected edition of the plays and poems of Charles Dickens was prefaced and annotated by Richard Herne Shepherd and published by W. H. Allen & Co. in 1882 in a limited and numbered edition. That edition included *The Loving Ballad of Lord Bateman*, which is almost certainly by Thackeray, but did not include *Aspire*, now regarded as one of Dickens's best poems.

THE STRANGE GENTLEMAN

A Comic Burletta

IN TWO ACTS

[1836]

CAST OF THE CHARACTERS

At St. James's Theatre, September 29, 1836

Mr. Owen Overton (*Mayor of a small town on the road to Gretna, and useful at the St. James's Arms*)	Mr. Hollingsworth.
John Johnson (*detained at the St. James's Arms*)	Mr. Sidney.
The Strange Gentleman (*just arrived at the St. James's Arms*)	Mr. Harley.
Charles Tomkins (*incognito at the St. James's Arms*)	Mr. Forester.
Tom Sparks (*a one-eyed 'Boots' at the St. James's Arms*)	Mr. Gardner.
John (*Waiters at the St. James's Arms*)	Mr. Williamson.
Tom (*Waiters at the St. James's Arms*)	Mr. May.
Will (*Waiters at the St. James's Arms*)	Mr. Coulson.
Julia Dobbs (*looking for a husband at the St. James's Arms*)	Madame Sala.
Fanny Wilson (*with an appointment at the St. James's Arms*)	Miss Smith.
Mary Wilson (*her sister, awkwardly situated at the St. James's Arms*)	Miss Julia Smith.
Mrs. Noakes (*the Landlady at the St. James's Arms*)	Mrs. W. Penson.
Chambermaid (*at the St. James's Arms*)	Miss Stuart.

Miss Smith and Miss Julia Smith will sing the duet of 'I know a Bank', in 'The Strange Gentleman'.

COSTUME

Mr. Owen Overton.—*Black smalls, and high black boots. A blue body coat, rather long in the waist, with yellow buttons, buttoned close up to the chin, white stock; ditto gloves. A broad-brimmed low-crowned white hat.*

Strange Gentleman.—*A light blue plaid French-cut trousers and vest. A brown cloth frock coat, with full skirts, scarcely covering the hips. A light handkerchief, and eccentric low-crowned broad-brimmed white hat. Boots.*

John Johnson.—*White fashionable trousers, boots, light vest, frock coat, black hat, gloves, etc.*

Charles Tomkins.—*Shepherd's plaid French-cut trousers; boots, mohair fashionable frock coat, buttoned up; black hat, gloves, etc.*

TOM SPARKS.—*Leather smalls, striped stockings, and lace-up half boots, red vest, and a Holland stable jacket; coloured kerchief, and red wig.*

THE WAITERS.—*All in black trousers, black stockings and shoes, white vests, striped jackets, and white kerchiefs.*

MARY WILSON.—*Fashionable walking dress, white silk stockings; shoes and gloves.*

FANNY WILSON.—*Precisely the same as Mary.*

JULIA DOBBS.—*A handsome white travelling dress, cashmere shawl, white silk stockings; shoes and gloves. A bonnet to correspond.*

MRS. NOAKES.—*A chintz gown, rather of a dark pattern, French apron, and handsome cap.*

SCENE.—A SMALL TOWN, ON THE ROAD TO GRETNA.

TIME.—PART OF A DAY AND NIGHT.

Time in acting.—One hour and twenty minutes.

THE STRANGE GENTLEMAN

ACT I

SCENE I.—*A Room at the St. James's Arms; Door in Centre, with a Bolt on it. A Table with Cover, and two Chairs,* R. H.

Enter MRS. NOAKES, C. DOOR.

MRS. NOAKES. Bless us, what a coachful! Four inside—twelve out; and the guard blowing the key-bugle in the fore-boot, for fear the informers should see that they have got one over the number. Post-chaise and a gig besides.—We shall be filled to the very attics. Now, look alive, there—bustle about.

Enter FIRST WAITER, *running,* C. DOOR.

Now, John.

FIRST WAITER (*coming down* L. H.). Single lady, inside the stage, wants a private room, ma'am.

MRS. NOAKES (R. H.). Much luggage?

FIRST WAITER. Four trunks, two bonnet-boxes, six brown-paper parcels, and a basket.

MRS. NOAKES. Give her a private room, directly. No. 1, on the first floor.

FIRST WAITER. Yes, ma'am. [*Exit* FIRST WAITER, *running,* C. DOOR.

Enter SECOND WAITER, *running,* C. DOOR.

Now, Tom.

SECOND WAITER (*coming down* R. H.). Two young ladies and one gentleman, in a post-chaise, want a private sitting-room d'rectly, ma'am.

MRS. NOAKES. Brother and sisters, Tom?

SECOND WAITER. Ladies are something alike, ma'am. Gentleman like neither of 'em.

MRS. NOAKES. Husband and wife and wife's sister, perhaps. Eh, Tom?

SECOND WAITER. Can't be husband and wife, ma'am, because I saw the gentleman kiss one of the ladies.

MRS. NOAKES. Kissing one of the ladies! Put them in the small sitting-room behind the bar, Tom, that I may have an eye on them through the little window, and see that nothing improper goes forward.

SECOND WAITER. Yes, ma'am. (*Going.*)

MRS. NOAKES. And Tom! (*Crossing to* L. H.)

SECOND WAITER (*coming down* R. H.). Yes, ma'am.

MRS. NOAKES. Tell Cook to put together all the bones and pieces that were left on the plates at the great dinner yesterday, and make some nice soup to feed the stage-coach passengers with.

SECOND WAITER. Very well, ma'am. [*Exit* SECOND WAITER, C. DOOR.

Enter THIRD WAITER, *running,* C. DOOR.

Now, Will.

THIRD WAITER (*coming down* L. H.). A strange gentleman in a gig, ma'am, wants a private sitting-room.

MRS. NOAKES. Much luggage, Will?

THIRD WAITER. One portmanteau, and a great-coat.

MRS. NOAKES. Oh! nonsense!—Tell him to go into the commercial room.

THIRD WAITER. I told him so, ma'am, but the Strange Gentleman says he *will* have a private apartment, and that it's as much as his life is worth, to sit in a public room.

MRS. NOAKES. As much as his life is worth?

THIRD WAITER. Yes, ma'am.—Gentleman says he doesn't care if it's a dark closet; but a private room of some kind he must and will have.

MRS. NOAKES. Very odd.—Did you ever see him before, Will?

THIRD WAITER. No, ma'am; he's quite a stranger here.—He's a wonderful man to talk, ma'am—keeps on like a steam engine. Here he is, ma'am.

STRANGE GENTLEMAN (*without*). Now don't tell me, because that's all gammon and nonsense; and gammoned I never was, and never will be, by any waiter that ever drew the breath of life, or a cork.—And just have the goodness to leave my portmanteau alone, because I can carry it very well myself; and show me a private room without further delay; for a private room I must and will have.—Damme, do you think I'm going to be murdered!—

Enter the three Waiters, C. DOOR—*they form down* L. H., *the* STRANGE GENTLEMAN *following, carrying his portmanteau and great-coat.*

There—this room will do capitally well. Quite the thing,—just the fit.—How are you, ma'am? I suppose you are the landlady of this place? Just order those very attentive young fellows out, will you, and I'll order dinner.

MRS. NOAKES (*to Waiters*). You may leave the room.

STRANGE GENTLEMAN. Hear that?—You may leave the room. Make yourselves scarce. Evaporate—disappear—come.

[*Exeunt Waiters,* C. DOOR.

That's right. And now, madam, while we're talking over this important matter of dinner, I'll just secure us effectually against further intrusion. (*Bolts the door.*)

MRS. NOAKES. Lor, sir! Bolting the door, and *me* in the room!

STRANGE GENTLEMAN. Don't be afraid—I won't hurt you. I have no designs against you, my dear ma'am: but *I must be private.* (*Sits on the portmanteau,* R. H.)

MRS. NOAKES. Well, sir—I have no objection to break through our rules for once; but it is not our way, when we're full, to give private rooms to solitary gentlemen, who come in a gig, and bring only one portmanteau. You're quite a stranger *here,* sir. If I'm not mistaken, it's your first appearance in this house.

STRANGE GENTLEMEN. You're right, ma'am. It *is* my first, my very first—but not my last, I can tell you.

MRS. NOAKES. No?

STRANGE GENTLEMAN. No (*looking round him*). I like the look of this place. Snug and comfortable—neat and lively. You'll very often find me at the St. James's Arms, I can tell you, ma'am.

MRS. NOAKES (*aside*). A civil gentleman. Are you a stranger in this town, sir?

STRANGE GENTLEMAN. Stranger! Bless you, no. I have been here for many years past, in the season.

MRS. NOAKES. Indeed!

STRANGE GENTLEMAN. Oh, yes. Put up at the Royal Hotel regularly for a long time; but I was obliged to leave it at last.

MRS. NOAKES. I have heard a good many complaints of it.

STRANGE GENTLEMAN. O! terrible! such a noisy house.

MRS. NOAKES. Ah!

STRANGE GENTLEMAN. Shocking! Din, din, din—Drum, drum, drum, all night. Nothing but noise, glare, and nonsense. I bore it a long time for old acquaintance sake; but what do you think they did at last, ma'am?

MRS. NOAKES. I can't guess.

STRANGE GENTLEMAN. Turned the fine Old Assembly Room into a stable, and took to keeping horses. I tried that too, but I found I couldnt' stand it; so I came away, ma'am, and—and —here I am. (*Rises.*)

MRS. NOAKES. And I'll be bound to say, sir, that you will have no cause to complain of the exchange.

STRANGE GENTLEMAN. I'm sure not, ma'am; I know it—I feel it, already.

MRS. NOAKES. About dinner, sir; what would you like to take?

STRANGE GENTLEMAN. Let me see; will you be good enough to suggest something, ma'am?

MRS. NOAKES. Why, a broiled fowl and mushrooms is a very nice dish.

STRANGE GENTLEMAN. You are right, ma'am; a broiled fowl and mushrooms form a very delightful and harmless amusement, either for one or two persons. Broiled fowl and mushrooms let it be, ma'am.

MRS. NOAKES. In about an hour, I suppose, sir?

STRANGE GENTLEMAN. For the second time, ma'am, you have anticipated my feelings.

MRS. NOAKES. You'll want a bed to-night, I suppose, sir; perhaps you'd like to see it? Step this way, sir, and—(*going* L. H.).

STRANGE GENTLEMAN. No, no, never mind. (*Aside.*) This is a plot to get me out of the room. She's bribed by somebody who wants to identify me. I must be careful; I am exposed to nothing but artifice and stratagem. Never mind, ma'am, never mind.

MRS. NOAKES. If you'll give me your portmanteau, sir, the Boots will carry it into the next room for you.

STRANGE GENTLEMAN (*aside*). Here's diabolical ingenuity; she thinks it's got the name upon it. (*To her.*) I'm very much obliged to the Boots for his disinterested attention, ma'am, but with your kind permission this portmanteau will remain just exactly where it is; consequently, ma'am, (*with greath warmth,*) if the aforesaid Boots wishes to succeed in removing this portmanteau, he must previously remove *me*, ma'am, *me*; and it will take a *pair* of very stout Boots to do that, ma'am, I promise you.

MRS. NOAKES. Dear me, sir, you needn't fear for your portmanteau in this house; I dare say nobody wants it.

STRANGE GENTLEMAN. I hope not, ma'am, because in that case nobody will be disappointed. (*Aside.*) How she fixes her old eyes on me!

MRS. NOAKES (*aside*). I never saw such an extraordinary person in all my life. What can he be? (*Looks at him very hard.*)

[*Exit* MRS. NOAKES, C. DOOR.

STRANGE GENTLEMAN. She's gone at last! Now let me commune with my own dreadful thoughts, and reflect on the best means of escaping from my horrible position. (*Takes a letter from his pocket.*) Here's an illegal death-warrant; a pressing invitation to be slaughtered; a polite request just to step out and be killed, thrust into my hand by some disguised assassin in a dirty black calico jacket, the very instant I got out of the gig at the door. I know the hand; there's a ferocious recklessness in the cross to this 'T,' and a baleful malignity in the dot of that 'I,' which warns me that it comes from my desperate rival. (*Opens it, and reads.*) 'Mr. Horatio Tinkles'—that's him —'presents his compliments to his enemy'—that's me—'and requests the pleasure of his company tomorrow morning, under the clump of trees, on Corpse Common,'—Corpse Common! —'to which any of the town's people will direct him, and where he hopes to have the satisfaction of giving him his gruel.' —Giving him his gruel! Ironical cut-throat!—'His punctuality will be esteemed a personal favour, as it will save Mr. Tinkles the trouble and inconvenience of calling with a horsewhip in his pocket. Mr. Tinkles has ordered breakfast at the Royal for *one*. It is paid for. The individual who returns alive can eat it. Pistols—half-past five—precisely.'—Bloodthirsty miscreant! *The* individual who returns alive! I have seen him hit the painted man at the shooting-gallery regularly every time in his centre shirt plait, except when he varied the entertainments, by lodging the ball playfully in his left eye. Breakfast! I shall want nothing beyond the gruel. What's to be done?

Escape! I can't escape; concealment's of no use, he knows I am here. He has dodged me all the way from London, and will dodge me all the way to the residence of Miss Emily Brown, whom my respected, but swine-headed parents have picked out for my future wife. A pretty figure I should cut before the old people, whom I have never beheld more than once in my life, and Miss Emily Brown, whom I have never seen at all, if I went down there, pursued by this Salamander, who, I suppose, is her accepted lover! What is to be done? I can't go back again; father would be furious. What can be done? nothing! (*Sinks into a chair.*) I must undergo this fiery ordeal, and submit to be packed up, and carried back to my weeping parents, like an unfortunate buck, with a flat piece of lead in my head, and a brief epitaph on my breast, 'Killed on Wednesday morning.' No, I won't (*starting up, and walking about*). I won't submit to it; I'll accept the challenge, but first I'll write an anonymous letter to the local authorities, giving them information of this intended duel, and desiring them to place me under immediate restraint. That's feasible; on further consideration, it's capital. My character will be saved—I shall be bound over—he'll be bound over—I shall resume my journey—reach the house—marry the girl—pocket the fortune, and laugh at him. No time to be lost; it shall be done forthwith. (*Goes to table and writes.*) There; the challenge accepted, with a bold defiance, that'll look very brave when it comes to be printed. Now for the other. (*Writes.*) 'To the Mayor—Sir—A strange Gentleman at the St. James's Arms, whose name is unknown to the writer of this communication, is bent upon committing a rash and sanguinary act, at an early hour tomorrow morning. As you value human life, secure the amiable youth, without delay. Think, I implore you, sir, think what would be the feelings of those to whom he is nearest and dearest, if any mischance befall the interesting young man. Do not neglect this solemn warning; the number of his room is seventeen.' There—(*folding it up*). Now if I can find any one who will deliver it secretly.—

TOM SPARKS, *with a pair of boots in his hand, peeps in at the* C. D.

TOM. Are these here your'n?
STRANGE GENTLEMAN. No.

TOM. Oh! (*going back*).

STRANGE GENTLEMAN. Hallo! stop, are you the Boots?

TOM (*still at the door*). I'm the head o' that branch o' the establishment. There's another man under me, as brushes the dirt off and puts the blacking on. The fancy work's my department. I do the polishing, nothing else.

STRANGE GENTLEMAN. You are the upper Boots, then?

TOM. Yes, I'm the reg'lar; t'other one's only the deputy; top boots and half boots, I calls us.

STRANGE GENTLEMAN. You're a sharp fellow.

TOM. Ah! I'd better cut then (*going*).

STRANGE GENTLEMAN. Don't hurry, Boots—don't hurry; I want you. (*Rises, and comes forward,* R. H.)

TOM (*coming forward,* L. H.). Well!

STRANGE GENTLEMAN. Can—can—you be secret, Boots?

TOM. That depends entirely on accompanying circumstances;—see the point?

STRANGE GENTLEMAN. I think I comprehend your meaning, Boots. You insinuate that you could be secret (*putting his hand in his pocket*) if you had—five shillings for instance—isn't that it, Boots?

TOM. That's the line o' argument I should take up; but that an't exactly my meaning.

STRANGE GENTLEMAN. No!

TOM. No. A secret's a thing as is always a rising to one's lips. It requires an astonishing weight to keep one on 'em down.

STRANGE GENTLEMAN. Ah!

TOM. Yes; I don't think I could keep one snug—reg'lar snug, you know——

STRANGE GENTLEMAN. Yes, regularly snug, of course.

TOM. —If it had a less weight a-top on it, than ten shillins.

STRANGE GENTLEMAN. You don't think three half-crowns would do it?

TOM. It might, I won't say it wouldn't, but I couldn't warrant it.

STRANGE GENTLEMAN. You could the other!

TOM. Yes.

STRANGE GENTLEMAN. Then there it is. (*Gives him four half-crowns.*) You see these letters?

TOM. Yes, I can manage that without my spectacles.

STRANGE GENTLEMAN. Well; that's to be left at the Royal Hotel.

This, *this*, is an anonymous one; and I want it to be delivered at the Mayor's house, without his knowing from whom it came, or seeing who delivered it.

TOM (*taking the letter*). I say—you're a rum 'un, you are.

STRANGE GENTLEMAN. Think so! Ha, ha! so are you.

TOM. Ay, but you're a rummer one than me.

STRANGE GENTLEMAN. No, no, that's your modesty.

TOM. No it an't. I say, how vell you did them last hay-stacks. How do you contrive that ere now, if it's a fair question. Is it done with a pipe, or do you use them Lucifer boxes?

STRANGE GENTLEMAN. Pipe—Lucifer boxes—hay-stacks! Why, what do you mean?

TOM (*looking cautiously round*). I know your name, old 'un.

STRANGE GENTLEMAN. You know my name! (*Aside.*) Now how the devil has he got hold of that, I wonder!

TOM. Yes, I know it. It begins with a 'S.'

STRANGE GENTLEMAN. Begins with an S!

TOM. And ends with a 'G' (*winking*). We've all heard talk of *Swing* down here.

STRANGE GENTLEMAN. Heard talk of Swing! Here's a situation! Damme, d'ye think I'm a walking carbois of vitriol, and burn everything I touch?—Will you go upon the errand you're paid for?

TOM. Oh, I'm going—I'm going. It's nothing to me, you know; I don't care. I'll only just give these boots to the deputy, to take them to whoever they belong to, and then I'll pitch this here letter in at the Mayor's office-window, in no time.

STRANGE GENTLEMAN. Will you be off?

TOM. Oh, I'm going, I'm going. Close, you knows, close!

[*Exit* TOM, C. DOOR.

STRANGE GENTLEMAN. In five minutes more the letter will be delivered; in another half hour, if the Mayor does his duty, I shall be in custody, and secure from the vengeance of this infuriated monster. I wonder whether they'll take me away? Egad! I may as well be provided with a clean shirt and a nightcap in case. Let's see, she said the next room was my bedroom, and as I have accepted the challenge, I may venture so far now. (*Shouldering the portmanteau.*) What a capital notion it is; there'll be all the correspondence in large letters, in the county paper, and my name figuring away in roman capitals, with a long story, how I was such a desperate dragon, and so bent upon fighting, that it took four constables to carry me to the Mayor, and one boy to carry my hat. It's a capital plan—must be done—the only way I have of escaping unpursued from this place, unless I could put myself in the General Post, and direct myself to a friend in town. And then it's a chance whether they'd take me in, being so much over weight.

[*Exit* STRANGE GENTLEMAN, *with portmanteau*, L. H.

MRS. NOAKES, *peeping in* C. DOOR, *then entering.*

MRS. NOAKES. This is the room, ladies, but the gentleman has stepped out somewhere, he won't be long, I dare say. Pray come in, Miss.

Enter MARY *and* FANNY WILSON, C. DOOR.

MARY (C.). This is the Strange Gentleman's apartment, is it?

MRS. NOAKES (R.). Yes, Miss; shall I see if I can find him, ladies, and tell him you are here?

MARY. No; we should prefer waiting till he returns, if you please.

MRS. NOAKES. Very well, ma'am. He'll be back directly, I dare say; for it's very near his dinner time.

[*Exit* MRS. NOAKES, C. DOOR.

MARY. Come, Fanny, dear; don't give way to these feelings of depression. Take pattern by me—I feel the absurdity of our situation acutely; but you see that I keep up, nevertheless.

FANNY. It is easy for you to do so. *Your* situation is neither so embarrassing, nor so painful a one as mine.

MARY. Well, my dear, it *may* not be, certainly; but the circumstances which render it less so are, I own, somewhat incomprehensible to me. My harebrained, mad-cap swain, John Johnson, implores me to leave my guardian's house, and accompany him on an expedition to Gretna Green. I with immense reluctance and after considerable pressing——

FANNY. Yield a very willing consent.

MARY. Well, we won't quarrel about terms; at all events I *do* consent. He bears me off, and when we get exactly half-way, discovers that his money is all gone, and that we must stop at this Inn, until he can procure a remittance from London, by post. I think, my dear, you'll own that *this* is rather an embarrassing position.

FANNY. Compare it with mine. Taking advantage of your flight, I send express to *my* admirer, Charles Tomkins, to say that I have accompanied you; first, because I should have been miserable if left behind with a peevish old man alone; secondly, because I thought it proper that your sister should accompany you——

MARY. And, thirdly, because you knew that he would immediately comply with this indirect assent to his entreaties of three months' duration, and follow you without delay, on the same errand. Eh, my dear?

FANNY. It by no means follows that such was my intention, or that I knew he would pursue such a course, but supposing he *has* done so; supposing this Strange Gentleman should be himself——

MARY. *Supposing!*—Why, you know it is. You told him not to disclose his name, on any account; and the *Strange Gentleman* is not a very common travelling name, I should imagine; besides the hasty note, in which he said he should join you here.

FANNY. Well, granted that it is he. In what a situation am I placed. You tell me, for the first time, that *my* violent intended must on no account be beheld by *your* violent intended, just now, because of some old quarrel between them, of long standing, which has never been adjusted to this day. What an appearance this will have! How am I to explain it, or relate your present situation? I should sink into the earth with shame and confusion.

MARY. Leave it to me. It arises from my heedlessness. I will take it all upon myself, and see him alone. But tell me, my dear—as you got up this love affair with so much secrecy and expedition during the four months you spent at Aunt Martha's, I have never yet seen Mr Tomkins, you know. Is he so very handsome?

FANNY. See him, and judge for yourself.

MARY. Well, I will; and you may retire, till I have paved the way for your appearance. But just assist me first, dear, in making a little noise to attract his attention, if he really be in the next room, or I may wait here all day.

DUET—*At end of which exit* FANNY, C. DOOR. MARY *retires up* R. H.

Enter STRANGE GENTLEMAN, L. H.

STRANGE GENTLEMAN. There; now with a clean shirt in one pocket and a night-cap in the other, I'm ready to be carried magnanimously to my dungeon in the cause of love.

MARY (*aside*). He says, he's ready to be carried magnanimously to a dungeon in the cause of love. I thought it was Mr. Tomkins! Hem! (*Coming down* L. H.)

STRANGE GENTLEMAN (*seeing her*). Hallo! Who's this! Not a disguised peace officer in petticoats. Beg your pardon, ma'am. (*Advancing towards her.*) What—did—you——

MARY. Oh, Sir; I feel the delicacy of my situation.

STRANGE GENTLEMAN (*aside*). Feels the delicacy of her situation; Lord bless us, what's the matter! Permit me to offer you a seat, ma'am, if you're in a delicate situation. (*He places chairs; they sit.*)

MARY. You are very good, Sir. You are surprised to see me here, Sir?

STRANGE GENTLEMAN. No, no, at least not very; rather, perhaps —rather. (*Aside.*) Never was more astonished in all my life!

MARY (*aside*). His politeness, and the extraordinary tale I have to tell him, overpower me. I must summon up courage. Hem!

STRANGE GENTLEMAN. Hem!

MARY. Sir!

STRANGE GENTLEMAN. Ma'am!

MARY. You have arrived at this house in pursuit of a young lady, if I mistake not?

STRANGE GENTLEMAN. You are quite right, ma'am. (*Aside.*) Mysterious female!

MARY. If you *are* the gentleman I'm in search of, you wrote a hasty note a short time since, stating that you would be found here this afternoon.

STRANGE GENTLEMAN (*drawing back his chair*). I—I—wrote a note, ma'am!

MARY. You need keep nothing secret from me, Sir. I know all.

STRANGE GENTLEMAN (*aside*). That villain, Boots, has betrayed me! Know all, ma'am?

MARY. Everything.

STRANGE GENTLEMAN (*aside*). It must be so. She's a constable's wife.

MARY. You *are* the writer of that letter, Sir? I think I am not mistaken.

STRANGE GENTLEMAN. You are not, ma'am; I confess I did write it. What was I to do, ma'am? Consider the situation in which I was placed.

MARY. In your situation, you had, as it appears to me, only one course to pursue.

STRANGE GENTLEMAN. You mean the course I adopted?

MARY. Undoubtedly.

STRANGE GENTLEMAN. I am very happy to hear you say so, though of course I should like it to be kept a secret.

MARY. Oh, of course.

STRANGE GENTLEMAN (*drawing his chair close to her, and speaking very softly*). Will you allow me to ask you, whether the constables are downstairs?

MARY (*surprised*). The constables!

STRANGE GENTLEMAN. Because if I am to be apprehended, I should like to have it over. I am quite ready, if it must be done.

MARY. No legal interference has been attempted. There is nothing to prevent your continuing your journey to-night.

STRANGE GENTLEMAN. But will not the other party follow?

MARY (*looking down*). The other party, I am compelled to inform you, is detained here by—by want of funds.

STRANGE GENTLEMAN (*starting up*). Detained here by want of funds! Hurrah! Hurrah! I have caged him at last. I'm revenged for all his blustering and bullying. This is a glorious triumph, ha, ha, ha! I have nailed him—nailed him to the spot!

MARY (*rising indignantly*). This exulting over a fallen foe, Sir, is mean and pitiful. In my presence, too, it is an additional insult.

STRANGE GENTLEMAN. Insult! I wouldn't insult you for the world, after the joyful intelligence you have brought me—I could hug you in my arms!—One kiss, my little constable's deputy. (*Seizing her.*)

MARY (*struggling with him*). Help! help!

Enter JOHN JOHNSON, C. DOOR.

JOHN. What the devil do I see! (*Seizes* STRANGE GENTLEMAN *by the collar.*)

MARY (L. H.). John, and Mr. Tomkins, met together! They'll kill each other.—Here, help! help!

[*Exit* MARY, *running*, C. DOOR.

JOHN (*shaking him*). What do you mean by that, scoundrel?

STRANGE GENTLEMAN. Come, none of your nonsense—there's no harm done.

JOHN. No harm done.—How dare you offer to salute that lady?

STRANGE GENTLEMAN. What did you send her here for?

JOHN. *I* send her here!

STRANGE GENTLEMAN. Yes, *you*; you gave her instructions, I suppose. (*Aside*.) Her husband, the constable, evidently.

JOHN. That lady, Sir, is attached to me.

STRANGE GENTLEMAN. Well, I know she is; and a very useful little person she must be, to be attached to anybody,—it's a pity she can't be legally sworn in.

JOHN. *Legally* sworn in! Sir, that is an insolent reflection upon the temporary embarrassment which prevents our taking the marriage vows. How dare you to insinuate——

STRANGE GENTLEMAN. Pooh! pooh!—don't talk about daring to insinuate; it doesn't become a man in your station of life——

JOHN. My station of life!

STRANGE GENTLEMAN. But as you have managed this matter very quietly, and say you're in temporary embarrassment—here—here's five shillings for you. (*Offers it*.)

JOHN. Five shillings! (*Raises his cane*.)

STRANGE GENTLEMAN (*flourishing a chair*). Keep off, sir!

Enter MARY, TOM SPARKS, *and two Waiters*.

MARY. Separate them, or there'll be murder! (TOM *clasps* STRANGE GENTLEMAN *round the waist—the Waiters seize* JOHN JOHNSON).

TOM. Come, none o' that 'ere, Mr. S. We don't let private rooms for such games as these.—If you want to try it on wery partickler, we don't mind making a ring for you in the yard, but you mustn't do it here.

JOHN. Let me get at him. Let me go; waiters—Mary, don't hold me. I insist on your letting me go.

STRANGE GENTLEMAN. Hold him fast.—Call yourself a *peace* officer, you prize-fighter!

JOHN (*struggling*). Let me go, I say!

STRANGE GENTLEMAN. Hold him fast! Hold him fast!

[TOM *takes* STRANGE GENTLEMAN *off*, R. H. *Waiters take* JOHN *off*, L. H., MARY *following*.

SCENE II.—*Another Room in the Inn.*

Enter JULIA DOBBS *and* OVERTON, L. H.

JULIA. You seem surprised, Overton.

OVERTON. Surprised, Miss Dobbs! Well I may be, when, after seeing nothing of you for three years and more, you come down here without any previous notice, for the express purpose of running away—positively running away, with a young man. I am astonished, Miss Dobbs!

JULIA. You would have had better reason to be astonished if I had come down here with any notion of positively running away with an old one, Overton.

OVERTON. Old or young, it would matter little to me, if you had not conceived the preposterous idea of entangling me—*me*, an attorney, and mayor of the town, in so ridiculous a scheme.—Miss Dobbs, I can't do it.—I really cannot consent to mix myself up with such an affair.

JULIA. Very well, Overton, very well. You recollect that in the lifetime of that poor old dear, Mr. Woolley, who——

OVERTON. —Who would have married you, if he hadn't died; and who, as it was, left you his property, free from all incumbrances, the incumbrance of himself, as a husband, not being among the least.

JULIA. Well, you may recollect, that in the poor old dear's lifetime, sundry advances of money were made to you, at my persuasion, which still remain unpaid. Oblige me by forwarding them to my agent in the course of the week, and I free you from any interference in this little matter. (*Crosses to* L. H *and is going.*)

OVERTON. Stay, Miss Dobbs, stay. As you say, we *are* old acquaintances, and there certainly *were* some small sums of money, which—which——

JULIA. Which certainly *are* still outstanding.

OVERTON. Just so, just so; and which, perhaps you would

be likely to forget, if you had a husband—eh, Miss Dobbs, eh?

JULIA. I have little doubt that I should. If I gained one through your assistance, indeed—I can safely say I should forget all about them.

OVERTON. My dear Miss Dobbs, we perfectly understand each other—Pray proceed.

JULIA. Well—dear Lord Peter——

OVERTON. That's the young man you're going to run away with, I presume?

JULIA. That's the young *nobleman* who's going to run away with me, Mr. Overton.

OVERTON. Yes, just so.—I beg your pardon—pray go on.

JULIA. Dear Lord Peter is young and wild, and the fact is, his friends do not consider him very sagacious or strong-minded. To prevent their interference, our marriage is to be a secret one. In fact, he is stopping now at a friend's hunting seat in the neighbourhood; he is to join me here; and we are to be married at Gretna.

OVERTON. Just so.—A matter, as it seems to me, which you can conclude without my interference.

JULIA. Wait an instant. To avoid suspicion, and prevent our being recognised and followed, I settled with him that you should give out in this house that he was a lunatic, and that I—his aunt—was going to convey him in a chaise, to-night, to a private asylum at Berwick. I have ordered the chaise at half-past one in the morning. You can see him, and make our final arrangements. It will avert all suspicion, if I have no communication with him, till we start. You can say to the people of the house that the sight of me makes him furious.

OVERTON. Where shall I find him?—Is he here?

JULIA. You know best.

OVERTON. I!

JULIA. I desired him, immediately on his arrival, to write you some mysterious nonsense, acquainting you with the number of his room.

OVERTON (*producing a letter*). Dear me, he has arrived, Miss Dobbs.

JULIA. No!

OVERTON. Yes—see here—a most mysterious and extraordinary

composition, which was thrown in at my office window this morning, and which I could make neither head nor tail of. Is that his handwriting? (*Giving her the letter.*)

JULIA (*taking letter*). I never saw it more than once, but I know he writes very large and straggling.—(*Looks at letter.*) Ha, ha, ha! This is capital, isn't it?

OVERTON. Excellent!—Ha, ha, ha!—So mysterious!

JULIA. Ha, ha, ha!—So very good.—'Rash act.'

OVERTON. Yes. Ha, ha!

JULIA. 'Interesting young man.'

OVERTON. Yes.—Very good.

JULIA. 'Amiable youth!'

OVERTON. Capital!

JULIA. 'Solemn warning!'

OVERTON. Yes.—That's best of all. (*They both laugh.*)

JULIA. Number seventeen, he says. See him at once, that's a good creature. (*Returning the letter.*)

OVERTON (*taking letter*). I will. (*He crosses to* L. H. *and rings a bell.*)

Enter WAITER, L. H.

Who is there in number seventeen, waiter?

WAITER. Number seventeen, sir?—Oh!—the strange gentleman, sir.

OVERTON. Show me the room. [*Exit* WAITER, L. H. (*Looking at* JULIA, *and pointing to the letter.*) 'The Strange Gentleman.'—Ha, ha, ha! Very good—very good indeed—Excellent notion! (*They both laugh.*) [*Exeunt severally.*

SCENE III.—*Same as the first.—A small table, with wine, dessert, and lights on it,* R. H. *of* C. DOOR; *two chairs.*

STRANGE GENTLEMAN *discovered seated at table.*

STRANGE GENTLEMAN. 'The other party is detained here, by want of funds.' Ha, ha, ha! I can finish my wine at my leisure, order my gig when I please, and drive on to Brown's in perfect security. I'll drink the other party's good health, and long may he be detained here. (*Fills a glass.*) Ha, ha, ha! The other party; and long may he—(*A knock at* C. DOOR.) Hallo! I hope *this* isn't the other party. Talk of the—(*A knock at* C. DOOR.)

Well—(*setting down his glass*)—this is the most extraordinary private room that was ever invented. I am continually disturbed by unaccountable knockings. (*A gentle tap at* C. DOOR.) There's another; that was a gentle rap—a persuasive tap—like a friend's fore-finger on one's coat-sleeve. It *can't* be Tinkles with the gruel.—Come in.

OVERTON *peeping in at* C. DOOR.

OVERTON. Are you alone, my Lord?

STRANGE GENTLEMAN (*amazed*). Eh!

OVERTON. Are you alone, my Lord?

STRANGE GENTLEMAN. My Lord!

OVERTON (*stepping in, and closing the door*). You are right, sir, we cannot be too cautious, for we do not know who may be within hearing. You are very right, sir.

STRANGE GENTLEMAN (*rising from table, and coming forward,* R. H.). It strikes me, sir, that you are very wrong.

OVERTON. Very good, very good; I like this caution; it shows me you are wide awake.

STRANGE GENTLEMAN. Wide awake!—damme, I begin to think I am fast asleep, and have been for the last two hours.

OVERTON (*whispering*). I—am—the mayor.

STRANGE GENTLEMAN (*in the same tone*). Oh!

OVERTON. This is your letter? (*Shows it;* STRANGE GENTLEMAN *nods assent solemnly.*) It will be necessary for you to leave here to-night, at half-past one o'clock, in a postchaise and four; and the higher you bribe the postboys to drive at their utmost speed, the better.

STRANGE GENTLEMAN. You don't say so?

OVERTON. I do indeed. You are not safe from pursuit here.

STRANGE GENTLEMAN. Bless my soul, can such dreadful things happen in a civilised community, Mr. Mayor?

OVERTON. It certainly does at first sight appear rather a hard case that people cannot marry whom they please, without being hunted down in this way.

STRANGE GENTLEMAN. To be sure. To be hunted down, and killed as if one was game, you know.

OVERTON. Certainly; and you *an't* game, you know.

STRANGE GENTLEMAN. Of course not. But can't you prevent it? can't you save me by the interposition of your power?

OVERTON. My power can do nothing in such a case.

STRANGE GENTLEMAN. Can't it, though?

OVERTON. Nothing whatever.

STRANGE GENTLEMAN. I never heard of such dreadful revenge, never! Mr. Mayor, I am a victim, I am the unhappy victim of parental obstinacy.

OVERTON. Oh, no; don't say that. You may escape yet.

STRANGE GENTLEMAN (*grasping his hand*). Do you think I may? Do you think I may, Mr. Mayor?

OVERTON. Certainly! certainly! I have little doubt of it, if you manage properly.

STRANGE GENTLEMAN. I thought I *was* managing properly. I understood the other party was detained here, by want of funds.

OVERTON. Want of funds!—There's no want of funds in that quarter, I can tell you.

STRANGE GENTLEMAN. An't there, though?

OVERTON. Bless you, no. Three thousand a year!—But who told you there was a want of funds?

STRANGE GENTLEMAN. Why, she did.

OVERTON. *She!* you *have* seen her then? She told me you had not.

STRANGE GENTLEMAN. Nonsense; don't believe her. She was in this very room half an hour ago.

OVERTON. Then I must have misunderstood her, and you must have misunderstood her too.—But to return to business. Don't you think it would keep up appearances if I had you put under some restraint.

STRANGE GENTLEMAN. I think it would. I am very much obliged to you. (*Aside.*) This regard for my character in an utter stranger, and in a Mayor too, is quite affecting.

OVERTON. I'll send somebody up, to mount guard over you.

STRANGE GENTLEMAN. Thank 'ee, my dear friend, thank 'ee.

OVERTON. And if you make a little resistance, when we take you upstairs to your bedroom, or away in the chaise, it will be keeping up the character, you know.

STRANGE GENTLEMAN. To be sure.—So it will.—I'll do it.

OVERTON. Very well, then. I shall see your Lordship again by and by.—For the present, my Lord, good evening. (*Going.*)

STRANGE GENTLEMAN. Lord!—Lordship!—Mr. Mayor!

OVERTON. Eh?—Oh!—I see. (*Comes forward.*) Practising the lunatic, my Lord. Ah, very good—very vacant look indeed.—Admirable, my Lord, admirable!—I say, my Lord—(*pointing to letter*)—'*Amiable youth!*'—'Interesting young man.'—'Strange Gentleman.'—Eh? Ha, ha, ha! Knowing trick in-indeed, my Lord, very! [*Exit* OVERTON, C. D.

STRANGE GENTLEMAN. That Mayor is either in the very last stage of mystified intoxication, or in the most hopeless state of in-curable insanity.—I have no doubt of it. A little touched here (*tapping his forehead*). Never mind, he is sufficiently sane to understand my business at all events. (*Goes to table and takes a glass.*) Poor fellow!—I'll drink his health, and speedy re-covery. (*A knock at* C. DOOR.) It is a most extraordinary thing, now, that every time I propose a toast to myself, some con-founded fellow raps at that door, as if he were receiving it with the utmost enthusiasm. Private room!—I might as well be sitting behind the little shutter of a Two-penny Post Office, where all the letters put in were to be post-paid. (*A knock at* C. DOOR.) Perhaps it's the guard! I shall feel a great deal safer if it is. Come in. (*He has brought a chair forward, and sits* L. H.)

Enter TOM SPARKS, C. DOOR, *very slowly, with an enormous stick. He closes the door, and, after looking at the* STRANGE GENTLE-MAN *very steadily, brings a chair down* L. H., *and sits opposite him.*

STRANGE GENTLEMAN. Are you sent by the mayor of this place, to mount guard over me?

TOM. Yes, yes.—It's all right.

STRANGE GENTLEMAN (*aside*). It's all right—I'm safe. (*To* TOM, *with affected indignation.*) Now mind, I have been insulted by receiving this challenge, and I want to fight the man who gave it me. I protest against being kept here. I denounce this treat-ment as an outrage.

TOM. Ay, ay. Anything you please—poor creature; don't put yourself in a passion. It'll only make you worse. (*Whistles*).

STRANGE GENTLEMAN. This is most extraordinary behaviour.—I don't understand it.—What d'ye mean by behaving in this manner? (*Rising.*)

TOM (*aside*). He's a getting wiolent. I must frighten him with a steady look.—I say, young fellow, do you see this here eye? (*Staring at him, and pointing at his own eye.*)

STRANGE GENTLEMAN (*aside*). Do I see his eye!—What can he mean by glaring upon me, with that large round optic!—Ha! a terrible light flashes upon me.—He thought I was 'Swing' this morning. It was an insane delusion.—That eye is an insane eye.—He's a madman!

TOM. Madman! Damme, I think he is a madman with a wengeance.

STRANGE GENTLEMAN. He acknowledges it. He is sensible of his misfortune!—Go away—leave the room instantly, and tell them to send somebody else.—Go away!

TOM. Oh, you unhappy lunatic!

STRANGE GENTLEMAN. What a dreadful situation!—I shall be attacked, strangled, smothered, and mangled, by a madman! Where's the bell?

TOM (*advancing and brandishing his stick*). Leave that 'ere bell alone—leave that 'ere bell alone—and come here!

STRANGE GENTLEMAN. Certainly, Mr. Boots, certainly.—He's going to strangle me. (*Going towards table.*) Let me pour you out a glass of wine, Mr. Boots—pray do! (*Aside.*) If he said 'Yes,' I'd throw the decanter at his temple.

TOM. None o' your nonsense.—Sit down there. (*Forces him into a chair,* L. H.) I'll sit here. (*Opposite him,* R. H.) Look me full in the face, and I won't hurt you. Move hand, foot, or eye, and you'll never want to move either of 'em again.

STRANGE GENTLEMAN. I'm paralysed with terror.

TOM. Ha! (*raising his stick in a threatening attitude*).

STRANGE GENTLEMAN. I'm dumb, Mr. Boots—dumb, sir.

They sit gazing intently on each other; TOM *with the stick raised, as the Act Drop slowly descends.*

END OF ACT FIRST

FIRST ACT FIFTY MINUTES

ACT II

SCENE I.—*The same as* SCENE III, ACT I.

TOM SPARKS *discovered in the same attitude watching the* STRANGE GENTLEMAN, *who has fallen asleep with his head over the back of his Chair.*

TOM. He's asleep; poor unhappy wretch! How very mad he looks with his mouth wide open and his eyes shut! (STRANGE GENTLEMAN *snores.*) Ah! there's a wacant snore; no meaning in it at all. I cou'd ha' told he was out of his senses from the very tone of it. (*He snores again.*) That's a wery insane snore. I should say he was melancholy mad from the sound of it.

Enter, through C. DOOR, OVERTON, MRS. NOAKES, *a Chambermaid, and two Waiters;* MRS. NOAKES *with a warming-pan, the Maid with a light.* STRANGE GENTLEMAN *starts up, greatly exhausted.*

TOM (*starting up in* C.). Hallo!—Hallo! keep quiet, young fellow. Keep quiet!

STRANGE GENTLEMAN (L. H.). Out of the way, you savage maniac. Mr. Mayor (*crossing to him,* R. H., the person you sent to keep guard over me is a madman, sir. What do you mean by shutting me up with a madman?—what do you mean, sir, I ask?

OVERTON, R. H. C. (*aside to* STRANGE GENTLEMAN). Bravo! bravo! very good indeed—excellent!

STRANGE GENTLEMAN. Excellent, sir!—It's horrible!—The bare recollection of what I have endured, makes me shudder, down to my very toe-nails.

MRS. NOAKES (R. H.). Poor dear!—Mad people always think other people mad.

STRANGE GENTLEMAN. Poor dear! Ma'am! What the devil do you mean by 'Poor dear'? How dare you have a madman here, ma'am, to assault and terrify the visitors to your establishment?

MRS. NOAKES. Ah! terrify indeed! I'll never have another, to please anybody, you may depend upon that, Mr. Overton. (*To* STRANGE GENTLEMAN.) There, there.—Don't exert yourself, there's a dear.

STRANGE GENTLEMAN (C.). Exert myself!—Damme! it's a mercy I have any life left to exert myself with. It's a special miracle, ma'am, that my existence has not long ago fallen a sacrifice to that sanguinary monster in the leather smalls.

OVERTON, R. C. (*aside to* STRANGE GENTLEMAN). I never saw any passion more real in my life. Keep it up, it's an admirable joke.

STRANGE GENTLEMAN. Joke!—joke!—Peril a precious life, and call it a joke,—you, a man with a sleek head and a broad-brimmed hat, who ought to know better, calling it a joke.—Are you mad too, sir,—are you mad? (*Confronting* OVERTON.)

TOM, L. H. (*very loud*). Keep your hands off. Would you murder the wery mayor, himself, you mis-rable being?

STRANGE GENTLEMAN. Mr. Mayor, I call upon you to issue your warrant for the instant confinement of that one-eyed Orson in some place of security.

OVERTON (*aside, advancing a little*). He reminds me that he had better be removed to his bedroom. He is right.—Waiters, carry the gentleman upstairs.—Boots, you will continue to watch him in his bedroom.

STRANGE GENTLEMAN. *He* continue!—What, am I to be boxed up again with this infuriated animal, and killed off, when he has done playing with me?—I won't go—I won't go—help there, help! (*The Waiters cross from* R. H. *to behind him.*)

Enter JOHN JOHNSON *hastily,* C. DOOR.

JOHN (*coming forward* L. H.). What on earth is the meaning of this dreadful outcry, which disturbs the whole house?

MRS. NOAKES. Don't be alarmed, sir, I beg.—They're only going to carry an unfortunate gentleman, as is out of his senses, to his bedroom.

STRANGE GENTLEMAN, C. (*to* JOHN). Constable—constable—do your duty—apprehend these persons—every one of them. Do you hear, officer, do you hear?—(*The Waiters seize him by the arms.*)—Here—here—you see this. You've seen the assault committed. Take them into custody—off with them.

MRS. NOAKES. Poor creature!—He thinks you are a constable, sir.

JOHN. Unfortunate man! It is the second time to-day that he has been the victim of this strange delusion.

STRANGE GENTLEMAN (*breaking from Waiters and going to*

JOHN). L. H. Unfortunate man!—What, do *you* think I am mad?

JOHN. Poor fellow! His hopeless condition is pitiable indeed. (*Goes up.*)

STRANGE GENTLEMAN (*returning to* C.). They're all mad!—Every one of 'em!

MRS. NOAKES. Come now, come to bed—there's a dear young man, do.

STRANGE GENTLEMAN. Who are you, you shameless old ghost, standing there before company, with a large warming-pan, and asking me to come to bed?—Are *you* mad?

MRS. NOAKES. Oh! he's getting shocking now. Take him away. —Take him away.

OVERTON. Ah, you had better remove him to his bedroom at once. (*The Waiters take him up by the feet and shoulders.*)

STRANGE GENTLEMAN. Mind, if I survive this, I'll bring an action of false imprisonment against every one of you. Mark my words—especially against that villainous old mayor.—Mind, I'll do it! (*They bear him off, struggling and talking—the others crowding round, and assisting.*)

OVERTON (*following*). How well he does it! [*Exeunt* L. H. 1*st* E.

Enter a Waiter, showing in CHARLES TOMKINS *in a travelling coat,* C. DOOR.

WAITER (L. H.). This room is disengaged now, sir. There *was* a gentleman in it, but he has just left it.

CHARLES. Very well, this will do. I may want a bed here to-night, perhaps, waiter.

WAITER. Yes, sir.—Shall I take your card to the bar, sir?

CHARLES. My card!—No, never mind.

WAITER. No name, sir?

CHARLES. No—it doesn't matter.

WAITER (*aside, as going out*). *Another* Strange Gentleman!

[*Exit Waiter,* C. DOOR.

CHARLES. Ah!—(*Takes off coat.*)—The sun and dust on this long ride have been almost suffocating. I wonder whether Fanny has arrived? If she has—the sooner we start forward on our journey further North the better. Let me see; she would be accompanied by her sister, she said in her note—and they would both be on the look-out for me. Then the best thing I can do is to ask no questions, for the present at all events, and to be on the look-out for them. (*Looking towards* C. DOOR.) Why here she comes, walking slowly down the long passage, straight towards this room—she can't have seen me yet.—Poor girl, how melancholy she looks! I'll keep in the background for an instant, and give her a joyful surprise. (*He goes up* R. H.)

Enter FANNY, C. DOOR.

FANNY (L. H.). Was ever unhappy girl placed in so dreadful a situation!—Friendless, and almost alone, in a strange place—my dear, dear Charles a victim to an attack of mental derangement, and I unable to avow my interest in him, or express my anxious sympathy and solicitude for his sufferings! I cannot bear this dreadful torture of agonising suspense. I must and will see him, let the cost be what it may. (*She is going* L. H.)

CHARLES (*coming forward* R. H.). Hist! Fanny!

FANNY (*starting and repressing a scream*). Ch—Charles—here in this room!

CHARLES. Bodily present, my dear, in this very room. My darling Fanny, let me strain you to my bosom. (*Advancing.*)

FANNY (*shrinking back*). N—n—no, dearest Charles, no, not now. —(*Aside.*)—How flushed he is!

CHARLES. No!—Fanny, this cold reception is a very different one to what I looked forward to meeting with, from you.

FANNY (*advancing, and offering the tip of her finger*). N—n—no —not cold, Charles; not cold. I do not mean it to be so, indeed.—How is your head, now dear?

CHARLES. How is my head! After days and weeks of suspense and anxiety, when half our dangerous journey is gained, and I meet you here, to bear you whither you can be made mine for life, you greet me with the tip of your longest finger, and inquire after my head,—Fanny, what can you mean?

FANNY. You—you have startled me rather, Charles.—I thought you had gone to bed.

CHARLES. Gone to bed!—Why I have but this moment arrived.

FANNY (*aside*). Poor, poor Charles!

CHARLES. Miss Wilson, what am I to——

FANNY. No, no; pray, pray, do not suffer yourself to be excited——

CHARLES. Suffer myself to be excited!—Can I possibly avoid it? can I do aught but wonder at this extraordinary and sudden change in your whole demeanour?—Excited! But five minutes since, I arrived here, brimful of the hope and expectation which had buoyed up my spirits during my long journey. I find you cold, reserved, and embarrassed—everything but what I expected to find you—and then you tell me not to be excited.

FANNY (*aside*). He is wandering again. The fever is evidently upon him.

CHARLES. This altered manner and ill-disguised confusion all convince me of what you would fain conceal. Miss Wilson, you repent of your former determination, and love another!

FANNY. Poor fellow!

CHARLES. Poor fellow!—What, am I pitied?

FANNY. Oh, Charles, do not give way to this. Consider how much depends upon your being composed.

CHARLES. I see how much depends upon my being composed, ma'am—well, very well.—A husband depends upon it, ma'am. Your new lover is in this house, and if he overhears my reproaches he will become suspicious of the woman who has jilted *another*, and may jilt *him*. That's it, madam—a great deal depends, as you say, upon my being composed.—A great deal, ma'am.

FANNY. Alas! these are indeed the ravings of frenzy!

CHARLES. Upon my word, ma'am, you must form a very modest estimate of your own power, if you imagine that disappointment has impaired my senses. Ha, ha, ha!—I am delighted. I am delighted to have escaped you, ma'am. I am glad, ma'am—damn'd glad! (*Kicks a chair over.*)

FANNY (*aside*). I must call for assistance. He grows more incoherent and furious every instant.

CHARLES. I leave you, ma'am.—I am unwilling to interrupt the tender *tête-à-tête* with the other gentleman, to which you are, no doubt, anxiously looking forward.—To you I have no more to say. To *him* I must beg to offer a few rather unexpected congratulations on his approaching marriage.

[*Exit* CHARLES *hastily,* C. DOOR.

FANNY. Alas! it is but too true. His senses have entirely left him.

[*Exit* L. H.

SCENE SECOND AND LAST.—*A Gallery in the Inn, leading to the Bedrooms. Four doors in the Flat, and one at each of the upper Entrances, numbered from* 20 *to* 25, *beginning at the* R. H. *A pair of boots at the door of* 23.

Enter Chambermaid with two lights; and CHARLES TOMKINS, R. H. 1*st* E.

MAID. This is your room, sir, No. 21. (*Opening the door.*)

CHARLES. Very well. Call me at seven in the morning.

MAID. Yes, sir. (*Gives him a light, and*

[*Exit Chambermaid,* R. H. 1*st* E.

CHARLES. And at nine, if I can previously obtain a few words of explanation with this unknown rival, I will just return to the place from whence I came, in the same coach that brought me down here. I wonder who he is and where he sleeps. (*Looking round.*) I have a lurking suspicion of those boots. (*Pointing to No.* 23.) They are an ill-looking, underhanded sort of pair, and an undefinable instinct tells me that they have clothed the feet of the rascal I am in search of. Besides myself, the owner of those ugly articles is the only person who has yet come up to bed. I will keep my eyes open for half an hour or so; and my ears too.

[*Exit* CHARLES *into No.* 21.

Enter R. H. 1*st* E. MRS. NOAKES *with two lights, followed by* MARY *and* FANNY.

MRS. NOAKES. Take care of the last step, ladies. This way, ma'am, if you please. No. 20 is your room, ladies: nice large double-bedded room, with coals and a rushlight.

FANNY, R. H. (*aside to* MARY). I must ask which is his room. I cannot rest unless I know he has at length sunk into the slumber he so much needs. (*Crosses to* MRS. NOAKES, *who is* L. H.) Which is the room in which the Strange Gentleman sleeps?

MRS. NOAKES. No. 23, ma'am. There's his boots outside the door. Don't be frightened of him, ladies. He's very quiet now, and our Boots is a watching him.

FANNY. Oh, no—we are not afraid of him. (*Aside.*) Poor Charles!

MRS. NOAKES (*going to door No.* 20, *which is* 3*rd* E. R. H.). This way, if you please; you'll find everything very comfortable, and there's a bell-rope at the head of the bed, if you want anything in the morning. Good night, ladies.

As MARY *and* FANNY *pass* MRS. NOAKES, FANNY *takes a light.*

[*Exeunt* FANNY *and* MARY *into No.* 20.

MRS. NOAKES (*tapping at No.* 23). Tom—Tom—

Enter TOM *from No.* 23.

TOM (*coming forward*, L. H.). Is that you, missis?

MRS. NOAKES (R. H.). Yes—How's the Strange Gentleman, Tom?

TOM. He was wery boisterous half an hour ago, but I punched his head a little, and now he's uncommon comfortable. He's fallen asleep, but his snores is still wery incoherent.

MRS. NOAKES. Mind you take care of him, Tom. They'll take him away in half an hour's time. It's very nearly one o'clock now.

TOM. I'll pay ev'ry possible attention to him. If he offers to call out, I shall whop him again. [*Exit* TOM *into No.* 23.

MRS. NOAKES (*looking off* R. H.). This way, ma'am, if you please. Up these stairs.

Enter JULIA DOBBS *with a light*, R. H. 1*st* E.

JULIA. Which did you say was the room in which I could arrange my dress for travelling?

MRS. NOAKES. No. 22, ma'am; the next room to your nephew's. Poor dear—he's fallen asleep, ma'am, and I dare say you'll be able to take him away very quietly by and by.

JULIA (*aside*). Not so quietly as you imagine, if he plays his part half as well as Overton reports he does. (*To* MRS. NOAKES.) Thank you.—For the present, good night.

[*Exit* JULIA *into No.* 22.

MRS. NOAKES. Wish you good night, ma'am. There.—Now I think I may go downstairs again, and see if Mr. Overton wants any more negus. Why who's this? (*Looking off* R. H.) Oh, I forgot—No. 24 an't a-bed yet.—It's him.

Enter JOHN JOHNSON *with a light*, R. H. 1*st* E.

MRS. NOAKES. No. 24, sir, if you please.

JOHN. Yes, yes, I know. The same room I slept in last night. (*Crossing* L. H.)

MRS. NOAKES. Yes, sir.—Wish you good night, sir.

[*Exit* MRS. NOAKES, R. H. 1*st* E.

JOHN. Good night, ma'am. The same room I slept in last night, indeed, and the same room I may sleep in to-morrow night, and the next night, and the night after that, and just as many more nights as I can get credit here, unless this remittance arrives. I could raise the money to prosecute my journey without difficulty were I on the spot; but my confounded thoughtless liberality to the post-boys has left me absolutely penniless. Well, we shall see what to-morrow brings forth. (*He goes into No.* 24, *but immediately returns and places his boots outside his room door, leaving it ajar.*) [*Exit* JOHN *into No.* 24.

CHARLES *peeping from No.* 21, *and putting out his boots.*

CHARLES. There's another pair of boots. Now I wonder which of these two fellows is the man. I can't help thinking it's No. 23. —Hallo! (*He goes in and closes his door.*)

The door of No. 20 *opens;* FANNY *comes out with a light in a night shade. No.* 23 *opens. She retires into No.* 20.

Enter TOM SPARKS, *with a stable lantern from No.* 23.

TOM (*closing the door gently*). Fast asleep still. I may as vell go my rounds, and glean for the deputy. (*Pulls out a piece of chalk from his pocket, and takes up boots from No.* 23.) Twenty-three. It's difficult to tell what a fellow is ven he han't got his senses, but I think this here twenty-three's a timorious faint-hearted genus. (*Examines the boots.*) You want new soleing, No. 23. (*Goes to No.* 24, *takes up boots and looks at them.*) Hallo! here's a *bust*: and there's been a piece put on in the corner.—I must let my missis know. The bill's always doubtful ven there's any mending. (*Goes to No.* 21, *takes up boots.*) French calf Vellingtons.—All's right here. These here French calves always comes it strong—light vines, and all that 'ere. (*Looking round.*) Werry happy to see there an't no high-lows —they never drinks nothing but gin-and-vater. Them and the cloth boots is the vurst customers an inn has.—The cloth boots is always obstemious, only drinks sherry vine and vater, and never eats no suppers. (*He chalks the No. of the room on each pair of boots as he takes them up.*) Lucky for you, my French calves, that you an't done with the patent polish, or you'd ha' been witrioled in no time. I don't like to put oil of witriol on a well-made pair of boots; but ven they're rubbed with that 'ere polish, it must be done, or the profession's ruined.

[*Exit* TOM *with boots*, R. H. 1*st* E.

Enter FANNY *from No.* 20, *with light as before.*

FANNY. I tremble at the idea of going into his room, but surely at a moment like this, when he is left to be attended by rude and uninterested strangers, the strict rules of propriety which regulate our ordinary proceedings may be dispensed with. I will but satisfy myself that he sleeps, and has those comforts which his melancholy situation demands, and return immediately. (*Goes to No.* 23, *and knocks.*)

CHARLES TOMKINS *peeping from No.* 21.

CHARLES. I'll swear I heard a knock.—A woman! Fanny Wilson —and at that door at this hour of the night!

FANNY *comes forward.*

Why what an ass I must have been ever to have loved that girl. —It *is* No. 23, though.—I'll throttle him presently. The next room door open—I'll watch there. (*He crosses to No.* 24, *and goes in.*)

FANNY *returns to No.* 23, *and knocks—the door opens and the* STRANGE GENTLEMAN *appears, night-cap on his head and a light in his hand.*—FANNY *screams and runs back into No.* 20.

STRANGE GENTLEMAN (*coming forward*). Well, of all the wonderful and extraordinary houses that ever did exist, this particular tenement is the most extraordinary. I've got rid of the madman at last—and it's almost time for that vile old mayor to remove me. But where?—I'm lost, bewildered, confused, and actually begin to think I am mad. Half these things I've seen to-day must be visions of fancy—they never could have really happened. No, no, I'm clearly mad!—I've not the least doubt of it now. I've caught it from that horrid Boots. He has inoculated the whole establishment. We're all mad together.— (*Looking off* R. H.) Lights coming upstairs!—Some more lunatics. [*Exit* STRANGE GENTLEMAN *in No.* 23.

Enter R. H. 1*st* E. OVERTON *with a cloak*, MRS. NOAKES, TOM SPARKS *with lantern, and three Waiters with lights. The Waiters range up* R. H. *side.* TOM *is in* R. H. *corner and* MRS. NOAKES *next to him.*

OVERTON. Remain there till I call for your assistance. (*Goes up to No.* 23 *and knocks.*)

Enter STRANGE GENTLEMAN *from No.* 23.

Now, the chaise is ready.—Muffle yourself up in this cloak. (*Puts it on the* STRANGE GENTLEMAN.—*They come forward.*)

STRANGE GENTLEMAN (L. H.). Yes.

OVERTON (C.). Make a little noise when we take you away, you know.

STRANGE GENTLEMAN. Yes—yes.—I say, what a queer room this is of mine. Somebody has been tapping at the wall for the last half hour, like a whole forest of woodpeckers.

OVERTON. Don't you know who that was?

STRANGE GENTLEMAN. No.

OVERTON. The other party.

STRANGE GENTLEMAN (*alarmed*). The other party!

OVERTON. To be sure.—The other party is going with you.

STRANGE GENTLEMAN. Going with me!—In the same chaise!

OVERTON. Of course.—Hush! (*Goes to No.* 22. *Knocks.*)

Enter JULIA DOBBS *from No.* 22, *wrapped up in a large cloak.*

Look here! (*Bringing her forward.* JULIA *is next to* MRS. NOAKES.)

STRANGE GENTLEMAN (*starting into* L. H. CORNER). I won't go—I won't go. This is a plot—a conspiracy. I won't go, I tell you. I shall be assassinated.—I shall be murdered!

FANNY *and* MARY *appear at No.* 20, JOHNSON *and* TOMKINS *at* 24.

JOHN (*at the door*). I told you he was mad.

CHARLES (*at the door*). I see—I see—poor fellow!

JULIA (*crossing to* STRANGE GENTLEMAN *and taking his arm*). Come, dear, come.

MRS. NOAKES. Yes, do go, there's a good soul. Go with your affectionate aunt.

STRANGE GENTLEMAN (*breaking from her*). My affectionate aunt!

JULIA *returns to her former position.*

TOM. He don't deserve no affection. I niver see such an unfectionate fellow to his relations.

STRANGE GENTLEMAN (L. H.). Take that wretch away, and smother him between two feather beds. Take him away, and make a sandwich of him directly.

JULIA (*to* OVERTON, *who is in* C.). What voice was that?—It was not Lord Peter's. (*Throwing off her cloak.*)

OVERTON. Nonsense—nonsense.—Look at him. (*Pulls cloak off* STRANGE GENTLEMAN.)

STRANGE GENTLEMAN (*turning round*). A woman!

JULIA. A stranger!

OVERTON. A stranger! What, an't he your husband that is to—your mad nephew, I mean?

JULIA. No!

ALL. No!

STRANGE GENTLEMAN. No!—no, I'll be damned if I am. I an't anybody's nephew.—My aunt's dead, and I never had an uncle.

MRS. NOAKES. And an't he mad, ma'am?

JULIA. No.

STRANGE GENTLEMAN. Oh, I'm *not* mad.—I was mistaken just now.

OVERTON. And isn't he going away with you?

JULIA. No.

MARY (*coming forward* R. H., *next to* MRS. NOAKES). And isn't his name Tomkins?

STRANGE GENTLEMAN (*very loud*). No!

(*All these questions and answers should be very rapid.* JOHNSON *and* TOMKINS *advance to the ladies, and they all retire up.*)

MRS. NOAKES. What *is* his name? (*Producing a letter.*) It an't Mr. Walker Trott, is it? (*She advances a little towards him.*)

STRANGE GENTLEMAN. Something so remarkably like it, ma'am, that, with your permission, I'll open that epistle. (*Taking letter*).

All go up, but JULIA *and* STRANGE GENTLEMAN.

(*Opening letter.*) Tinkle's hand. (*Reads.*) 'The challenge was a *ruse.* By this time I shall have been united at Gretna Green to the charming Emily Brown.'—Then, through a horror of duels, I have lost a wife!

JULIA (R. H. *with her handkerchief to her eyes*). And through Lord Peters' negligence, I have lost a husband!

STRANGE GENTLEMAN. Eh! (*Regards her a moment, then beckons* OVERTON, *who comes forward*, L. H.) I say, didn't you say something about three thousand a year this morning?

OVERTON. I did.

STRANGE GENTLEMAN. You alluded to that party? (*Nodding towards* JULIA.)

OVERTON. I did.

STRANGE GENTLEMAN. Hem! (*Puts* OVERTON *back.*) Permit me, ma'am (*going to her*), to sympathise most respectfully with your deep distress.

JULIA. Oh, sir! your kindness penetrates to my very heart.

STRANGE GENTLEMAN (*aside*). Penetrates to her heart!—It's taking the right direction.—If I understand your sorrowing murmur, ma'am, you contemplated taking a destined husband away with you, in the chaise at the door?

JULIA. Oh! sir,—spare my feelings—I did.—The horses were ordered and paid for; and everything was ready. (*Weeps.*)

STRANGE GENTLEMAN (*aside*). She weeps.——Expensive thing, posting, ma'am.

JULIA. Very, sir.

STRANGE GENTLEMAN. Eighteen-pence a mile, ma'am, not including the boys.

JULIA. Yes, sir.

STRANGE GENTLEMAN. *You've* lost a husband, ma'am—*I* have lost a wife.—Marriages are made above—I'm quite certain ours is booked.—Pity to have all this expense for nothing—let's go together.

JULIA (*drying her eyes*). The suddenness of this proposal, sir——

STRANGE GENTLEMAN. Requires a sudden answer, ma'am.—You don't say no—you mean yes. Permit me to—(*kisses her*).—All right! Old one (*to* OVERTON, *who comes down* L. H.), I've done it.—Mrs. Noakes (*she comes down* R. H.), don't countermand the chaise.—We're off directly.

CHARLES (*who with* FANNY *comes down* L. H. C.). So are we.

JOHN (*who with* MARY *comes down* R. H. C.). So are we, thanks to a negotiated loan, and an explanation as hasty as the quarrel that gave rise to it.

STRANGE GENTLEMAN. Three post-chaises and four, on to Gretna, directly. [*Exeunt Waiters,* R. H. 1*st* E.
I say—we'll stop here as we come back?

JOHN *and* CHARLES. Certainly.

STRANGE GENTLEMAN. But before I go, as I fear I have given a great deal of trouble here to-night—permit me to inquire whether you will view my mistakes and perils with an indulgent eye, and consent to receive '*The Strange Gentleman*' again to-morrow.

JOHN. JULIA. STRANGE GENTLEMAN.
MARY. FANNY.
MRS. NOAKES. CHARLES.
TOM. OVERTON.
R. H. L. H.

CURTAIN

THE END

SECOND ACT THIRTY MINUTES.

THE VILLAGE COQUETTES

A Comic Opera

IN TWO ACTS

[1836]

DEDICATION

To J. P. HARLEY, ESQ.

MY DEAR SIR,

My dramatic bantlings are no sooner born, than you father them. You have made my 'Strange Gentleman' exclusively your own; you have adopted Martin Stokes with equal readiness; and you still profess your willingness to do the same kind office for all future scions of the same stock.

I dedicate to you the first play I ever published; and you made for me the first play I ever produced:—the balance is in your favour, and I am afraid it will remain so.

That you may long contribute to the amusement of the public, and long be spared to shed a lustre, by the honour and integrity of your private life, on the profession which for many years you have done so much to uphold, is the sincere and earnest wish of, my dear Sir,

Yours most faithfully,

CHARLES DICKENS.

December 15*th*, 1836.

PREFACE

'Either the Honourable Gentleman is in the right, or he is not,' is a phrase in very common use within the walls of Parliament. This drama may have a plot, or it may not; and the songs may be poetry, or they may not; and the whole affair, from beginning to end, may be great nonsense, or it may not, just as the honourable gentleman or lady who reads it may happen to think. So, retaining his own private and particular opinion upon the subject (an opinion which he formed upwards of a year ago, when he wrote the piece), the Author leaves every such gentleman or lady, to form his or hers, as he or she may think proper, without saying one word to influence or conciliate them.

All he wishes to say is this;—That he hopes Mr. Braham, and all the performers who assisted in the representation of this opera, will accept his warmest thanks for the interest they evinced in it, from its very first rehearsal, and for their zealous efforts in his behalf—efforts which have crowned it with a degree of success far exceeding his most sanguine anticipations; and of which no form of words could speak his acknowledgement.

It is needless to add that the *libretto* of an opera must be, to a certain extent, a mere vehicle for the music; and that it is scarcely fair or reasonable to judge it by those strict rules of criticism which would be justly applicable to a five-act tragedy, or a finished comedy.

DRAMATIS PERSONÆ

AT ST. JAMES'S THEATRE, DECEMBER 6, 1836

SQUIRE NORTON	MR. BRAHAM.
THE HON. SPARKINS FLAM (*his friend*) . . .	MR. FORESTER.
OLD BENSON (*a small farmer*)	MR. STRICKLAND.
MR. MARTIN STOKES (*a very small farmer with a very large circle of particular friends*)	MR. HARLEY.
GEORGE EDMUNDS (*betrothed to Lucy*)	MR. BENNETT.
YOUNG BENSON	MR. J. PARRY.
JOHN MADDOX (*attached to Rose*)	MR. GARDNER.
LUCY BENSON	MISS RAINFORTH.
ROSE (*her cousin*)	MISS J. SMITH.

Time occupied in Representation.—Two hours and a half.

PERIOD.—THE AUTUMN OF 1729.

SCENE.—AN ENGLISH VILLAGE.

THE VILLAGE COQUETTES

ACT I

SCENE I.—*A Rick-yard, with a cart laden with corn-sheaves.* JOHN MADDOX, *and labourers, unloading it. Implements of husbandry, etc., lie scattered about. A gate on one side.* JOHN MADDOX *is in the cart, and dismounts at the conclusion of the Chorus.*

Round.

Hail to the merry Autumn days, when yellow cornfields shine,
Far brighter than the costly cup that holds the monarch's wine!
Hail to the merry harvest time, the gayest of the year,
The time of rich and bounteous crops, rejoicing, and good cheer!

'Tis pleasant on a fine Spring morn to see the buds expand,
'Tis pleasant in the Summer time to view the teeming land;
'Tis pleasant on a Winter's night to crouch around the blaze,—
But what are joys like these, my boys, to Autumn's merry days!

Then hail to merry Autumn days, when yellow corn-fields shine,
Far brighter than the costly cup that holds the monarch's wine!
And hail to merry harvest time, the gayest of the year,
The time of rich and bounteous crops, rejoicing, and good cheer!

JOHN. Well done, my lads; a good day's work, and a warm one. Here, Tom (*to Villager*), run into the house, and ask Miss Rose to send out some beer for the men, and a jug for Master Maddox; and d'ye hear, Tom, tell Miss Rose it's a fine evening, and that if she'll step out herself, it'll do her good, and do me good into the bargain. (*Exit Villager.*) That's right, my lads, stow these sheaves away, before the sun goes down. Let's begin fresh in the morning, without any leavings of to-day. By this time to-morrow the last load will have been carried, and then for our Harvest-Home!

VILLAGERS. Hurrah! Hurrah!

(*First four lines of Round repeated.*)

Enter MARTIN STOKES.

MARTIN. Very good! very good, indeed!—always sing while you work—capital custom! I always do when I work, and I never work at all when I can help it;—another capital custom. John, old fellow, how are you?—give us your hand,—hearty squeeze,—good shake,—capital custom number three. Fine dry weather for the harvest, John. Talking of that, I'm dry too: you always give away plenty of beer, here;—capital custom number four. Trouble you for the loan of that can, John.

JOHN (*taking it from the cart*). Here's the can, but as to there being anything good in it it's as dry as the weather, and as empty as you. Hoo! hoo! (*laughing boisterously, is suddenly checked by a look from* MARTIN).

MARTIN. Hallo, John, hallo! I have often told you before, Mr. Maddox, that I don't consider you in a situation of life which entitles you to make jokes, far less to laugh at 'em. If you must make a joke, do it solemnly, and respectfully. If *I* laugh, that's quite enough, and it must be far more gratifying to your feelings than any contortions of that enormous mouth of yours.

JOHN. Well, perhaps, as you say, I oughtn't to make jokes till I arrive, like you, at the dignity of a small piece of ground and a cottage; but I must laugh at a joke, sometimes.

MARTIN. Must, must you!—Rather presuming fellow, this Maddox. (*Aside.*)

JOHN. Why, when you make one of them rum jokes of yours,—'cod, I must laugh then!

MARTIN. Oh! ah! you may laugh then, John; always laugh at my jokes,—capital custom number five; no harm in that, because you can't help it, you know.—Knowing fellow, though. (*Aside.*)

JOHN. Remember that joke about the old cow, as you made five years ago?—'cod, that was a joke! Hoo! hoo! hoo!—I never shall forget that joke. I never see a cow, to this day, without laughing.

MARTIN. Ha! ha! ha! very good, very good!—Devilish clever

fellow this! (*Aside.*) Well, Jack, you behave yourself well, all the evening, and perhaps I may make that joke again before the day's out.

JOHN. Thank 'ee, that's very kind.

MARTIN. Don't mention it, don't mention it; but I say, John I called to speak to you about more important matters.—Something wrong here, an't there? (*Mysteriously.*)

JOHN. Wrong! you're always fancying something wrong.

MARTIN. Fancying,—come, I like that. I say, why don't you keep your harvest-home at home, to-morrow night? Why are we all to go up to the Squire's, as if we couldn't be merry in Benson's barn? And why is the Squire always coming down here, looking after some people, and cutting out other people? —an't that wrong? Where's George Edmunds—old Benson's so fond of, and that Lucy *was* fond of too, once upon a time, —eh? An't that wrong? Where's your sweetheart, Rose?—An't her walkings, and gigglings, and whisperings, and simperings, with the Squire's friend, Mr. Sparkins Flam, the talk of the whole place? Nothing wrong there—eh? (MADDOX *goes up.*) Had him there; I knew there was something wrong. I'll keep a sharp eye upon these doings, for I don't like these new-fangled customs. It was all very well in the old time, to see the Squire's father come riding among the people on his bay cob, nodding to the common folks, shaking hands with me, and all that sort of thing; but when you change the old country-gentleman into a dashing fop from London, and the steady old steward into Mr. Sparkins Flam, the case is very different. We shall see,—but if I might tell Miss Lucy Benson a bit of my mind, I should say, 'Stick to an independent young fellow, like George Edmunds, and depend upon it you will be happier than you would with all the show and glitter of a squire's lady.' And I should say to Rose, very solemn, 'Rose——'

ROSE *enters unperceived, with beer.*

'Rose——'

ROSE (*starting*). Lord bless us! What a hollow voice!—Why, it's Mr. Stokes!—What on earth is the matter with him?

MARTIN (*not seeing her*). Rose,—if you would be happy and contented, if you would escape destruction, shield yourself from dangerous peril, and save yourself from horrid ruin!—

ROSE. What dreadful words!—

MARTIN. You will at once, and without delay, bestow your hand on John Maddox; or if you would aspire to a higher rank in life, and a loftier station in society, you will cultivate the affections of Mr. Stokes,—Mr. Martin Stokes,—a young gentleman of great mental attractions, and very considerable personal charms; leaving the false and fatal Flam to the ignominious fate which——

ROSE. Why, Mr. Stokes.—

MARTIN. Ignominious fate which——

ROSE. Dear, he must be in a fit! Mr. Stokes!

MARTIN. Eh?—Ah! Miss Rose,—It's you, is it?

ROSE. Me! Yes, and here have I been waiting all this time, while you were talking nonsense to yourself. Here, I have brought you some beer.

MARTIN. Oh! Miss Rose, if you go on in this way, you'll bring us to our bier, instead of bringing our beer to us. (*Looking round.*) You may laugh, if you want to, very much, John.

JOHN. Hoo! hoo! hoo!

ROSE. Be quiet, oaf! And pray, sir (*to* MARTIN), to what may your most humorous observation refer?

MARTIN. Why, my dear Miss Rose, you know my way,—always friendly,—always thinking of the welfare of those I like best, and very seldom receiving any gratitude in return.

ROSE. I know you very seldom deserve any.

MARTIN. Ah! that's exactly my meaning; that's the way, you see. The moment I begin to throw out a hint to one of my dear friends, out comes some unkind and rude remark. But I bear it all for their sakes. I won't allow you to raise my ill nature,—you shan't stop me. I was going to say,—don't you think—now *don't* you think—that you—don't be angry—make rather—don't colour up,—*rather* too free with Mr. Sparkins Flam?

ROSE. *I* make free with Mr. Sparkins Flam! Why you odious, insolent creature!

MARTIN. Ah, of course—always the way—I told you so—I knew you'd say that.

ROSE. And you, John, you mean-spirited scarecrow; will you stand there, and see me insulted by an officious, impertinent——

MARTIN. Go on, go on! (*A gun fired.*) Hallo! (*Looking off.*) Here they are, the Squire and Mr. Sparkins Flam.

ROSE (*hastily adjusting her dress*). My goodness! Mr. Spar—— run, John, run, there's a dear!

JOHN (*not moving*). Very dear, I dare say.

ROSE. Run, and tell my uncle and Lucy, that Mr. Spar——I mean that the Squire's coming.

JOHN. I wouldn't ha' gone anyhow; but nobody need go now, for here they are. Now, I'm extinguished for the rest of the day.

Enter through the gate SQUIRE NORTON *and* MR. SPARKINS FLAM, *dressed for sporting, with guns, etc., and two Gamekeepers. On the other side, Old* BENSON *and* LUCY. MARTIN, *during the whole scene, thrusts himself in the* SQUIRE'S *way, to be taken notice of.*

SQUIRE (*to Gamekeeper, and putting down his gun*). Take the birds into the house. Benson, we have had a good day's sport, but a tiring one; and as the load is heavy for my fellows, you'll let our game remain where it is. I could not offer it to a better friend.

BENSON. Your honour's very good, but——

SQUIRE. Nay, you make a merit of receiving the smallest favour.

BENSON. Not a merit of receiving, nor a boast of refusing it; but a man in humble station should be cautious how he receives favours from those above him, which he never asks, and can never return. I have had too many such favours forced upon me by your honour, lately, and would rather not increase the number.

SQUIRE. But such a trifle——

BENSON. A trifle from an equal, but a condescension from a superior. Let your men carry your birds up to the Hall, sir, or, if they are tired, mine shall do it for them, and welcome. (*Retires up.*)

FLAM (*aside*). Swine and independence! Leather breeches and liberty!

SQUIRE. At least I may be permitted to leave a few brace, as a present to the ladies. Lucy, I hope, will not object. (*Crosses to her.*)

LUCY. I feel much flattered by your honour's politeness—and—and—and——

ROSE. My cousin means to say, sir, that we're very much obliged to your honour and Mr. Flam for your politeness, and that we are very willing to accept of anything, your honour.

FLAM (*aside*). Condescending little savage.

SQUIRE. You have spoken well, both for yourself and your cousin Flam, this is Rose—the pretty little Rose, you know.

FLAM. Know! can I ever forget the charming Rose—the beautiful—the—the—(*aside*) the Cabbage Rose!

SQUIRE (*aside*). Keep that girl engaged, while I talk to the other one.

ROSE. Oh, Mr. Flam!

FLAM. Oh, Miss Rose! (*He salutes her.*)

BENSON. Your honour will not object to taste our ale, after your day's sport. The afternoon is fresh and cool, and 'twill be pleasant here in the air. Here, Ben, Thomas, bring mugs here —quick—quick—and a seat for his honour.

[*Exeunt* BENSON, MADDOX, *etc.*

SQUIRE. It will be delightful—won't it, Flam?

FLAM. Inexpressibly charming! (*Aside.*) An amateur tea-garden. (*He retires a little up with* ROSE—*she coquetting.*)

SQUIRE (*to* LUCY). And in such society, how much the pleasure will be enhanced!

LUCY. Your honour knows I ought not to listen to you—George Edmunds would——

SQUIRE. Edmunds! a rustic!—you cannot love that Edmunds, Lucy. Forget him—remember your own worth.

LUCY. I wish I could, sir. My heart will tell me though, weak and silly as I am, that I cannot better show the consciousness of my own worth, than by remaining true to my first and early love. Your honour rouses my foolish pride; but real true love is not to be forgotten easily.

Song.—LUCY.

Love is not a feeling to pass away,
Like the balmy breath of a summer day;
It is not—it cannot be—laid aside;
It is not a thing to forget or hide.
It clings to the heart, ah, woe is me!
As the ivy clings to the old oak tree.

Love is not a passion of earthly mould,
As a thirst for honour, or fame, or gold:
For when all these wishes have died away,
The deep strong love of a brighter day,
Though nourish'd in secret, consumes the more,
As the slow rust eats to the iron's core.

Re-enter OLD BENSON, JOHN MADDOX, *and Villagers, with jugs, seats, etc.*; SQUIRE NORTON *seats himself next* LUCY, *and* ROSE *contrives to sit next* MR. SPARKINS FLAM, *which* MARTIN *and* MADDOX *in vain endeavour to prevent.*

SQUIRE. Flam, you know these honest people? all tenants of my own.

FLAM. Oh, yes, I know 'em—pleasant fellows! This—this is—what's his name?

BENSON. Martin, sir,—Martin Stokes.

MARTIN (*starting forward*). A—a—*Mr.* Stokes, at your service, sir,—how do you do, sir? (*shaking* FLAM *by the hand, while speaking*). I hope you are quite well, sir; I am delighted to see you looking so well, sir. I hope your majestic father, and your fashionable mother, are in the enjoyment of good health, sir. I should have spoken to you before, sir, only you have been so very much engaged, that I couldn't succeed in catching your honourable eye;—very happy to see you, sir.

FLAM. Ah. Pleasant fellow, this Martin!—agreeable manners,—no reserve about him.

MARTIN. Sir, you do me a great deal of honour. Mr. Norton, sir, I have the honour of drinking your remarkably good health,—I admire you, sir.

SQUIRE (*laughing*). Sir, I feel highly gratified, I'm sure.

MARTIN (*aside*). He's gratified!—I flatter myself I have produced a slight impression here. (*Drinks.*)

FLAM (*turns round, sees* MADDOX). Ah, Ox!

JOHN. *Ox!* Who do you call Ox? Maddox is my name.

FLAM. Oh, mad Ox! true; I forgot the lunacy:—your health, mad Ox.

SQUIRE (*rising and coming forward*). Come, Flam, another glass. Here, friends, is success to our Harvest-Home!

MARTIN. Hear, hear! a most appropriate toast, most eloquently given,—a charming sentiment, delightfully expressed. Gentleman (*to Villagers*), allow me to have the pleasure of proposing Mr. Norton, if you please. Take your time from me. (*He gives the time, and they all cheer.*) Mr. Norton, sir, I beg to call upon you for a song.

Song.—SQUIRE NORTON.

That very wise head, old Æsop, said,
  The bow should be sometimes loose;
Keep it tight for ever, the string you sever:—
  Let's turn his old moral to use.
The world forget, and let us yet,
  The glass our spirits buoying,
Revel to-night in those moments bright
  Which make life worth enjoying.
The cares of the day, old moralists say,
  Are quite enough to perplex one;
Then drive to-day's sorrow away till to-morrow,
  And then put it off till the next one.
    Chorus.—The cares of the day, etc.

Some plodding old crones, the heartless drones!
  Appeal to my cool reflection,
And ask me whether such nights can ever
  Charm sober recollection.
Yes, yes! I cry, I'll grieve and die,
  When those I love forsake me;
But while friends so dear surround me here,
  Let Care. if he can, o'ertake me.
    Chorus.—The cares of the day, etc.

(*During the Chorus,* SQUIRE NORTON *and* FLAM *resume their guns, and go up the stage, followed by the various characters. The Chorus concludes as the Scene closes.*)

SCENE II.—*An open spot near the village, with stile and pathway leading to the church, which is seen in the distance.*

GEORGE EDMUNDS *enters, with a stick in his hand.*

EDMUNDS. How thickly the fallen leaves lie scattered at the feet of that old row of elm-trees! When I first met Lucy on this spot, it was a fine spring day, and those same leaves were trembling in the sunshine, as green and bright as if their beauty would last for ever. What a contrast they present now, and how true an emblem of my own lost happiness!

Song.—GEORGE EDMUNDS.

Autumn leaves, autumn leaves, lie strewn around me here;
Autumn leaves, autumn leaves, how sad, how cold, how drear!
How like the hopes of childhood's day,
Thick clustering on the bough!
How like those hopes is their decay,—
How faded are they now!
Autumn leaves, autumn leaves, lie strewn around me here;
Autumn leaves, autumn leaves, how sad, how cold, how drear!

Wither'd leaves, wither'd leaves, that fly before the gale;
Wither'd leaves, wither'd leaves, ye tell a mournful tale,
Of love once true, and friends once kind,
And happy moments fled:
Dispersed by every breath of wind,
Forgotten, changed, or dead!
Autumn leaves, autumn leaves, lie strewn around me here;
Autumn leaves, autumn leaves, how sad, how cold, how drear!

An hour past the old time, and still no Lucy! 'Tis useless lingering here: I'll wait no longer. A female crossing the meadow!—'Tis Rose, the bearer of a letter or a message perhaps.

Enter ROSE. (*She avoids him.*)

No! Then I will see Lucy at once, without a moment's delay. (*Going.*)

ROSE. No, no, you can't. (*Aside.*) There'll certainly be bloodshed! I am quite certain Mr. Flam will kill him. He offered me, with the most insinuating speeches, to cut John's throat at a moment's notice: and when the Squire complimented him on being a good shot, he said he should like to 'bag' the whole male population of the village. (*To him.*) You can't see her.

EDMUNDS. Not see her, and she at home! Were you instructed to say this, Rose?

ROSE. I say it, because I know you can't see her. She is not well; and—and——

EDMUNDS. And Mr. Norton is there, you would say.

ROSE. Mr. Norton!

EDMUNDS. Yes, Mr. Norton. Was he not there last evening? Was he not there the evening before? Is he not there at this moment?

Enter JOHN MADDOX.

JOHN. There at this moment?—of course he is.

ROSE (*aside*). John here!

JOHN. Of course he is; of course he was there last night; and of course he was there the evening before. He's always there, and so is his bosom friend and confidential demon, Mr. Sparkins Flam. Oh! George, we're injured men, both of us.

EDMUNDS. Heartless girl! (*Retires up.*)

JOHN (*to* ROSE). Faithless person!

ROSE. Don't call me a person.

JOHN. You *are* a person, perjured, treacherous and deceiving! Oh! George, if you had seen what I have seen to-day. Soft whisperings and loving smiles, gentle looks and encouraging sighs,—such looks and sighs as used once upon a time to be bestowed on us. George! If you had seen the Squire making up to Lucy, and Rose making up to Flam:—but I am very glad you did not see it, George, very. It would have broken your heart, as it has broken mine! Oh, Rose! could you break my heart?

ROSE. I could break your head with the greatest pleasure, you mischief-making booby; and if you don't make haste to whereever you're going, somebody that I know of will certainly do so, very quickly.

JOHN. Will he, will he?—your friend, Mr. Flam, I suppose! Let him—that's all; let him! (*Retires up.*)

ROSE. Oh! I'll let him: you needn't be afraid of my interfering. Dear, dear, I wish Mr. Flam would come, for I will own, notwithstanding what graver people may say, that I enjoy a little flirtation as much as any one.

Song.—ROSE.

Some folks who have grown old and sour,
Say love does nothing but annoy.
The fact is, they have had their hour,
So envy what they can't enjoy.
I like the glance—I like the sigh—
That does of ardent passion tell!

If some folks were as young as I,
I'm sure they'd like it quite as well.
Old maiden aunts so hate the men,
So well know how wives are harried,
It makes them sad—not jealous—when
They see their poor dear nieces married.
All men are fair and false, they know,
And with deep sighs they assail 'em,
It's so long since they tried men, though,
I rather think their memories fail 'em.

—Here comes Mr. Flam. You'd better go, John. I know you'll be murdered.

JOHN. Here I shall stop; let him touch me, and he shall feel the weight of my indignation.

Enter FLAM.

FLAM. Ah, my charmer! Punctual to my time, you see, my sweet little Damask Rose!

JOHN (*coming down*). A great deal more like a monthly one,—constantly changing, and gone the moment you wear it.

ROSE. Impertinent creature!

FLAM. Who is this poetical cauliflower?

JOHN. Don't pretend not to know me. You know who I am, well enough.

FLAM. As I live, it's the Ox!—retire, Ox, to your pasture, and don't rudely disturb the cooing of the doves. Go and graze, Ox!

JOHN. Suppose I choose to remain here, what then?

FLAM. Why then you must be driven off, mad Ox. (*To* ROSE.) Who is that other grasshopper?

ROSE. Hush, hush! for Heaven's sake don't let him hear you! It's young Edmunds.

FLAM. Young Edmunds? And who the devil is young Edmunds? For beyond the natural inference that young Edmunds is the son of old Edmunds, curse me if the fame of young Edmunds has ever reached my ears.

ROSE (*in a low tone*). It's Lucy's former lover, whom she has given up for the squire.

FLAM. The rejected cultivator?

ROSE. The same.

FLAM. Ah! I guessed as much from his earthy appearance. But, my darling Rose, I must speak with you,—I must—(*putting his arm round her waist, sees* John). Good-bye, Ox!

John. Good-bye!

Flam. Pleasant walk to you, Ox!

John (*not moving*). Thank'ee;—same to you!

Flam. That other clodpole must not stay here either.

Rose. Yes, yes! he neither sees nor hears us. Pray let him remain.

Flam (*to* John). You understand, Ox, that it is my wish that you forthwith retire and graze,—or in other words, that you at once, and without delay, betake yourself to the farm, or the devil, or any other place where you are in your element, and won't be in the way.

John. Oh yes, I understand that.

Flam. Very well; then the sooner you create a scarcity of such animals in this market, the better. Now, my dear Rose (*puts his arm round her waist again*). Are you gone, Ox?

John. No.

Flam. Are you going?

John. By no means.

Flam. This insolence is not to be borne.

Rose. Oh, pray don't hurt him,—pray don't. Go away, you stupid creature, if you don't want to be ruined.

John. That's just the very advice I would give you, Rose; do *you* go away, if you don't want to be ruined. As for me, this is a public place, and here I'll remain just as long as I think proper.

Flam (*quitting* Rose, *and advancing towards him*). You will?

John. I will.

Rose. Oh, dear, dear! I knew he'd be murdered all along. I was quite certain of it.

John. Don't frown and scowl at me,—it won't do,—it only makes me smile; and when you talk of insolence and put my blood up, I tell you at once, that I am not to be bullied.

Flam. Bullied?

John. Ay, bullied was the word,—bullied by a coward, if you like that better.

Flam. Coward! (*Seizes his gun by the barrel, and aims a blow at him, with the butt-end*; Edmunds *rushes forward, and strikes it up with his stick.*)

Edmunds. Hold your hand, sir,—hold your hand, or I'll fell you to the ground. Maddox, leave this place directly: take the opposite path, and I'll follow you. (*Exit* MADDOX.) As for you, sir, who by the way of vindicating yourself from the charge of cowardice, raise your gun against an unarmed man, tell your protector, the Squire, from me, that he and his companions might content themselves with turning the heads of our farmers' daughters, and endeavouring to corrupt their hearts, without wantonly insulting the men they have most injured. Let this be a lesson to you, sir,—although you were armed, you would have had the worst of a scuffle, and you may not have the benefit of a third person's interference at so critical a moment, another time;—remember this warning, sir, and benefit by it. [*Exit.*

FLAM (*aside*). If Norton does not take a dear revenge for this insult, I have lost my influence with him. Bully! coward! They shall rue it.

ROSE (*with her apron to her eyes*). Oh, Mr. Flam! I can't bear to think that you should have suffered all this, on my account.

FLAM (*aside*). On her account!—a little vanity! (*To her.*) Suffered! Why, my dear, it was the drollest and most humorous affair that ever happened. Here stand I,—the Honourable Sparkins Flam,—on this second day of September, one thousand seven hundred and twenty-nine; and positively and solemnly declare that all the coffee-houses, play-houses, faro-tables, brag-tables, assemblies, drums and routs of a whole season put together, could not furnish such a splendid piece of exquisite drollery. The idea is admirable. My affecting to quarrel with a ploughman, and submitting to be lectured by another caterpillar, whom I suffer to burst into a butterfly importance!

ROSE. Then you were not really quarrelling?

FLAM. Bless you, no! I was only acting.

ROSE. Lor'! how well you do act, to be sure.

FLAM. Come, let us retire into the house, or after this joke we shall be the gaze of all the animated potatoes that are planted in this hole of a village. Why do you hesitate, Damask?

ROSE. Why, I have just been thinking that if you go to all these coffee-houses, and play-houses, and fairs, and brags, and keep playing drums, and routing people about, you'll forget me, when you go back to London.

FLAM (*aside*). More than probable. (*To her.*) Never fear; you will be generally known as Rose the lovely, and I shall be universally denominated Flam the constant.

Duet.—ROSE *and* SPARKINS FLAM.

FLAM. 'Tis true I'm caress'd by the witty,
The envy of all the fine beaux,
The pet of the court and the city,
But still I'm the lover of Rose.

ROSE. Country sweethearts, oh, how I despise!
And oh! how delighted I am
To think that I shine in the eyes
Of the elegant—sweet—Mr. Flam.

FLAM. Allow me (*offers to kiss her*).
ROSE. Pray don't be so bold, sir. (*Kisses her.*)
FLAM. What sweets on that honey'd lip hang!
ROSE. Your presumption, I know, I should scold, sir,
But I really *can't* scold Mr. Flam.

BOTH. Then let us be happy together,
Content with the world as it goes,
An unchangeable couple for ever,
Mr. Flam and his beautiful Rose. [*Exeunt.*

SCENE III.—*The Farmer's Kitchen. A table and chairs.*

Enter OLD BENSON *and* MARTIN.

BENSON. Well, Stokes. Now you have the opportunity you have desired, and we are alone, I am ready to listen to the information which you wished to communicate to my private ear.
MARTIN. Exactly;—you said information, I think?
BENSON. *You* said information, or I have forgotten.
MARTIN. Just so, exactly; I said information. I *did* say information, why should I deny it?
BENSON. I see no necessity for your doing so, certainly. Pray go on.
MARTIN. Why, you see, my dear Mr. Benson, the fact is—won't you be seated? Pray sit down (*brings forward two chairs;—they sit*). There, now,—let me see,—where was I?

BENSON. You were going to begin, I think.

MARTIN. Oh,—ah!—so I was;—I hadn't begun, had I?

BENSON. No, no! Pray begin again, if you had.

MARTIN. Well, then, what I have got to say it not so much information, as a kind of advice, or suggestion, or hint, or something of that kind; and it relates to—eh?—(*looking very mysterious*).

BENSON. What?

MARTIN. Yes (*nodding*). Don't you think there's something wrong there?

BENSON. Where?

MARTIN. In that quarter.

BENSON. In what quarter? Speak more plainly, sir.

MARTIN. You know what a friendly feeling I entertain to your family. You know what a very particular friend of mine you are. You know how anxious I always am to prevent anything going wrong.

BENSON. Well! (*abruptly*).

MARTIN. Yes, I see you're very sensible of it, but I'll take it for granted: you needn't bounce and fizz about, in that way, because it makes one nervous. Don't you think, now, *don't* you think, that ill-natured people may say;—don't be angry, you know, because if I wasn't a very particular friend of the family, I wouldn't mention the subject on any account;—don't you think that ill-natured people may say there's something wrong in the frequency of the Squire's visits here?

BENSON (*starting up furiously*). What!

MARTIN (*aside*). Here he goes again!

BENSON. Who dares suspect my child?

MARTIN. Ah, to be sure, that's exactly what I say. Who dares? Damme, I should like to see 'em!

BENSON. Is it you?

MARTIN. I! Bless you, no, not for the world! I!—Come, that's a good one. I only say what other people say, you know; that's all.

BENSON. And what are these tales, that idle busy fools prate of with delight, among themselves, caring not whose ears they reach, so long as they are kept from the old man, whose blindness—the blindness of a fond and doting father—is subject for their rude and brutal jeering. What are they?

MARTIN. Dear me, Mr. Benson, you keep me in a state of perpetual excitement.

BENSON. Tell me, without equivocation, what do they say?

MARTIN. Why, they say they think it—not exactly wrong, perhaps; don't fly out, now—but among those remarkable coincidences which do occur sometimes, that whenever you go out of your house, the Squire and his friend should come into it; that Miss Lucy and Miss Rose, in the long walks they take every day, should be met and walked home with by the same gentlemen; that long after you have gone to bed at night, the Squire and Mr. Sparkins Flam should still be seen hovering about the lane and meadow; and that one of the lattice windows should be always open, at that hour.

BENSON. This is all?

MARTIN. Ye—yes,—yes, that's all.

BENSON. Nothing beside?

MARTIN. Eh?

BENSON. Nothing beside?

MARTIN. Why, there *is* something else, but I know you'll begin to bounce about again, if I tell it you.

BENSON. No, no! let me hear it all.

MARTIN. Why, then, they do say that the Squire has been heard to boast that he had practised on Lucy's mind—that when he bid her, she would leave her father and her home, and follow him over the world.

BENSON. They lie! Her breast is pure and innocent! Her soul is free from guilt; her mind from blemish. They lie! I'll not believe it. Are they mad? Do they think that I stand tamely by, and look upon my child's disgrace? Heaven! do they know of what a father's heart is made?

MARTIN. My dear Mr. Benson, if you——

BENSON. This coarse and brutal boast shall be disowned. (*Going*; MARTIN *stops him.*)

MARTIN. My dear Mr. Benson, you know it may not have been made after all,—my dear sir,—

BENSON (*struggling*). Unhand me, Martin! Made or not made, it has gone abroad, fixing an infamous notoriety on me and mine. I'll hear its truth or falsehood from himself. (*Breaks from him and exit.*)

MARTIN (*solus*). There'll be something decidedly wrong here presently. Hallo! here's another very particular friend in a fume.

Enter YOUNG BENSON *hastily.*

MARTIN. Ah! my dear fellow, how——

YOUNG BENSON. Where is Lucy?

MARTIN. I don't know, unless she has walked out with the Squire

YOUNG BENSON. The Squire!

MARTIN. To be sure; she very often walks out with the Squire. Very pleasant recreation walking out with the Squire;—capital custom, an't it?

YOUNG BENSON. Where's my father?

MARTIN. Why, upon my word, I am unable to satisfy your curiosity in that particular either. All I know of him is that he whisked out of this room in a rather boisterous and turbulent manner for an individual at his time of life, some few seconds before you whisked in. But what's the matter?—you seem excited. Nothing wrong, is there?

YOUNG BENSON (*aside*). This treatment of Edmunds, and Lucy's altered behaviour to him, confirm my worst fears. Where is Mr. Norton?

MARTIN (*calling off*). Ah! to be sure,—where is Mr. Norton?

Enter SQUIRE.

SQUIRE. Mr. Norton is here. Who wishes to see him?

MARTIN. To be sure, sir. Mr. Norton is here: who wishes to see him?

YOUNG BENSON. I do.

MARTIN. I don't. Old fellow, good-bye! Mr. Norton, good evening! (*Aside.*) There'll be something wrong here, in a minute. [*Exit.*

SQUIRE. Well, young man?

YOUNG BENSON. If you contemplate treachery here, Mr. Norton, look to yourself. My father is an old man; the chief prop of his declining years is his child,—my sister. For your actions here, sir, you shall render a dear account to me.

SQUIRE. To *you*, peasant!

YOUNG BENSON. To me, sir. One other scene like that enacted by your creature, at your command, to-night, may terminate more seriously to him. For your behaviour here you are responsible to me.

SQUIRE. Indeed! Anything more, sir?

YOUNG BENSON. Simply this:—after injuring the old man beyond reparation, and embittering the last moments of his life, you may possibly attempt to shield yourself under the paltry excuse, that, as a gentleman, you cannot descend to take the consequences from my hand. You *shall t*ake them from me, sir, if I strike you to the earth first. [*Exit.*

SQUIRE. Fiery and valorous, indeed! As the suspicions of the family are aroused, no time is to be lost: the girl must be carried off to-night, if possible. With Flam's assistance and management, she may be speedily removed from within the reach of these rustic sparks. In my cooler moments, the reflection of the misery I may inflict upon the old man makes my conduct appear base and dishonourable, even to myself. Pshaw! hundreds have done the same thing before me, who have been lauded and blazoned forth as men of honour. Honour in such cases,—an idle tale!—a by-word! Honour! There is much to be gleaned from old tales; and the legend of the child and the old man speaks but too truly.

Song.—SQUIRE NORTON.

The child and the old man sat alone
  In the quiet peaceful shade
Of the old green boughs, that had richly grown
  In the deep thick forest glade.
It was a soft and pleasant sound,
  That rustling of the oak;
And the gentle breeze play'd lightly round,
  As thus the fair boy spoke:—

'Dear father, what can honour be,
  Of which I hear men rave?
Field, cell and cloister, land and sea,
  The tempest and the grave:—
It lives in all, 'tis sought in each,
  'Tis never heard or seen:
Now tell me, father, I beseech,
  What can this honour mean?'

'It is a name,—a name, my child,—
  It lived in other days,

When men were rude, their passions wild,
  Their sport, thick battle-frays.
When in armour bright, the warrior bold,
  Knelt to his lady's eyes:
Beneath the abbey-pavement old
  That warrior's dust now lies.

'The iron hearts of that old day
  Have moulder'd in the grave;
And chivalry has pass'd away,
  With knights so true and brave;
The honour, which to them was life,
  Throbs in no bosom now;
It only gilds the gambler's strife,
  Or decks the worthless vow.'

Enter Lucy.

Squire. Lucy, dear Lucy.

Lucy. Let me entreat you not to stay here, sir! you will be exposed to nothing but insult and attack. Edmunds and my brother have both returned, irritated at something that has passed with my cousin Rose:—for my sake,—for my sake, Mr. Norton, spare me the pain of witnessing what will ensue, if they find you here. You little know what I have borne already.

Squire. For your sake, Lucy. I would do much; but why should I leave you to encounter the passion and ill-will, from which you would have me fly?

Lucy. Oh, I can bear it, sir; I deserve it but too well.

Squire. Deserve it!—you do yourself an injustice, Lucy. No; rather let me remove you from a house where you will suffer nothing but persecution, and confer upon you a title which the proudest lady in the land might wear. Here—here, on my knees (*he bends on his knee, and seizes her hand*).

Enter Flam.

Squire (*rising*). Flam here!

Flam (*aside*). Upon my word!—I thought we had been getting on pretty well in the open air, but they're beating us hollow here, under cover.

SQUIRE. Lucy, but one word, and I understand your decision.

LUCY. I—I cannot subdue the feelings of uneasiness and distrust which the great difference between your honour's rank and mine awakens in my mind.

SQUIRE. Difference! Hundreds of such cases happen every day.

LUCY. Indeed!

SQUIRE. Oh, 'tis a matter of general notoriety,—isn't it, Flam?

FLAM. No doubt of it. (*Aside.*) Don't exactly know yet what they are talking about, though.

SQUIRE. A relation of my own, a man of exalted rank, courted a girl far his inferior in station, but only beneath him in that respect. In all others she was on a footing of equality with himself, if not far above him.

LUCY. And were they married?

FLAM (*aside*). Rather an important circumstance in the case. I *do* remember that.

SQUIRE. They were,—after a time, when the resentment of his friends, occasioned by his forming such an attachment, had subsided, and he was able to acknowledge her, without involving the ruin of both.

LUCY. They were married privately at first, then?

FLAM (*aside*). I must put in a word here. Oh, yes, it was all comfortably arranged to everybody's satisfaction,—wasn't it, Norton?

SQUIRE. Certainly. And a happy couple they were, weren't they, Flam?

FLAM. Happiest of the happy. As happy as (*aside*)—a separation could make them.

SQUIRE. Hundreds of great people have formed similar attachments,—haven't they, Flam?

FLAM. Undoubtedly. There was the Right Honourable Augustus Frederick Charles Thomson Camharado, and the German Baron Hyfenstyfenlooberhausen, and they were both married —(*aside*) to somebody else, first. Not to mention Damask and I, who are models of constancy. By the bye, I have lost sight of her, and I am interrupting you. (*Aside to* SQUIRE, *as he goes out.*) I came to tell you that she is ripe for an elopement, if you urge her strongly. Edmunds has been reproaching her to my knowledge. She'll consent while her passion lasts. [*Exit.*

SQUIRE. Lucy, I wait your answer. One word from you, and a

few hours will place you far beyond the reach of those who would fetter your choice and control your inclinations. You hesitate. Come, decide. The Squire's lady, or the wife of Edmunds!

Duet.—LUCY *and* SQUIRE NORTON.

SQUIRE. In rich and lofty station shine,
Before his jealous eyes:
In golden splendour, lady mine,
This peasant youth despise.

LUCY (*apart: the* SQUIRE *regarding her attentively*).
Oh! it would be revenge indeed
With scorn his glance to meet.
I, I, his humble pleading heed!
I'd spurn him from my feet.

SQUIRE. With love and rage her bosom's torn,
And rash the choice will be;
LUCY. With love and rage my bosom's torn,
And rash the choice will be.

SQUIRE. From hence she quickly must be borne,
Her home, her home, she'll flee.
LUCY. Oh! long shall I have cause to mourn
My home, my home, for thee!

Enter OLD BENSON.

BENSON. What do I see! The Squire and Lucy.

SQUIRE. Listen. A chaise and four fleet horses, under the direction of a trusty friend of mine, will be in waiting on the high road, at the corner of the Elm-Tree avenue, to-night, at ten o'clock. They shall bear you whither we can be safe, and in secret, by the first light of morning.

LUCY. His cruel harshness;—it would be revenge, indeed. But my father—my poor old father!

SQUIRE. Your father is prejudiced in Edmunds' favour; and so long as he thinks there is any chance of your being his, he will oppose your holding communication with me. Situated as you are now, you only stand in the way of his wealth and advancement. Once fly with me, and in four-and-twenty hours you will be his pride, his boast, his support.

OLD BENSON *coming forward.*

BENSON. It is a lie, a base lie!—(LUCY *shrieks and throws herself at his feet.*) My pride! my boast! She would be my disgrace, my shame: an outcast from her father's roof, and from the world. Support!—support *me* with the gold coined in her infamy and guilt! Heaven help me! Have I cherished her for this!

LUCY (*clinging to him*). Father!—dear, dear father!

SQUIRE. Hear me speak, Benson. Be calm.

BENSON. Calm!—Do you know that from infancy I have almost worshipped her, fancying that I saw in her young mind the virtues of a mother, to whom the anguish of this one hour would have been worse than death! Calm!—do you know that I have a heart and soul within me; or do you believe that because I am of lower station, I am a being of a different order from yourself, and that Nature has denied me thought and feeling! Calm! Man, do you know that I am this girl's father?

SQUIRE. Benson, if you will not hear me, at least do not, by hastily exposing this matter, deprive me of the inclination of making you some reparation.

BENSON. Reparation! You need be thankful, sir, for the grasp she has upon my arm. Money! If she were dying for want, and the smallest coin from you could restore her to life and health, sooner than she should take it from your hand, I would cast her from a sick bed to perish on the road-side.

SQUIRE. Benson, a word.

BENSON. Do not, I caution you; do not talk to me, sir. I am an old man, but I do not know what passion may make me do.

SQUIRE. These are high words, Benson. A farmer!

BENSON. Yes, sir; a farmer, one of the men on whom you, and such as you, depend for the money they squander in profligacy and idleness. A farmer, sir! I care not for your long pedigree of ancestors,—my forefathers made them all. Here, neighbours, friends! (ROSE, MADDOX, STOKES, *Villagers, etc., crowd on the stage.*) Hear this, hear this! your landlord, a high-born gentleman, entering the houses of your humble farmers, and tempting their daughters to destruction!

Enter YOUNG BENSON *and* GEORGE EDMUNDS.

YOUNG BENSON. What's that I hear? (*rushing towards the* SQUIRE, STOKES *interposes*).

MARTIN. Hallo, hallo! Take hold of the other one, John. (MADDOX *and he remove them to opposite sides of the stage.*) Hold him tight, John, hold him tight. Stand still, there's a good fellow. Keep back, Squire. Knew there'd be something wrong,—ready to come in at the nick of time,—capital custom.

FLAM *enters and stands next the* SQUIRE.

SQUIRE. Exposed, baited! Benson, are you mad? Within the last few hours my friend here has been attacked and insulted on the very land you hold, by a person in your employ and young Edmunds there. I, too, have been threatened and insulted in the presence of my tenantry and workmen. Take care you do not drive me to extremities. Remember—the lease of this farm for seventy years, which your father took of mine, expires to-morrow; and that I have the power to refuse its renewal. Again I ask you, are you mad?

BENSON. Quit my house, villain!

SQUIRE. Villain! quit *my* house, then. This farm is mine: and you and yours shall depart from under its roof, before the sun has set to-morrow. (BENSON *sinks into a chair in centre, and covers his face with his hands.*)

Sestet and Chorus.

LUCY—ROSE—EDMUNDS—SQUIRE NORTON—FLAM—
YOUNG BENSON—*and Chorus.*

YOUNG BENSON. Turn him from the farm! From his home will you cast
The old man who has till'd it for years?
Every tree, every flower, is link'd with the past,
And a friend of his childhood appears.
Turn *him* from the farm! O'er its grassy hill-side,
A gay boy he once loved to range;
His boyhood has fled, and its dear friends are dead,
But these meadows have never known change.

EDMUNDS. Oppressor, hear me.

LUCY. On my knees I implore.

SQUIRE. I command it, and you will obey.
ROSE. Rise, dear Lucy, rise; you shall not kneel before
The tyrant who drives us away.
SQUIRE. Your sorrows are useless, your prayers are in vain;
I command it and you will begone.
I'll hear no more.
EDMUNDS. No, they shall not beg again,
Of a man whom I view with deep scorn.
FLAM. Do not yield.
YOUNG BENSON.
SQUIRE
LUCY.
ROSE.
} Leave the farm!
EDMUNDS. Your power I despise.
SQUIRE. And your threats, boy, I disregard, too.
FLAM. Do not yield.
YOUNG BENSON.
SQUIRE.
LUCY.
ROSE.
} Leave the farm!
ROSE. If he leaves it, he dies.
EDMUNDS. This base act, proud man, you shall rue.
YOUNG BENSON Turn him from the farm! From his home will you cast
The old man who has till'd it for years?
Every tree, every flower, is link'd with the past,
And a friend of his childhood appears.
SQUIRE. Yes, yes, leave the farm! From his home I will cast
The old man who has till'd it for years;
Though each tree and flower is link'd with the past,
And a friend of his childhood appears.

Chorus.

He has turn'd from his farm, from his home he has cast
The old man who has till'd it for years;
Though each tree and flower is link'd with the past,
And a friend of his childhood appears.

END OF THE FIRST ACT

ACT II

SCENE I.—*An Apartment in the Hall. A breakfast-table, with urn and tea-service. A Livery Servant arranging it.* FLAM, *in a morning gown and slippers, reclining on the sofa.*

FLAM. Is the Squire out of bed yet?

SERVANT. Yes, sir, he will be down directly.

FLAM. Any letters from London?

SERVANT. One for your honour, that the man brought over from the market-town, this morning.

FLAM. Give it me, blockhead! (*Servant gives it and exit.*) Never like the look of a great official-folded letter, with a large seal, it's always an unpleasant one. Talk of discovering a man's character from his handwriting!—I'll back myself against any odds to form a very close guess at the contents of a letter from the form into which it is folded. This, now, I should say, is a decidedly hostile fold. Let us see—'King's Bench Walk—September 1st, 1729. Sir, I am instructed by my client, Mr. Edward Montague, to apply to you—(the old story—for the immediate payment, I suppose—what's this?)—to apply to you for the instant restitution of the sum of two hundred and fifty pounds, his son lost to you at play; and to acquaint you, that unless it is immediately forwarded to my office, as above, the circumstances of the transaction will be made known; and the unfair and fraudulent means by which you deprived the young man of his money, publicly advertised.—I am, Sir, your obedient Servant, John Ellis.' The devil! who would believe now, that such a trifling circumstance as the mere insinuation of a small piece of gold into the corner of two dice would influence a man's destiny! What's to be done? If, by some dextrous stroke, I could manage to curry favour with Norton, and procure some handsome present in return for services rendered,—for, 'work and labour done and performed,' as my obedient servant, John Ellis, would say, I might keep my head above water yet. I have it! He shall have a joyful surprise. I'll carry this girl off for him, and he shall know nothing of the enterprise until it is completed, or at least till she is fairly off. I have been well rewarded for similar services before, and may securely calculate on his gratitude in the present instance. He is here. (*Puts up the letter.*)

Enter SQUIRE NORTON.

SQUIRE (*seating himself at table*). Has any application for permission to remain on the farm been made from Benson, this morning, Flam?

FLAM. None.

SQUIRE. I am very sorry for it, although I admire the old man's independent spirit. I am very sorry for it. Wrong as I know I have been, I would rather that the first concession came from him.

FLAM. Concession!

SQUIRE. The more I reflect upon the occurrences of yesterday, Flam, the more I regret that, under the influence of momentary passion and excitement, I should have used so uncalled-for a threat against my father's oldest tenant. It is an act of baseness to which I look back with abhorrence.

FLAM (*aside*). What weathercock morality is this!

SQUIRE It was unnecessary violence.

FLAM. Unnecessary! Oh, certainly; no doubt you could have attained your object without it, and can still. There is no occasion to punish the old man.

SQUIRE. Nor will I. He shall not leave the farm, if I myself implore, and beg him to remain.

Enter Servant.

SERVANT. Two young women to speak with your honour.

Enter LUCY *and* ROSE.

SQUIRE. Lucy!

FLAM (*aside*). She must be carried off to-night, or she certainly will save me the trouble, and I shall lose the money.

LUCY. Your honour may be well surprised to see me here, after the events of yesterday. It has cost me no trifling struggle to take this step, but I hope my better feelings have at length prevailed, and conquered my pride and weakness. I wish to speak to your honour, with nobody by.

FLAM (*aside*). Nobody by! I rather suspect I'm not particularly wanted here. (*To them.*) Pray allow us to retire for a few moments. Rose, my dear.

ROSE. Well!

FLAM. Come along.

LUCY. Rose will remain here, I brought her for that purpose.

FLAM. Bless me! that's very odd. As you please, of course, but I really think you'll find her very much in the way. (*Aside.*) Acting propriety! So much the better for my purpose; a little coyness will enhance the value of the prize. [*Exit* FLAM.

LUCY. Mr. Norton, I come here to throw myself upon your honourable feelings, as a man and as a gentleman. Oh, sir! now that my eyes are opened to the misery into which I have plunged myself, by my own ingratitude and treachery, do not —do not add to it the reflection that I have driven my father in his old age from the house where he was born, and in which he hoped to have died.

SQUIRE. Be calm, Lucy; your father shall continue to hold the farm; the lease shall be renewed.

LUCY. I have more to say to your honour still, and what I have to add may even induce your honour to retract the promise you have just now made me.

SQUIRE. Lucy! what can you mean?

LUCY. Oh, sir! call me coquette, faithless, treacherous, deceitful, what you will; I deserve it all;—but believe me, I speak the truth when I make the humiliating avowal. A weak, despicable vanity induced me to listen with a ready ear to your honour's addresses, and to cast away the best and noblest heart that ever woman won.

SQUIRE. Lucy, 'twas but last night you told me that your love for Edmunds had vanished into air; that you hated and despised him.

LUCY. I know it, sir, too well. He laid bare my own guilt, and showed me the ruin which impended over me. He spoke the truth. Your honour more than confirmed him.

SQUIRE (*after pause*). Even the avowal you have just made, unexpected as it is, shall not disturb my resolution. Your father shall not leave the farm.

Quartet

LUCY—ROSE—SQUIRE NORTON, *and afterwards* YOUNG BENSON.

SQUIRE. Hear me, when I swear that the farm is your own
Through all changes Fortune may make;
The base charge of falsehood I never have known;
This promise I never will break.

ROSE *and* LUCY. Hear him, when he swears that the farm is our own
Through all changes Fortune may make;
The base charge of falsehood he never has known;
This promise he never will break.

Enter YOUNG BENSON.

YOUNG BENSON. My sister here! Lucy! begone, I command.

SQUIRE. To your home I restore you again.

YOUNG BENSON. No boon I'll accept from that treacherous hand
As the price of my sister's fair fame.

SQUIRE. To your home!

YOUNG BENSON (*to* LUCY). Hence away!

LUCY. Brother dear, I obey.

SQUIRE. I restore.

YOUNG BENSON. Hence away!

YOUNG BENSON, ROSE, *and* LUCY. Let us leave.

LUCY. He swears it, dear brother.

SQUIRE. I swear it.

YOUNG BENSON. Away!

SQUIRE. I swear it.

YOUNG BENSON. You swear to deceive.

SQUIRE. Hear me, when I swear that the farm is your own
Through all changes Fortune may make.

LUCY *and* ROSE. Hear him when he swears that the farm is our own
Through all changes Fortune may make.

YOUNG BENSON. Hear him swear, hear him swear, that the farm is our own
Through all changes Fortune may make.

SQUIRE. The base charge of falsehood I never have known,
This promise I never will break.

LUCY *and* ROSE. The base charge of falsehood he never has known,
This promise he never will break.

YOUNG BENSON. The base charge of falsehood he often has known,
This promise he surely will break.
[*Exeunt omnes.*

Re-enter FLAM, *in a walking-dress.*

FLAM. The coast is clear at last. What on earth the conversation can have been, at which Rose *was* wanted, and I was not, I confess my inability to comprehend; but away with speculation, and now to business.—(*Rings.*)

Enter Servant.

Pen and ink.

SERVANT. Yes, sir. [*Exit Servant.*

FLAM (*solus*). Nearly all the tenantry will be assembled here at the ball to-night; and if the father of this rustic Dulcinea is reinstated in his farm, he and his people will no doubt be among the number. It will be easy enough to entice the girl into the garden, through the window opening on the lawn; a chaise can be waiting in the quiet lane at the side, and some trusty fellow can slip a hasty note into Norton's hands informing him of the flight, and naming the place at which he can join us. (*Re-enter Servant with pen, ink, taper, and two sheets of notepaper; he places them on the table and exit.*) I may as well reply to my friend Mr. John Ellis's obliging favour now, too, by promising that the money shall be forwarded in the course of three days' post. (*Takes the letter from his pocket, and lays it on the table.*) Lie you there. First, for Norton's note. —'Dear Norton,—knowing your wishes—seized the girl—no blame attach to you. Join us as soon as people have dispersed in search of her in all directions but the right one,—fifteen miles off.' (*Folds it ready for an envelope and lays it by the side of the other letter.*) Now for John Ellis. Why, what does the rascal mean by bringing but two sheets of paper? No matter: that affair will keep cool till to-morrow, when I have less business on my hands, and more money in my pockets, I hope. (*Crumples the letter he has just written, hastily up, thrusts it into his pocket, and folds the wrong one in the envelope. As he is sealing it—*

Enter MARTIN, *very cautiously.*

MARTIN (*peeping*). There he is, hatching some mysterious and diabolical plot. If I can only get to the bottom of these dreadful designs, I shall immortalise myself. What a lucky dog I am, to be such a successful gleaner of news, and such a confidential person into the bargain, as to be the first to hear that he wanted some trustworthy person. All comes of talking to everybody I meet, and drawing out everything they hear. Capital custom! He don't see me. Hem! (*Coughs very loud, and when* FLAM *looks round, nods familiarly.*) How are you again?

FLAM. How am I again! Who the devil are you?—and what do you want here?

MARTIN. Hush!

FLAM. Eh?

MARTIN. Hush! I'm the man.

FLAM. *The* man!

MARTIN. Yes, the man that you asked the ostler at the George to recommend you; the trustworthy man that knows all the by-roads well, and can keep a secret; the man that you wanted to lend you a hand in a job that——

FLAM. Hush, hush!

MARTIN. Oh! you're beginning to hush now, are you?

FLAM. Haven't I seen your face before?

MARTIN. To be sure you have. You recollect admiring my manners at Benson's yesterday. You must remember Mr. Martin Stokes. You *can't* have forgotten him—not possible!

FLAM (*aside*). A friend of Benson!—a dangerous rencontre. Another moment, and our conversation might have taken an awkward turn. (*To him.*) So you are Stokes, eh? Benson's friend Stokes?

MARTIN. To be sure. Ha, ha! I knew you couldn't have forgotten me. Pleasant Stokes they call me, clever Stokes sometimes;—but that's flattery.

FLAM. No, surely.

MARTIN. Yes, 'pon my life! it is. Can't bear flattery,—don't like it at all.

FLAM. Well, Mr. Stokes——

MARTIN (*aside*). Now for the secret.

FLAM. I am very sorry you have had the trouble of coming up

here, Mr. Stokes, because I have changed my plan, and shall not require your valuable services. (*Goes up to the table.*)

MARTIN (*aside*). Something wrong here: try him again. You're sure you don't want me?

FLAM. Quite.

MARTIN. That's unlucky, because, as I have quarrelled with Benson——

FLAM. Quarrelled with Benson!

MARTIN. What! didn't you know that?

FLAM. Never heard of it. Now I think of it, Mr. Stokes, I *shall* want your assistance. Pray, sit down, Mr. Stokes.

MARTIN. With pleasure. (*They sit.*) I say, I *thought* you wanted me.

FLAM. Ah! you're a sharp fellow.

MARTIN. You don't mean that?

FLAM. I do, indeed.

MARTIN (*aside*). You would, if you knew all.

FLAM (*aside*). Conceited hound!

MARTIN (*aside*). Poor devil!

FLAM. Mr. Stokes, I needn't impress upon a gentleman of your intelligence, the necessity of secrecy in this matter.

MARTIN. Of course not: see all—say nothing. Capital custom:—(*aside*) not mine though. Go on.

FLAM. You wouldn't mind playing Benson a trick,—just a harmless trick?

MARTIN. Certainly not. Go on.

FLAM. I'll trust you.

MARTIN. So you may. Go on.

FLAM. A chaise and four will be waiting to-night, at ten o'clock precisely, at the little gate that opens from the garden into the lane.

MARTIN. No: will it though? Go on.

FLAM. Don't interrupt me, Stokes. Into that chaise you must assist me in forcing as quickly as possible and without noise——

MARTIN. Yes. Go on.

FLAM. Whom do you think?

MARTIN. Don't know.

FLAM. Can't you guess whom?

MARTIN. No.

FLAM. Try.

MARTIN. Eh! what!—Miss——

FLAM. Hush, hush! You understand me, I see. Not another word; not another syllable.

MARTIN. But do you really mean to run away with——

FLAM (*stopping his mouth*). You understand me;—that's quite sufficient.

MARTIN (*aside*). He's going to run away with Rose. Why, if I hadn't found this out, John Maddox,—one of my most particular friends,—would have gone stark, staring, raving mad with grief. (*To him.*) But what will become of Miss Lucy, when she has lost Rose?

FLAM. No matter. We cannot take them both, without the certainty of an immediate discovery. Meet me at the corner of the avenue, before the ball commences, and I will communicate any further instructions I may have to give you. Meanwhile, take this (*gives him money*) as an earnest of what you shall receive when the girl is secured. Remember, silence and secrecy.

MARTIN. Silence and secrecy, (*exit* FLAM)—confidence and two guineas. I am perfectly bewildered with this tremendous secret. What shall I do? Where shall I go?—To my particular friend, old Benson, or young Benson, or George Edmunds? or—no; I'll go and paralyse my particular friend, John Maddox. Not a moment is to be lost. I am all in a flutter. Run away with Rose! I suppose he'll run away with Lucy next. *I* shouldn't wonder. Run away with Rose! I never did——

[*Exit hastily.*

SCENE II.—*An open spot in the Village.*

Enter SQUIRE NORTON.

SQUIRE. My mind is made up. This girl has opened her whole heart to me; and it would be worse than villainy to pursue her further. I will seek out Benson and Edmunds, and endeavour to repair the mischief my folly has occasioned. I have sought happiness in the dissipation of crowded cities, in vain. A country life offers health and cheerfulness; and a country life shall henceforth be mine, in all seasons.

Song.—SQUIRE NORTON.

There's a charm in Spring, when everything
  Is bursting from the ground;
When pleasant showers bring forth the flowers,
  And all is life around.

In summer day, the fragrant hay
  Most sweetly scents the breeze;
And all is still, save murmuring rill,
  Or sound of humming bees.

Old Autumn come, with trusty gun
  In quest of birds we roam:
Unerring aim, we mark the game,
  And proudly bear it home.

A winter's night has its delight,
  Well warm'd to bed we go;
A winter's day, we're blithe and gay,
  Snipe-shooting in the snow.

A country life without the strife
  And noisy din of town,
Is all I need, I take no heed
  Of splendour or renown.

And when I die, oh, let me lie
  Where trees above me wave;
Let wild plants bloom, around my tomb,
  My quiet country grave! [*Exit.*

SCENE III.—*The Rick-yard. Same as* ACT I, SCENE I.

EDMUNDS *and* MADDOX *meeting.*

JOHN. Ah, George! Why this is kind to come down to the old farm to-day, and take one peep at us, before we leave it for ever. I suppose it's fancy, now, George, but to my thinking I never saw the hedges look so fresh, the fields so rich, or the old house so pretty and comfortable, as they do this morning. It's fancy that, George—an't it?

EDMUNDS. It's a place you may well be fond of, and attached to, for it's the prettiest spot in all the country round.

JOHN. Ah! you always enter into my feelings; and speaking of that, I want to ask your advice about Rose. I meant to come up to you to-day, on purpose. Do you think she is fond of me, George?

EDMUNDS (*smiling*). What do *you* think? She has not shown any desperate warmth of affection, of late, has she?

JOHN. No—no, she certainly has not, but she used to once, and the girl has got a good heart after all; and she came crying to me, this morning, in the little paddock, and somehow or other, my heart melted towards her; and—and—there's something very pleasant about her manner,—isn't there, George?

EDMUNDS. No doubt of it, as other people besides ourselves would appear to think.

JOHN. You mean Mr. Flam? (EDMUNDS *nods assent.*) Ah! it's a bad business, altogether; but still there are some excuses to be made for a young country girl, who has never seen a town gentleman before, and can't be expected to know as well as you and I, George, what the real worth of one is. However that may be, Rose came into the little paddock this morning, as I was standing there, looking at the young colts, and thinking of all our misfortunes; and first of all she walked by me, and then she stopped at a little distance, and then she walked back, and stopped again; and I heard her sobbing as if her heart would burst: and then she came a little nearer, and at last she laid her hand upon my arm, and looked up in my face: and the tears started into my eyes, George, and I couldn't bear it any longer, for I thought of the many pleasant days we had been happy together, and it hurt me to think that she should ever have done anything to make her afraid of me, or me unkind to her.

EDMUNDS. You're a good fellow, John, an excellent fellow. Take her; I believe her to have an excellent disposition, though it is a little disguised by girlish levity sometimes;—you may safely take her,—if she had far less good feeling than she actually possesses, she could never abuse your kind and affectionate nature.

JOHN. Is that your advice? Give me your hand, George (*they shake hands*), I will take her. You shall dance at our wedding, and I don't quite despair yet of dancing at yours, at the same time.

EDMUNDS. At mine! Where is the old man? I came here to offer him the little cottage in the village, which belongs to me. There is no tenant in it now: it has a pretty garden, of which I know he is fond, and it may serve his turn till he has had time to look about him.

JOHN. He is somewhere about the farm; walk with me across the yard, and perhaps we may meet him—this way. [*Exeunt.*

Enter YOUNG BENSON.

YOUNG BENSON. The worst portion of the poor old man's hard trial is past. I have lingered with him in every field on the land, and wandered through every room in the old house. I can neither blame his grief, nor console him in his affliction, for the farm has been the happy scene of my birth and boyhood; and I feel, in looking on it, for the last time, as if I were leaving the dearest friends of my youth, for ever.

Song.—YOUNG BENSON.

My fair home is no longer mine;
  From its roof-tree I'm driven away,
Alas! who will tend the old vine,
  Which I planted in infancy's day!
The garden, the beautiful flowers,
  The oak with its branches on high,
Dear friends of my happiest hours,
  Among ye, I long hoped to die.
The briar, the moss, and the bramble,
  Along the green paths will run wild:
The paths where I once used to ramble,
  An innocent, light-hearted child.

At the conclusion of the song enter to the symphony OLD BENSON, *with* LUCY *and* ROSE.

YOUNG BENSON (*advancing to meet him*). Come, father, come!

OLD BENSON. I am ready, boy. We have but to walk a few steps, and the pang of leaving is over. Come, Rose, bring on that unhappy girl; come!

As they are going, enter the SQUIRE, *who meets them.*

SQUIRE. I am in time.

BENSON (*to* YOUNG BENSON, *who is advancing*). Harry, stand back. Mr. Norton, if by this visit you intend to mock the misery you have inflicted here, it is a heartless insult that might have been spared.

SQUIRE. You do me an injustice, Benson. I come here,—not to insult your grief, but to entreat, implore you, to remain. The lease of this farm shall be renewed;—I beseech you to remain here.

BENSON. It is not the quitting even the home of my infancy, which most men love, that bows my spirit down to-day. Here, in this old house, for near two hundred years, my ancestors have lived and died, and left their names behind them free from spot or blemish. I am the first to cross its threshold with the brand of infamy upon me. Would to God I had been borne from its porch a senseless corpse many weary years ago, so that I had been spared this hard calamity! You have moved an old man's weakness, but not with your revenge, sir. You implore me to remain here. I spurn your offer. *Here!* A father yielding to the destroyer of his child's good name and honour! Say no more, sir. Let me pass.

Enter, behind, STOKES *and* EDMUNDS.

SQUIRE. Benson, you are guilty of the foulest injustice, not to me, but to your daughter. After her fearless confession to me this morning of her love for Edmunds, and her abhorrence of my professions, I honour her too much to injure her, or you.

LUCY. Dear father, it is true indeed. The noble behaviour of his honour to me, this morning, I can never forget, or be too grateful for.

BENSON. Thank God! thank God! I can look upon her once again. My child! my own child! (*he embraces her with great emotion.*) I have done your honour wrong, and I hope you'll forgive me. (*They shake hands.*)

MARTIN (*running forward*). So have I! so have I! I have done his honour wrong, and I hope he'll forgive me too. You don't leave the farm, then? Hurrah! (*A man carrying a pail, some harness, etc., crosses the stage.*) Hallo, young fellow! go back, go back! don't take another thing away, and bring back all you have carried off; they are going to stop in the farm. Hallo! you fellows! (*Calling off.*) Leave the barn alone, and put everything in its place. They are going to stop in the farm. [*Exit bawling.*

BENSON (*seeing* EDMUNDS). What! George here, and turning away from his old friend, too, without a look of congratulation or a shake of the hand, just at the time, when of all others, he had the best right to expect it! For shame, George, for shame!

EDMUNDS. My errand here is rendered useless. By accident, and not intentionally, I partly overheard just now the nature of the avowal made by your daughter to Mr. Norton this morning.

BENSON. You believe it, George. You cannot doubt its truth.

EDMUNDS. I *do* believe it. But I have been hurt, slighted, set aside for another. My honest love has been despised; my affection has been remembered, only to be tried almost beyond endurance. Lucy, all this from *you* I freely forgive. Be what you have been once, and what you may so well become again. Be the high-souled woman; not the light and thoughtless trifler that disgraces the name. Let me see you this, and you are mine again. Let me see you what you have been of late, and I never can be yours!

BENSON. Lead her in, Rose. Come, dear, come. (*The* BENSONS *and* ROSE *lead her slowly away.*)

EDMUNDS. Mr. Norton, if this altered conduct be sincere, it deserves a much better return than my poor thanks can ever be to you. If it be feigned, to serve some purposes of your own, the consequences will be upon your head.

SQUIRE. And I shall be prepared to meet them.

Duet.—SQUIRE NORTON *and* EDMUNDS.

SQUIRE. Listen, though I do not fear you,
Listen to me, ere we part.
EDMUNDS. List to *you*! Yes, I will hear you.
SQUIRE. Yours alone is Lucy's heart,
I swear it, by that Heaven above me.
EDMUNDS. What! can I believe my ears!
Could I hope that she still loves me!
SQUIRE. Banish all these doubts and fears,
If a love were e'er worth gaining,
If love were ever fond and true,
No disguise or passion feigning,

Such is her young love for you.
Listen, though I do not fear you,
Listen to me ere we part.

EDMUNDS. List to you! yes, I will hear you,
Mine alone is her young heart. [*Exeunt severally.*

SCENE IV.—*The avenue leading to the Hall, by moonlight. The house in the distance, gaily illuminated.*

Enter FLAM *and* MARTIN.

FLAM. You have got the letter I gave you for the Squire?

MARTIN. All right. Here it is.

FLAM. The moment you see me leave the room, slip it into the Squire's hand; you can easily do so, without being recognised, in the confusion of the dance, and then follow me. You perfectly understand your instructions?

MARTIN. Oh, yes,—I understand them well enough.

FLAM. There's nothing more, then, that you want to know?

MARTIN. No, nothing,—oh, yes there is. I want to know whether —whether——

FLAM. Well, go on.

MARTIN. Whether you could conveniently manage to let me have another couple of guineas, before you go away in the chaise. Payment beforehand,—capital custom. And if you don't, perhaps I may not get them at all, you know: (*aside*) seeing that I don't intend to go at all, I think it's very likely.

FLAM. You're a remarkably pleasant fellow, Stokes, in general conversation,—very,—but when you descend into particularities, you become excessively prosy. On some points,—money-matters for instance,—you have a very grasping imagination, and seem disposed to dilate upon them at too great a length. You must cure yourself of this habit,—you must indeed. Good-bye, Stokes; you shall have the two guineas doubled when the journey is completed. Remember,—ten o'clock. [*Exit* FLAM.

MARTIN. I shan't forget ten o'clock depend upon it. Now to burst upon my particular friend, Mr. John Maddox, with the awful disclosure. He must pass this way on his road to the Hall. Here they come,—don't see him though. (*Groups of male and female Villagers in cloaks, etc., cross the stage on their way to the Hall.*)

MARTIN. How are you, Tom? How do, Will?

VILLAGERS. How do, Mas'r Stokes?

MARTIN (*shaking hands with them*). How do, Susan? Mind, Cary, you're my first partner. Always kiss your first partner,—capital custom. (*Kisses her.*) Good-bye! See you up at the Hall.

VILLAGERS. Ay, ay, Mas'r Stokes. [*Exeunt Villagers.*

MARTIN. Not among them. (*More Villagers cross.*) Nor them. Here he comes:—Rose with him too,—innocent little victim, little thinking of the atrocious designs that are going on against her!

Enter MADDOX *and* ROSE, *arm-in-arm.*

JOHN. Ha, ha, ha! that was a good 'un,—wasn't it? Ah! Martin, I wish I'd seen you a minute ago. I made such a joke! How you would ha' laughed!

MARTIN (*mysteriously beckoning* MADDOX *away from* ROSE, *and whispering*). I want to speak to you

JOHN (*whispering*). What about?

ROSE. Lor'! don't stand whispering there, John. If you have anything to say, Mr. Stokes, say it before me.

JOHN (*taking her arm*). Ah! say it before her! Don't mind her, Martin; she's to be my wife, you know, and we're to be on the mutual-confidence principle; an't we,—Rose?

ROSE. To be sure. Why don't you speak, Mr. Stokes? I suppose it's the old story,—something wrong.

MARTIN. Something wrong! I rather think there is; and you little know what it is, or you wouldn't look so merry. What I have got to say—don't be frightened, Miss Rose,—relates to—don't alarm yourself, Master Maddox.

JOHN. I an't alarming myself; you're alarming me. Go on!

ROSE. Go on!—can't you?

MARTIN. Relates to Mr. Flam.

JOHN (*dropping* ROSE'S *arm*). Mr. Flam!

MARTIN. Hush!—and Miss Rose.

ROSE. Me! Me and Mr. Flam!

MARTIN. Mr. Flam intends at ten o'clock, this very night,—don't be frightened, Miss,—by force, in secret, and in a chaise and four, too,—to carry off, against her will, and elope with, Miss Rose.

ROSE. Me! Oh! (*Screams, and falls into the arms of* MADDOX.)

JOHN. Rub her hands, Martin, she's going off in a fit.

MARTIN. Never mind; she'd better go off in a fit than a chaise.

ROSE (*recovering*). Oh, John! don't let me go.

JOHN. Let you go!—not if I set the whole Hall on fire.

ROSE. Hold me fast, John.

JOHN. I'll hold you fast enough, depend upon it.

ROSE. Come on the other side of me, Mr. Stokes: take my arm; hold me tight, Mr. Stokes.

MARTIN. Don't be frightened, I'll take care of you. (*Takes her arm.*)

ROSE. Oh! Mr. Stokes.

MARTIN. Oh, indeed! Nothing wrong,—eh?

ROSE. Oh! Mr. Stokes,—pray forgive my having doubted that there was——Oh! what a dreadful thing! What is to be done with me?

MARTIN. Upon my word, I don't know. I think we had better shut her up in some place under ground,—hadn't we, John? —or, stay,—suppose we borrow the keys of the family vault, and lock her up there, for an hour or two.

JOHN. Capital!

ROSE. Lor'! surely you may find out some more agreeable place than that, John.

MARTIN. I have it.—I'm to carry her off.

BOTH. You!

MARTIN. Me,—don't be afraid of me:—all my management. You dance with her all the evening, and I'll keep close to you. If anybody tries to get her away, you knock him down,—and I'll help you.

JOHN. That's the plan;—come along.

ROSE. Oh, I am so frightened! Hold me fast, Mr. Stokes,— Don't let me go, John! [*Exeunt, talking.*

Enter LUCY.

LUCY. Light-hearted revellers! how I envy them! How painful is my situation,—obliged with a sad heart to attend a festivity, from which the only person I would care to meet will, I know, be absent. But I will not complain. He shall see that I can become worthy of him, once again. I have lingered here so long, watching the soft shades of evening as they closed around me, that I cannot bear the thought of exchanging this beautiful scene for the noise and glare of a crowded room.

Song.—LUCY.

How beautiful at even-tide
To see the twilight shadows pale,
Steal o'er the landscape, far and wide,
O'er stream and meadow, mound and dale.
How soft is Nature's calm repose
When evening skies their cool dews weep:
The gentlest wind more gently blows,
As if to soothe her in her sleep!
The gay morn breaks,
Mists roll away,
All Nature awakes
To glorious day.
In my breast alone
Dark shadows remain;
The peace it has known
It can never regain.

SCENE THE LAST.—*A spacious ball-room, brilliantly illuminated. A window at the end, through which is seen a moonlit landscape. A large concourse of country people, discovered.—The* SQUIRE,—FLAM,—*the* BENSONS,—LUCY,—ROSE,—MARTIN, *and* MADDOX.

SQUIRE. Welcome, friends, welcome all! Come, choose your partners, and begin the dance.

FLAM (*to Lucy*). Your hand, for the dance?

LUCY. Pray excuse me, sir; I am not well. My head is oppressed and giddy. I would rather sit by the window which looks into the garden, and feel the cool evening air. (*She goes up. He follows her.*)

JOHN (*aside*). Stand by me, Martin. He's gone to order the chaise, perhaps.

ROSE. Oh! pray don't let me be taken away, Mr. Stokes.

MARTIN. Don't be frightened,—don't be frightened. Mr. Flam is gone. I'll give the Squire the note in a minute.

SQUIRE. Now,—begin the dance.

A Country Dance.

(MARTIN *and* MADDOX, *in their endeavours to keep close to* ROSE, *occasion great confusion. As the* SQUIRE *is looking at some par-*

ticular couple in the dance, MARTIN *steals behind him, thrusts the letter in his hands, and resumes his place. The* SQUIRE *looks round as if to discover the person who has delivered it; but being unsuccessful, puts it up, and retires among the crowd of dancers. Suddenly a violent scream is heard, and the dance abruptly ceases. Great confusion.* MARTIN *and* MADDOX *hold* ROSE *firmly.*)

SQUIRE. What has happened? Whence did that scream proceed?

SEVERAL VOICES. From the garden!—from the garden!

EDMUNDS (*without*). Raise him, and bring him here. Lucy,—dear Lucy!

BENSON. Lucy! My child! (*Runs up the stage, and exit into garden.*)

MARTIN. *His* child! Damme! they can't get this one, so they're going to run away with the other. Here's some mistake here. Let me go, Rose. Come along, John. Make way there,—make way!

(*As they run towards the window,* EDMUNDS *appears at it, without a hat, and his dress disordered, with* LUCY *in his arms. He delivers her to her father and* ROSE.)

ROSE. Lucy,—dear Lucy,—look up!

BENSON. Is she hurt, George?—is the poor child injured?

EDMUNDS. No, it is nothing but terror; she will be better instantly. See! she is recovering now. (LUCY *gradually recovers, as* FLAM, *his clothes torn, and face disfigured, is led in by* MADDOX *and* MARTIN.)

BENSON. Mr. Norton, this is an act of perjury and baseness, of which another instant would have witnessed the completion.

SQUIRE (*to* FLAM). Rascal! this is your deed.

FLAM (*aside to* NORTON). That's right, Norton, keep it up.

SQUIRE. Do not address me with your odious familiarity, scoundrel!

FLAM. You don't really mean to give me up?

SQUIRE. I renounce you from this instant.

FLAM. You do?—then take the consequences.

SQUIRE. Benson,—Edmunds,—friends,—I declare to you most solemnly that I had neither hand nor part in this disgraceful outrage. It has been perpetrated without my knowledge, wholly by that scoundrel.

FLAM. 'Tis false; it was done with his consent. He has in his pocket, at this moment, a letter from me, acquainting him with my intention.

ALL. A letter!

SQUIRE. A letter *was* put into my hands five minutes since; but it acquainted me, not with this fellow's intention, but with his real dishonourable and disgraceful character, to which I had hitherto been a stranger. (*To* FLAM.) Do you know that handwriting, sir? (*Showing him the letter.*)

FLAM. Ellis's letter! (*searching his pockets, and producing the other*). I must,—ass that I was!—I did—enclose the wrong one.

SQUIRE. You will quit my house this instant; its roof shall not shelter you another night. Take that with you, sir, and begone. (*Throws him a purse.*)

FLAM (*taking it up*). Ah! I suppose you think this munificent, now—eh? I could have made twice as much of you in London, Norton, I could indeed, to say nothing of my exhibiting myself for a whole week to these clods of earth, which would have been cheap, dirt-cheap, at double the money. Bye-bye, Norton! Farewell, grubs! [*Exit.*

SQUIRE. Edmunds, you have rescued your future wife from brutal violence; you will not leave her exposed to similar attempts in future?

EDMUNDS. Even if I would, I feel, now that I have preserved her, that I could not.

SQUIRE. Then take her, and with her the old farm, which from henceforth is your own. *You* will not turn the old man out, I suppose?

EDMUNDS (*shaking* BENSON *by the hand*). I don't think we are very likely to quarrel on that score; and most gratefully do we acknowledge your honour's kindness. Maddox!

JOHN. Hallo!

EDMUNDS. I shall not want that cottage and garden we were speaking of, this morning, now. Let me imitate a good example, and bestow it on *your* wife, as *her* marriage portion.

ROSE. Oh, delightful! Say certainly, John,—can't you?

JOHN. Thank'ee, George, thank'ee! I say, Martin, I have arrived at the dignity of a cottage and a piece of ground, at last.

MARTIN. Yes, you may henceforth consider yourself on a level with me.

SQUIRE. Resume the dance.

MARTIN. I beg your pardon. One word. (*Whispers the* SQUIRE.)

SQUIRE. I hope not. Recollect, you have been mistaken before, to-day. You had better inquire.

MARTIN. I will. (*To the audience.*) My very particular friend, if he will allow me to call him so,——

SQUIRE. Oh, certainly.

MARTIN. My very particular friend, Mr. Norton, wishes me to ask my other particular friends here, whether there's—anything wrong? We are delighted to hear your approving opinion in the old way. You *can't* do better. It's a capital custom.

Dance and Finale.—Chorus.

Join the dance, with step as light
As every heart should be to-night;
Music, shake the lofty dome,
In honour of our Harvest Home.

Join the dance, and banish care,
All are young, and gay, and fair;
Even age has youthful grown,
In honour of our Harvest Home.

Join the dance, bright faces beam,
Sweet lips smile, and dark eyes gleam;
All these charms have hither come,
In honour of our Harvest Home.

Join the dance, with step as light,
As every heart should be to-night;
Music, shake the lofty dome,
In honour of our Harvest Home.

Quintet.

LUCY—ROSE—EDMUNDS—*The* SQUIRE—YOUNG BENSON.

No light bound
Of stag or timid hare,
O'er the ground
Where startled herds repair,

Do we prize
So high, or hold so dear,
As the eyes
That light our pleasures here.

No cool breeze
That gently plays by night,
O'er calm seas,
Whose waters glisten bright;
No soft moan
That sighs across the lea,
Harvest Home,
Is half so sweet as thee!

Chorus.

Hail to the merry autumn days, when yellow cornfields shine,
Far brighter than the costly cup that holds the monarch's wine!
Hail to the merry harvest time, the gayest of the year,
The time of rich and bounteous crops, rejoicing, and good cheer.
Hail! Hail! Hail!

CURTAIN

THE END

IS SHE HIS WIFE?
OR, SOMETHING SINGULAR!

A Comic Burletta

IN ONE ACT

[1837]

DRAMATIS PERSONÆ

AT ST. JAMES'S THEATRE, MARCH 6, 1837

ALFRED LOVETOWN, ESQ.	MR. FORESTER.
MR. PETER LIMBURY	MR. GARDNER.
FELIX TAPKINS, ESQ. (*formerly of the India House, Leadenhall Street, and Prospect Place, Poplar; but now of the Rustic Lodge, near Reading*) . .	MR. HARLEY.
JOHN (*servant to Lovetown*)	———
MRS. LOVETOWN	MISS ALLISON.
MRS. PETER LIMBURY	MADAME SALA.

IS SHE HIS WIFE?

OR, SOMETHING SINGULAR!

SCENE I.—*A Room opening into a Garden. A Table laid for Breakfast; Chairs, etc.* MR. *and* MRS. LOVETOWN, C., *discovered at Breakfast,* R. H. *The former in a dressing-gown and slippers, reading a newspaper. A Screen on one side.*

LOVETOWN (L. H. *of table, yawning*). Another cup of tea, my dear,—O Lord!

MRS. LOVETOWN (R. H. *of table*). I wish, Alfred, you would endeavour to assume a more cheerful appearance in your wife's society. If you are perpetually yawning and complaining of *ennui* a few months after marriage, what am I to suppose you'll become in a few years? It really is very odd of you.

LOVETOWN. Not at all odd, my dear, not the least in the world; it would be a great deal more odd if I were not. The fact is, my love, I'm tired of the country; green fields, and blooming hedges, and feathered songsters, are fine things to talk about and read about and write about; but I candidly confess that I prefer paved street, area railings and dustman's bells, after all.

MRS. LOVETOWN. How often have you told me that, blessed with my love, you could live contented and happy in a desert?

LOVETOWN (*reading*). 'Artful imposter!'

MRS. LOVETOWN. Have you not over and over again said that fortune and personal attractions were secondary considerations with you? That you loved me for those virtues which, while they gave additional lustre to public life, would adorn and sweeten retirement?

LOVETOWN (*reading*). 'Soothing syrup!'

MRS. LOVETOWN. You complain of the tedious sameness of a country life. Was it not you yourself who first proposed our residing permanently in the country? Did you not say that I should then have an ample sphere in which to exercise those charitable feelings which I have so often evinced, by selling at those benevolent fancy fairs?

LOVETOWN (*reading*). 'Humane man-traps!'

MRS. LOVETOWN. He pays no attention to me,—Alfred dear,——

LOVETOWN (*stamping his foot*). Yes, my life.

MRS. LOVETOWN. Have you heard what I have just been saying, dear?

LOVETOWN. Yes, love.

MRS. LOVETOWN. And what can you say in reply?

LOVETOWN. Why, really, my dear, you've said it so often before in the course of the last six weeks, that I think it quite unnecessary to say anything more about it. (*Reads.*) 'The learned judge delivered a brief but impressive summary of the unhappy man's trial.'

MRS. LOVETOWN (*aside*). I could bear anything but this neglect. He evidently does not care for me.

LOVETOWN (*aside*). I could put with anything rather than these constant altercations and little petty quarrels. I repeat, my dear that I am very dull in this out-of-the-way villa—confoundedly dull, horridly dull.

MRS. LOVETOWN. And *I* repeat that if you took any pleasure in your wife's society, or felt for her as you once professed to feel, you would have no cause to make such a complaint.

LOVETOWN. If I did not know you to be one of the sweetest creatures in existence, my dear, I should be strongly disposed to say that you were a very close imitation of an aggravating female.

MRS. LOVETOWN. That's very curious, my dear, for I declare that if I hadn't known *you* to be such an exquisite, good-tempered, attentive husband, I should have mistaken you for a very great brute.

LOVETOWN. My dear, you're offensive.

MRS. LOVETOWN. My love, you're intolerable. (*They turn their chairs back to back.*)

MR. FELIX TAPKINS *sings without.*

'The wife around her husband throws
Her arms to make him stay;
"My dear, it rains, it hails, it blows,
And you cannot hunt to-day."

But a hunting we will go,
And a hunting we will go,—wo—wo—wo!
And a hunting we will go.'

MRS. LOVETOWN. There's that dear, good-natured creature, Mr. Tapkins,—do you ever hear *him* complain of the tediousness of a country life? Light-hearted creature,—his lively disposition and rich flow of spirits are wonderful, even to me. (*Rising.*)

LOVETOWN. They need not be a matter of astonishment to anybody, my dear,—he's a bachelor.

MR. FELIX TAPKINS *appears at window*, L. H.

TAPKINS. Ha, ha! How are you both?—Here's a morning! Bless my heart alive, *what* a morning! I've been gardening ever since five o'clock, and the flowers have been actually growing before my very eyes. The London Pride is sweeping everything before it, and the stalks are half as high again as they were yesterday. They're all run up like so many tailors' bills, after that heavy dew of last night broke down half my rosebuds with the weight of its own moisture,—something like a dew that!—reg'lar *doo*, eh?—come, that's not so bad for a before-dinner one.

LOVETOWN. Ah, you happy dog, Felix!

TAPKINS. Happy! of course I am,—Felix by name, Felix by nature—what the deuce should I be unhappy for, or anybody be unhappy for? What's the use of it, that's the point?

MRS. LOVETOWN. Have you finished your improvements yet, Mr. Tapkins?

TAPKINS. At Rustic Lodge? (*She nods assent.*) Bless your heart and soul! you never saw such a place,—cardboard chimneys, Grecian balconies,—Gothic parapets, thatched roof.

MRS. LOVETOWN. Indeed!

TAPKINS. Lord bless you, yes,—green verandah, with ivy twining round the pillars.

MRS. LOVETOWN. How very rural!

TAPKINS. Rural, my dear Mrs. Lovetown! delightful! The French windows, too! Such an improvement!

MRS. LOVETOWN. I should think they were!

TAPKINS. Yes, *I* should think they were. Why, on a fine summer's evening the frogs hop off the grass-plot into the very sitting-room.

MRS. LOVETOWN. Dear me!

TAPKINS. Bless you, yes! Something like the country,—quite a little Eden. Why, when I'm smoking under the verandah, after a shower of rain, the black beetles fall into my brandy-and-water.

MR. *and* MRS. LOVETOWN. No!—Ha! ha! ha!

TAPKINS. Yes. And I take 'em out again with the teaspoon, and lay bets with myself which of them will run away the quickest. Ha! ha! ha! (*They all laugh.*) Then the stable, too. Why, in Rustic Lodge the stables are close to the dining-room window.

LOVETOWN. No!

TAPKINS. Yes. The horse can't cough but I hear him. There's compactness. Nothing like the cottage style of architecture for comfort, my boy. By the bye, I have left the new horse at your garden-gate this moment.

MRS. LOVETOWN. The new horse!

TAPKINS. The new horse! Splendid fellow,—such action! Puts out its feet like a rocking-horse, and carries its tail like a hat-peg. Come and see him.

LOVETOWN (*laughing*). I can't deny you anything.

TAPKINS. No, that's what they all say, especially the—eh! (*Nodding and winking.*)

LOVETOWN. Ha! ha! ha!

MRS. LOVETOWN. Ha! ha! ha! I'm afraid you're a very bad man, Mr. Tapkins; I'm afraid you're a shocking man, Mr. Tapkins.

TAPKINS. Think so? No, I don't know,—not worse than other people similarly situated. Bachelors, my dear Mrs. Lovetown, bachelors—eh! old fellow? (*Winking to* LOVETOWN.)

LOVETOWN. Certainly, certainly.

TAPKINS. *We* know—eh? (*They all laugh.*) By the bye, talking of bachelors puts me in mind of Rustic Lodge, and talking of Rustic Lodge puts me in mind of what I came here for. You must come and see me this afternoon. Little Peter Limbury and his wife are coming.

MRS. LOVETOWN. I detest that man.

LOVETOWN. The wife is supportable, my dear.

TAPKINS. To be sure, so she is. You'll come, and that's enough. Now come and see the horse.

LOVETOWN. Give me three minutes to put on my coat and boots, and I'll join you. I won't be three minutes.

[*Exit* LOVETOWN, R. H.

TAPKINS. Look sharp, look sharp!—Mrs. Lovetown, will you excuse me one moment? (*Crosses to* L.; *calling off.*) Jim,—these fellows never know how to manage horses,—walk him gently up and down,—throw the stirrups over the saddle to show the people that his master's coming, and if anybody asks what the fine animal's pedigree is, and who he belongs to, say he's the property of Mr. Felix Tapkins of Rustic Lodge, near Reading, and that he's the celebrated horse who ought to have won the Newmarket Cup last year, only he didn't.

[*Exit* TAPKINS.

MRS. LOVETOWN. My mind is made up,—I can bear Alfred's coldness and insensibility no longer, and come what may I will endeavour to remove it. From the knowledge I have of his disposition I am convinced that the only mode of doing so will be by rousing his jealousy and wounding his vanity. This thoughtless creature will be a very good instrument for my scheme. He plumes himself on his gallantry, has no very small share of vanity, and is easily led. I see him crossing the garden. (*She brings a chair hastily forward and sits* R. H.)

Enter FELIX TAPKINS, L. H. *window.*

TAPKINS (*singing*). 'My dear, it rains, it hails, it blows'——

MRS. LOVETOWN (*tragically*). Would that I had never beheld him!

TAPKINS (*aside*). Hallo! She's talking about her husband. I knew by their manner there had been a quarrel, when I came in this morning.

MRS. LOVETOWN. So fascinating, and yet so insensible to the tenderest of passions as not to see how devotedly I love him.

TAPKINS (*aside*). I thought so.

MRS. LOVETOWN. That he should still remain unmarried is to me extraordinary.

TAPKINS. Um!

MRS. LOVETOWN. He ought to have married long since.

TAPKINS (*aside*). Eh! Why, they aren't married!—'ought to have married long since.'—I rather think he ought.

MRS. LOVETOWN. And, though I am the wife of another,——

TAPKINS (*aside*). Wife of another!

MRS. LOVETOWN. Still, I grieve to say that I cannot be blind to his extraordinary merits.

TAPKINS. Why, he's run away with somebody else's wife! The villain!—I must let her know I'm in the room, or there's no telling what I may hear next. (*Coughs.*)

MRS. LOVETOWN (*starting up in affected confusion*). Mr. Tapkins! (*They sit.*) Bring your chair nearer. I fear, Mr. Tapkins, that I have been unconsciously giving utterance to what was passing in my mind. I trust you have not overheard my confession of the weakness of my heart.

TAPKINS. No—no—not more than a word or two.

MRS. LOVETOWN. That agitated manner convinces me that you have heard more than you are willing to confess. Then why—why should I seek to conceal from you—that though I esteem my husband, I—I—love—another?

TAPKINS. I heard you mention that little circumstance.

MRS. LOVETOWN. Oh! (*Sighs.*)

TAPKINS (*aside*). What the deuce is she Oh-ing at? She looks at me as if I were Lovetown himself.

MRS. LOVETOWN (*putting her hand on his shoulder with a languishing air*). Does my selection meet with your approbation?

TAPKINS (*slowly*). It doesn't.

MRS. LOVETOWN. No!

TAPKINS. Decidedly not. (*Aside.*) I'll cut that Lovetown out, and offer myself. Hem! Mrs. Lovetown.

MRS. LOVETOWN. Yes, Mr. Tapkins.

TAPKINS. I know an individual——

MRS. LOVETOWN. Ah! an individual!

TAPKINS. An individual,—I may, perhaps, venture to say an estimable individual,—who for the last three months has been constantly in your society, who never yet had courage to disclose his passion, but who burns to throw himself at your feet. Oh! (*Aside.*) I'll try an Oh or two now,—Oh! (*Sighs.*) That's a capital Oh!

MRS. LOVETOWN (*aside*). He must have misunderstood me before, for he is evidently speaking of himself. Is the gentleman you speak of handsome, Mr. Tapkins?

TAPKINS. He is generally considered remarkably so.

MRS. LOVETOWN. Is he tall?

TAPKINS. About the height of the Apollo Belvidere.

MRS. LOVETOWN. Is he stout?

TAPKINS. Of nearly the same dimensions as the gentleman I have just named.

MRS. His figure is——

TAPKINS. Quite a model.

MRS. LOVETOWN. And he is——

TAPKINS. Myself. (*Throws himself on his knees and seizes her hand.*)

Enter LOVETOWN, R H.

TAPKINS *immediately pretends to be diligently looking for something on the floor.*

MRS. LOVETOWN. Pray don't trouble yourself. I'll find it. Dear me! how could I lose it?

LOVETOWN. What have you lost, love? I should almost imagine that you had lost yourself, and that our friend Mr. Tapkins here had just found you.

TAPKINS (*aside*). Ah! you always will have your joke,—funny dog! funny dog! Bless my heart and soul, there's that immortal horse standing outside all this time! He'll catch his death of cold! Come and see him at once,—come—come.

LOVETOWN. No. I can't see him to-day. I had forgotten. I've letters to write,—business to transact,—I'm engaged.

TAPKINS (*to* MRS. LOVETOWN). Oh! if he's engaged, you know, we'd better not interrupt him.

MRS. LOVETOWN. Oh! certainly! Not by any means.

TAPKINS (*taking her arm*). Good-bye, old fellow.

LOVETOWN (*seating himself at table*). Oh!—good-bye.

TAPKINS (*going*). Take care of yourself. I'll take care of Mrs. L.
[*Exeunt* TAPKINS *and* MRS. LOVETOWN, C.

LOVETOWN. What the deuce does that fellow mean by laying such emphasis on Mrs. L.? What's my wife to him, or he to my wife? Very extraordinary! I can hardly believe that even if he had the treachery to make any advances, she would encourage such a preposterous intrigue. (*Walks to and fro.*) She spoke in his praise at breakfast-time, though,—and they have gone away together to see that confounded horse. But stop, I must keep a sharp eye upon them this afternoon, without appearing to do so. I would not appear unnecessarily suspicious for the world. Dissembling in such a case, though, is difficult—very difficult.

Enter a Servant, L. H.

SERVANT. Mr. and Mrs. Peter Limbury.

LOVETOWN. Desire them to walk in. [*Exit Servant*, L. H. A lucky visit! it furnishes me with a hint. This Mrs. Limbury is a vain, conceited woman, ready to receive the attentions of anybody who feigns admiration for her, partly to gratify herself, and partly to annoy the jealous little husband whom she keeps under such strict control. If I pay particular attention to *her*, I shall lull my wife and that scoundrel Tapkins into a false security, and have better opportunities of observation. They are here.

Enter MR. *and* MRS. LIMBURY, L. H.

LOVETOWN. My dear Mrs. Limbury. (*Crosses to* C.)

LIMBURY. Eh?

LOVETOWN (*not regarding him*). How charming—how delightful —how divine you look to-day.

LIMBURY (*aside*). Dear Mrs. Limbury,—charming,—divine and beautiful look to-day! They are smiling at each other,—he squeezes her hand. I see how it is. I always thought he paid her too much attention.

LOVETOWN. Sit down,—sit down.

(LOVETOWN *places the chairs so as to sit between them, which* LIMBURY *in vain endeavours to prevent.*)

MRS. LIMBURY. Peter and I called as we passed in our little pony-chaise, to inquire whether we should have the pleasure of seeing you at Tapkins's this afternoon.

LOVETOWN. Is it possible you can ask such a question? Do you think I could stay away?

MRS. LIMBURY. Dear Mr. Lovetown! (*Aside.*) How polite,—he's quite struck with me.

LIMBURY (*aside*). Wretched miscreant! a regular assignation before my very face.

LOVETOWN (*to* MRS. LIMBURY). Do you know I entertained some apprehensions—some dreadful fears—that you might not be there.

LIMBURY. Fears that we mightn't be there? Of course we shall be there.

MRS. LIMBURY. Now don't talk, Peter.

LOVETOWN. I thought it just possible, you know, that you might not be agreeable——

MRS. LIMBURY. O, Peter is always agreeable to anything that is agreeable to me. Aren't you, Peter?

LIMBURY. Yes, dearest. (*Aside.*) Agreeable to anything that's agreeable to her! O Lor'!

MRS. LIMBURY. By the bye, Mr. Lovetown, how do you like this bonnet?

LOVETOWN. O, beautiful!

LIMBURY (*aside*). I must change the subject. Do you know, Mr. Lovetown, I have often thought, and it has frequently occurred to me—when——

MRS. LIMBURY. Now don't talk, Peter. (*To* LOVETOWN.) The colour is so bright, is it not?

LOVETOWN. It might appear so elsewhere, but the brightness of those eyes casts it quite into shade.

MRS. LIMBURY. I know you are a connoisseur in ladies' dresses: how do you like those shoes?

LIMBURY (*aside*). Her shoes! What will she ask his opinion of next?

LOVETOWN. O, like the bonnet, you deprive them of their fair chance of admiration. That small and elegant foot engrosses all the attention which the shoes might otherwise attract. That taper ankle, too——

LIMBURY (*aside*). Her taper ankle! My bosom swells with the rage of an ogre. Mr. Lovetown,—I——

MRS. LIMBURY. Now, pray do not talk so, Limbury. You've put Mr. Lovetown out as it is.

LIMBURY (*aside*). Put him out! I wish I could put him out, Mrs. Limbury. I must.

Enter Servant, hastily.

SERVANT. I beg your pardon, sir, but the bay pony has got his hind leg over the traces, and he's kicking the chaise to pieces!

LIMBURY. Kicking the *new* chaise to pieces!

LOVETOWN. Kicking the new chaise to pieces! The bay pony! Limbury, my dear fellow, fly to the spot! (*Pushing him out.*)

LIMBURY. But, Mr. Lovetown, I——

MRS. LIMBURY. Oh! he'll kick somebody's brains out, if Peter don't go to him.

LIMBURY. But perhaps he'll kick my brains out if I do go to him.

LOVETOWN. Never mind, don't lose an instant,—not a moment. (*Pushes him out, both talking together.*) [*Exit* LIMBURY. (*Aside.*) Now for it,—here's my wife. Dearest Mrs. Limbury— (*Kneels by her chair, and seizes her hand.*)

Enter MRS. LOVETOWN, C.

MRS. LOVETOWN (*aside*). Can I believe my eyes? (*Retires behind the screen.*)

MRS. LIMBURY. Mr. Lovetown!

LOVETOWN. Nay. Allow me in one hurried interview, which I have sought for in vain for weeks,—for months,—to say how devotedly, how ardently I love you. Suffer me to retain this hand in mine. Give me one ray of hope.

MRS. LIMBURY. Rise, I entreat you,—we shall be discovered.

LOVETOWN. Nay, I will not rise till you promise me that you will take an opportunity of detaching yourself from the rest of the company and meeting me alone in Tapkins's grounds this evening. I shall have no eyes, no ears for any one but yourself.

MRS. LIMBURY. Well,—well,—I will—I do——

LOVETOWN. Then I am blest indeed!

MRS. LIMBURY. I am so agitated. If Peter or Mrs. Lovetown— were to find me thus—I should betray all. I'll teach my husband to be jealous! (*Crosses to* L. H.) Let us walk round the garden.

LOVETOWN. With pleasure,—take my arm. Divine creature! (*Aside.*) I'm sure she is behind the screen. I saw her peeping. Come.

[*Exit* LOVETOWN *and* MRS. LIMBURY, L. H.

MRS. LOVETOWN (*coming forward*). Faithless man! His coldness and neglect are now too well explained. O Alfred! Alfred! how little did I think when I married you, six short months since, that I should be exposed to so much wretchedness! I begin to tremble at my own imprudence, and the situation in which it may place me; but it is now too late to recede. I must be firm. This day will either bring my project to the explanation I so much desire, or convince me of what I too much fear,—my husband's aversion. Can this woman's husband suspect their intimacy? If so, he may be able to prevent this assignation taking place. I will seek him instantly. If I can but meet him at once, he may prevent her going at all.

[*Exit* MRS. LOVETOWN, R. H.

Enter TAPKINS, L. H. *window.*

TAPKINS. This, certainly, is a most extraordinary affair. Not her partiality for me,—that's natural enough,—but the confession I overhead about her marriage to another. I have been thinking that, after such a discovery, it would be highly improper to allow Limbury and his wife to meet her without warning him of the fact. The best way will be to make him acquainted with the real state of the case. Then he must see the propriety of not bringing his wife to my house to-night. Ah! here he is. I'll make the awful disclosure at once, and petrify him.

Enter LIMBURY, L. H. *window.*

LIMBURY. That damned little bay pony is as bad as my wife. There's no curbing either of them; and as soon as I have got the traces of the one all right, I lose all traces of the other.

TAPKINS (R.). Peter!

LIMBURY (L.). Ah! Tapkins!

TAPKINS. Hush! Hush! (*Looking cautiously round.*) If you have a moment to spare, I've got something of great importance to communicate.

LIMBURY. Something of great importance, Mr. Tapkins! (*Aside.*) What can he mean? Can it relate to Mrs. Limbury? The thought is dreadful. You horrify me!

TAPKINS. You'll be more horrified presently. What I am about to tell you concerns yourself and your honour very materially; and I beg you to understand that I communicate it—in the strictest confidence.

LIMBURY. Myself and my honour! I shall dissolve into nothing with horrible anticipations!

TAPKINS (*in a low tone*). Have you ever observed anything remarkable about Lovetown's manner?

LIMBURY. Anything remarkable?

TAPKINS. Ay,—anything very odd, and rather unpleasant?

LIMBURY. Decidedly! No longer than half an hour ago,—in this very room, I observed something in his manner particularly odd and exceedingly unpleasant.

TAPKINS. To your feelings as a husband?

LIMBURY. Yes, my friend, yes, yes;—you know it all, I see!

TAPKINS. What! Do *you* know it?

LIMBURY. I'm afraid I do; but go on—go on.

TAPKINS (*aside*). How the deuce can he know anything about it? Well, this oddness arises from the peculiar nature of his connexion with—— You look very pale.

LIMBURY. No, no,—go on,—'connexion with——'

TAPKINS. A certain lady,—you know whom I mean.

LIMBURY. I do, I do! (*Aside.*) Disgrace and confusion! I'll kill her with a look! I'll wither her with scornful indignation! Mrs. Limbury!—viper!

TAPKINS (*whispering with caution*). They—aren't—married.

LIMBURY. *They* aren't married! *Who* aren't?

TAPKINS. Those two, to be sure!

LIMBURY. *Those* two! *What* two?

TAPKINS. Why them. And the worst of it is she's—she's married to somebody else.

LIMBURY. Well, of course I know that.

TAPKINS. You know it?

LIMBURY. Of course I do. Why, how you talk! Isn't she my wife?

TAPKINS. *Your* wife! Wretched bigamist! Mrs. Lovetown your wife?

LIMBURY. Mrs. Lovetown! What! Have you been talking of Mrs. Lovetown all this time? My dear friend! (*Embraces him.*) The revulsion of feeling is almost insupportable. I thought you were talking about Mrs. Limbury.

TAPKINS. No!

LIMBURY. Yes. Ha! ha! But I say, what a dreadful fellow this is —another man's wife! Gad, I think he wants to run away with every man's wife he sees. And Mrs. Lovetown, too—horrid!

TAPKINS. Shocking!

LIMBURY. I say, I oughtn't to allow Mrs. Limbury to associate with her, ought I?

TAPKINS. Precisely my idea. You had better induce your wife to stay away from my house to-night.

LIMBURY. I'm afraid I can't do that.

TAPKINS. What, has she any particular objection to staying away?

LIMBURY. She has a very strange inclination to go, and 'tis much the same; however, I'll make the best arrangement I can!

TAPKINS. Well, so be it. Of course I shall see *you*?

LIMBURY. Of course.

TAPKINS. Mind the secret,—close—close—you know, as a Cabinet Minister answering a question.

LIMBURY. You may rely upon me.

[*Exit* LIMBURY, L. H., TAPKINS, R. H.

SCENE II.—*A Conservatory on one side. A Summer-house on the other.*

Enter LOVETOWN *at* L. H.

LOVETOWN. So far so good. My wife has not dropped the slightest hint of having overheard the conversation between me and Mrs. Limbury; but she cannot conceal the impression it has made upon her mind, or the jealousy it has evidently excited in her breast. This is just as I wished. I made Mr. Peter Limbury's amiable helpmate promise to meet me here. I know that refuge for destitute reptiles (*pointing to summer-house*) is Tapkins's favourite haunt, and if he has any assignation with my wife, I have no doubt he will lead her to this place. A woman's coming down the walk. Mrs. Limbury, I suppose,—no, my wife, by all that's actionable. I must conceal myself here, even at the risk of a shower of black beetles, or a marching regiment of frogs. (*Goes into conservatory,* L. H.)

Enter MRS. LOVETOWN *from top,* L. H.

MRS. LOVETOWN. I cannot have been mistaken. I am certain I saw Alfred here; he must have secreted himself somewhere to avoid me. Can his assignation with Mrs. Limbury have been discovered? Mr. Limbury's behaviour to me just now was strange in the extreme; and after a variety of incoherent expressions he begged me to meet him here, on a subject, as he said, of great delicacy and importance to myself. Alas! I fear that my husband's neglect and unkindness are but too well

Enter MR. LIMBURY *at top*, L. H.

known. The injured little man approaches. I summon all my fortitude to bear the disclosure.

LIMBURY (*aside*). Now as I could not prevail on Mrs. Limbury to stay away, the only distressing alternative I have is to inform Mrs. Lovetown that I know her history, and to put it to her good feeling whether she hadn't better go.

LOVETOWN. (*peeping*). Limbury! what the deuce can that little wretch want here?

LIMBURY. I took the liberty, Mrs. Lovetown, of begging you to meet me in this retired spot, because the esteem I still entertain for you, and my regard for your feelings, induce me to prefer a private to a public disclosure.

LOVETOWN (*peeping*). 'Public disclosure!' what on earth is he talking about? I wish he'd speak a little louder.

MRS. LOVETOWN. I am sensible of your kindness, Mr. Limbury, and believe me most grateful for it. I am fully prepared to hear what you have to say.

LIMBURY. It is hardly necessary for me, I presume, to say, Mrs. Lovetown, that I have accidentally discovered the whole secret.

MRS. LOVETOWN. The whole secret, sir?

LOVETOWN (*peeping*). Whole secret! What secret?

LIMBURY. The whole secret, ma'am, of this disgraceful—I must call it disgraceful—and most abominable intrigue.

MRS. LOVETOWN (*aside*). My worst fears are realised,—my husband's neglect is occasioned by his love for another.

LOVETOWN (*peeping*). Abominable intrigue! My first suspicions are too well founded. He reproaches my wife with her infidelity, and she cannot deny it,—that villain Tapkins!

MRS. LOVETOWN (*weeping*). Cruel—cruel—Alfred!

LIMBURY. You may well call him cruel, unfortunate woman. His usage of you is indefensible, unmanly, scandalous.

MRS. LOVETOWN. It is. It is, indeed.

LIMBURY. It's very painful for me to express myself in such plain terms, Mrs. Lovetown; but allow me to say, as delicately as possible, that you should not endeavour to appear in society under such unusual and distressing circumstances.

MRS. LOVETOWN. Not appear in society! Why should I quit it?

LOVETOWN (*peeping*). Shameful woman!

LIMBURY. Is it possible you can ask such a question?

MRS. LOVETOWN. What should I do? Where can I go?

LIMBURY. Gain permission to return once again to your husband's roof.

MRS. LOVETOWN. My husband's roof?

LIMBURY. Yes, the roof of your husband, your wretched, unfortunate husband!

MRS. LOVETOWN. Never!

LIMBURY (*aside*). She's thoroughly hardened, steeped in vice beyond redemption. Mrs. Lovetown, as you reject my well-intentioned advice in this extraordinary manner, I am reduced to the painful necessity of expressing my hope that you will,—now pray don't think me unkind,—that you will never attempt to meet Mrs. Limbury more.

MRS. LOVETOWN. What! Can you suppose I am so utterly dead to every sense of feeling and propriety as to meet that person,—the destroyer of my peace and happiness,—the wretch who has ruined my hopes and blighted my prospects for ever? Ask your own heart, sir,—appeal to your own feelings. *You* are naturally indignant at her conduct. *You* would hold no further communication with her. Can you suppose, then, *I* would deign to do so? The mere supposition is an insult!

[*Exit* MRS. LOVETOWN *hastily at top*, L. H.

LIMBURY. What can all this mean? I am lost in a maze of astonishment, petrified at the boldness with which she braves it out. Eh! it's breaking upon me by degrees. I see it. What did she say? 'Destroyer of peace and happiness,—person—ruined hopes and blighted prospects—*her*.' I see it all. That atrocious Lovetown, that Don Juan multiplied by twenty, that unprecedented libertine, has seduced Mrs. Limbury from her allegiance to her lawful lord and master. He first of all runs away with the wife of another man, and he is no sooner tired of her, than he runs away with another wife of another man. I thirst for his destruction. I—(LOVETOWN *rushes from the conservatory and embraces* LIMBURY, *who disengages himself*.) Murderer of domestic happiness! behold your victim!

LOVETOWN. Alas! you speak but too truly. (*Covering his face with his hands*.) I am the victim.

LIMBURY. I speak but too truly!—He avows his own criminality. I shall throttle him. I know I shall. I feel it.

Enter MRS. LIMBURY *at back*, L. H.

MRS. LIMBURY (*aside*). My husband here! (*Goes into conservatory.*)

Enter TAPKINS *at back*, L. H.

TAPKINS (*aside*). Not here, and her husband with Limbury. I'll reconnoitre. (*Goes into summer-house*, R. H.)

LIMBURY. Lovetown, have you the boldness to look an honest man in the face?

LOVETOWN. O, spare me! I feel the situation in which I am placed acutely, deeply. Feel for me when I say that from that conservatory I overheard the greater part of what passed between you and Mrs. Lovetown.

LIMBURY. You did?

LOVETOWN. Need I say how highly I approve both of the language you used, and the advice you gave her?

LIMBURY. What! you want to get rid of her, do you?

LOVETOWN. Can you doubt it?

TAPKINS (*peeping*). Hallo! he wants to get rid of her. Queer!

LOVETOWN. Situated as I am, you know, I have no other resource, after what has passed. I must part from her.

MRS. LIMBURY (*peeping*). What can he mean?

LIMBURY (*aside*). I should certainly throttle him, were it not that the coolness with which he refers to the dreadful event paralyses me. Mr. Lovetown, look at me! Sir, consider the feelings of an indignant husband, sir!

LOVETOWN. Oh, I thank you for those words. Those strong expressions prove the unaffected interest you take in the matter.

LIMBURY. Unaffected interest! I shall go raving mad with passion and fury! Villain! Monster! To embrace the opportunity afforded him of being on a footing of friendship.

LOVETOWN. To take a mean advantage of his being a single man.

LIMBURY. To tamper with the sacred engagements of a married woman.

LOVETOWN. To place a married man in a disgraceful and humiliating situation.

LIMBURY. Scoundrel! Do you mock me to my face?

LOVETOWN. Mock *you*! What d'ye mean? Who the devil are you talking about?

LIMBURY. Talking about—*you*!

LOVETOWN. Me!

LIMBURY. Designing miscreant! Of whom do *you* speak?

LOVETOWN. Of whom should I speak but that scoundrel Tapkins?

TAPKINS (*coming forward*, R.). Me! What the devil do you mean by that?

LOVETOWN. Ha! (*Rushing at him, is held back by* LIMBURY.)

LIMBURY (*to* TAPKINS). Avoid him. Get out of his sight. He's raving mad with conscious villainy.

TAPKINS. What are you all playing at *I spy I* over my two acres of infant hay for?

LOVETOWN (*to* TAPKINS). How dare you tamper with the affections of Mrs. Lovetown?

TAPKINS. O, is that all? Ha! ha! (*Crosses to* C.)

LOVETOWN. All!

TAPKINS. Come, come, none of your nonsense.

LOVETOWN. Nonsense! Designate the best feelings of our nature nonsense!

TAPKINS. Pooh! pooh! Here, I know all about it.

LOVETOWN (*angrily*). And so do I, sir. And so do I.

TAPKINS. Of course you do. And you've managed very well to keep it quiet so long. But you're a deep fellow, by Jove! you're a deep fellow!

LOVETOWN. Now, mind! I restrain myself sufficiently to ask you once again before I knock you down, by what right dare you tamper with the affections of Mrs. Lovetown?

TAPKINS. Right! O, if you come to strict right, you know, nobody has a right but her husband.

LOVETOWN. And who is her husband? Who is her husband?

TAPKINS. Ah! to be sure, that's the question. Nobody that I know. I hope—poor fellow——

LOVETOWN. I'll bear these insults no longer! (*Rushes towards* TAPKINS. LIMBURY *interposes.* LOVETOWN *crosses to* R. H. *A scream is heard from the conservatory—a pause.*)

TAPKINS. Something singular among the plants! (*He goes into the conservatory and returns with* MRS. LIMBURY.) A flower that wouldn't come out of its own accord. I was obliged to force it. Tolerably full blown now, at all events.

LIMBURY. My wife! Traitoress! (*Crosses to* L. H.) Fly from my presence! Quit my sight! Return to the conservatory with that demon in a frock-coat!

Enter MRS. LOVETOWN *at top*, L. H., *and comes down* C.

TAPKINS. Hallo! Somebody else!

LOVETOWN (*aside*). My wife here!

MRS. LOVETOWN (*to* LIMBURY). I owe you some return for the commiseration you expressed just now for my wretched situation. The best, the only one I can make you is, to entreat you to refrain from committing any rash act, however excited you may be, and to control the feelings of an injured husband.

TAPKINS. Injured husband! Decidedly singular!

LOVETOWN. The allusion of that lady I confess my utter inability to understand. Mr. Limbury, to you an explanation is due, and I make it more cheerfully, as my abstaining from doing so might involve the character of your wife. Stung by the attentions which I found Mrs. Lovetown had received from a scoundrel present,——

TAPKINS (*aside*). That's me.

LOVETOWN. I—partly to obtain opportunities of watching her closely, under an assumed mask of levity and carelessness, and partly in the hope of awakening once again any dormant feelings of affection that might still slumber in her breast, affected a passion for your wife which I never felt, and to which she never really responded. The second part of my project, I regret to say, has failed. The first has succeeded but too well.

LIMBURY. Can I believe my ears? But how came Mrs. Peter Limbury to receive those attentions?

MRS. LIMBURY. Why, not because I liked them, of course, but to assist Mr. Lovetown in his project, and to teach you the misery of those jealous fears. Come here, you stupid little jealous insinuating darling. (*They retire up* L. H., *she coaxing him.*)

TAPKINS (*aside*). It strikes me very forcibly that I have made a slight mistake here, which is something particularly singular. (*Turns up* R. H.)

MRS. LOVETOWN. Alfred, hear me! I am as innocent as yourself. Your fancied neglect and coldness hurt my weak vanity, and roused some foolish feelings of angry pride. In a moment of irritation I resorted to some such retaliation as you have yourself described. That I did so from motives as guiltless as your own I call Heaven to witness. That I repent my fault I solemnly assure you.

LOVETOWN. Is this possible?

TAPKINS. Very possible indeed! Believe your wife's assurance and my corroboration. Here, give and take is all fair, you know. Give me your hand and take your wife's. Here, Mr. and Mrs. L. (*To* LIMBURY.) Double L,—I call them. (*To* LOVETOWN.) Small italic and Roman capital. (*To* MR. *and* MRS. LIMBURY, *who come forward.*) Here, it's all arranged. The key to the whole matter is, that I've been mistaken, which is something singular. If I have made another mistake in calculating on *your* kind and lenient reception of our last half-hour's misunderstanding (*to the audience*), I shall have done something more singular still. Do you forbid me committing any more mistakes, or may I announce my intention of doing something singular again?

CURTAIN

THE END

THE LAMPLIGHTER

A Farce

IN ONE ACT

[1838]

DRAMATIS PERSONÆ

MR. STARGAZER.
MASTER GALILEO ISAAC NEWTON FLAMSTEAD STARGAZER (*his son*).
TOM GRIG (*the Lamplighter*).
MR. MOONEY (*an astrologer*).
SERVANT.
BETSY MARTIN.
EMMA STARGAZER.
FANNY BROWN.

THE LAMPLIGHTER

SCENE I.—*The Street, outside of* MR. STARGAZER'S *house. Two street Lamp-posts in front.*

TOM GRIG (*with ladder and lantern, singing as he enters*).

Day has gone down o'er the Baltic's proud bil-ler;
Evening has sigh'd, alas! to the lone wil-ler;
Night hurries on, night hurries on, earth and ocean to kiv-ver;
Rise, gentle moon, rise, gentle moon, and guide me to my——

That ain't a rhyme, that ain't—kiv-ver and lover! I ain't much of a poet; but if I couldn't make better verse than that, I'd undertake to be set fire to, and put up, instead of the lamp, before Alderman Waithman's obstacle in Fleet Street. Bil-ler, wil-ler, kiv-ver—shiver, obviously. That's what *I* call poetry. (*Sings.*)

Day has gone down o'er the Baltic's proud bil-ler—

(*During the previous speech he has been occupied in lighting one of the lamps. As he is about to light the other,* MR. STARGAZER *appears at window, with a telescope.*)

MR. STARGAZER (*after spying most intently at the clouds*). Holloa!

TOM (*on ladder*). Sir, to you! And holloa again, if you come to that.

MR. STARGAZER. Have you seen the comet?

TOM. What Comet—the Exeter Comet?

MR. STARGAZER. What comet? *The* comet—Halley's comet!

TOM. Nelson's you mean. I saw it coming out of the yard, not five minutes ago.

MR. STARGAZER. Could you distinguish anything of a tail?

TOM. Distinguish a tail? I believe you—four tails?

MR. STARGAZER. A comet with four tails; and all visible to the naked eye! Nonsense! it couldn't be.

TOM. You wouldn't say that again if you was down here, old bantam. (*Clock strikes five.*) You'll tell me next, I suppose, that that isn't five o'clock striking, eh?

MR. STARGAZER. Five o'clock—five o'clock! Five o'clock P.M. on the thirtieth day of November, one thousand eight hundred and thirty-eight! Stop till I come down—stop! Don't go away on any account—not a foot, not a step. (*Closes window.*)

TOM (*descending, and shouldering his ladder*). Stop! stop, to a lamplighter, with three hundred and seventy shops and a hundred and twenty private houses waiting to be set a light to! Stop, to a lamplighter!

As he is running off, enter MR. STARGAZER *from his house, hastily.*

MR. STARGAZER (*detaining him*). Not for your life!—not for your life! The thirtieth day of November, one thousand eight hundred and thirty-eight! Miraculous circumstance! extraordinary fulfilment of a prediction of the planets!

TOM. What are you talking about?

MR. STARGAZER (*looking about*). Is there nobody else in sight, up the street or down? No, not a soul! This, then, is the man whose coming was revealed to me by the stars, six months ago!

TOM. What do you mean?

MR. STARGAZER. Young man, that I have consulted the Book of Fate with rare and wonderful success,—that coming events have cast their shadows before.

TOM. Don't talk nonsense to me,—I ain't an event; I'm a lamplighter!

MR. STARGAZER (*aside*). True!—Strange destiny that one, announced by the planets as of noble birth, should be devoted to so humble an occupation. (*Aloud.*) But you were not *always* a lamplighter?

TOM. Why, no. I wasn't born with a ladder on my left shoulder, and a light in my other hand. But I took to it very early, though,—I had it from my uncle.

MR. STARGAZER (*aside*). He had it from his uncle! How plain, and yet how forcible, is his language! He speaks of lamplighting, as though it were the whooping-cough or measles! (*To him.*) Ay!

TOM. Yes, he was the original. You should have known him!—'cod! he was a genius, if ever there was one. Gas was the death of him! When gas lamps was first talked of, my uncle draws himself up, and says, 'I'll not believe it, there's no sich a thing,' he says. 'You might as well talk of laying on an everlasting succession of glow-worms!' But when they made the experiment of lighting a piece of Pall Mall——

MR. STARGAZER. That was when it first came up?

TOM. No, no, that was when it was first laid down. Don't mind me; I can't help a joke, now and then. My uncle was sometimes took that way. When the experiment was made of lighting a piece of Pall Mall, and he had actually witnessed it, with his own eyes, you should have seen my uncle then!

MR. STARGAZER. So much overcome?

TOM. Overcome, sir! He fell off his ladder, from weakness, fourteen times that very night; and his last fall was into a wheelbarrow that was going his way, and humanely took him home. 'I foresee in this,' he says, 'the breaking up of our profession; no more polishing of the tin reflectors,' he says; 'no more fancy-work, in the way of clipping the cottons at two o'clock in the morning; no more going the rounds to trim by daylight, and dribbling down of the *ile* on the hats and bonnets of the ladies and gentlemen, when one feels in good spirits. Any low fellow can light a gas-lamp, and it's all up!' So he petitioned the Government for—what do you call that that they give to people when it's found out that they've never been of any use, and have been paid too much for doing nothing?

MR. STARGAZER. Compensation?

TOM. Yes, that's the thing,—compensation. They didn't give him any, though! And then he got very fond of his country all at once, and went about, saying how that the bringing in of gas was a death-blow to his native land, and how that its *ile* and cotton trade was gone for ever, and the whales would go and kill themselves, privately, in spite and vexation at not being caught! After this, he was right-down cracked, and called his 'bacco pipe a gas pipe, and thought his tears was lamp *ile*, and all manner of nonsense. At last, he went and hung himself on a lamp iron, in St. Martin's Lane, that he'd always been very fond of; and as he was a remarkably good husband, and had never had any secrets from his wife, he put a note in the two-penny post, as he went along, to tell the widder where the body was.

MR. STARGAZER (*laying his hand upon his arm, and speaking mysteriously*). Do you remember your parents?

TOM. My mother I do, very well!

MR. STARGAZER. Was she of noble birth?

TOM. Pretty well. She was in the mangling line. Her mother came of a highly respectable family,—such a business, in the sweet-stuff and hardbake way!

MR. STARGAZER. Perhaps your father was——

TOM. Why, I hardly know about him. The fact is, there was some little doubt, at the time, who *was* my father. Two or three young gentlemen were paid the pleasing compliment; but their incomes being limited, they were compelled delicately to decline it.

MR. STARGAZER. Then the prediction is not fulfilled merely in part, but entirely and completely. Listen, young man,—I am acquainted with all the celestial bodies——

TOM. Are you, though?—I hope they are quite well,—every body.

MR. STARGAZER. Don't interrupt me. I am versed in the great sciences of astronomy and astrology; in my house there I have every description of apparatus for observing the course and motion of the planets. I'm writing a work about them, which will consist of eighty-four volumes, imperial quarto; and an appendix, nearly twice as long. I read what's going to happen in the stars.

TOM. Read what's going to happen in the stars! Will anything particular happen in the stars in the course of next week, now?

MR. STARGAZER. You don't understand me. I read in the stars what's going to happen here. Six months ago I derived from this source the knowledge that, precisely as the clock struck five, on the afternoon of this very day, a stranger would present himself before my enraptured sight,—that stranger would be a man of illustrious and high descent,—that stranger would be the destined husband of my young and lovely niece, who is now beneath that roof (*points to his house*);—that stranger is yourself: I receive you with open arms!

TOM. Me! I, the man of illustrious and high—I, the husband of a young and lovely—Oh! it can't be, you know! the stars have made a mistake—the comet has put 'em out!

MR. STARGAZER. Impossible! The characters were as plain as pikestaves. The clock struck five; you were here; there was not a soul in sight; a mystery envelopes your birth; you are a man of noble aspect. Does not everything combine to prove the accuracy of my observations?

TOM. Upon my word, it looks like it! And now I come to think of it, I have very often felt as if I wasn't the small beer I was taken for. And yet I don't know,—you're quite sure about the noble aspect?

MR. STARGAZER. Positively certain.

TOM. Give me your hand.

MR. STARGAZER. And my heart, too! (*They shake hands heartily.*)

TOM. The young lady is tolerably good-looking, is she?

MR. STARGAZER. Beautiful! A graceful carriage, an exquisite shape, a sweet voice; a countenance beaming with animation and expression; the eye of a startled fawn.

TOM. I see; a sort of game eye. Does she happen to have any of the—this is quite between you and me, you know,—and I only ask from curiosity,—not because I care about it,—any of the ready?

MR. STARGAZER. Five thousand pounds! But what of that? what of that? A word in your ear. I'm in search of the philosopher's stone! I have very nearly found it—not quite. It turns everything to gold; that's its property.

TOM. What a lot of property it must have!

MR. STARGAZER. When I get it, we'll keep it in the family. Not a word to any one! What will money be to us? We shall never be able to spend it fast enough.

TOM. Well, you know, we can but try,—I'll do my best endeavours.

MR. STARGAZER. Thank you,—thank you! But I'll introduce you to your future bride at once:—this way, this way!

TOM. What, without going my rounds first?

MR. STARGAZER. Certainly. A man in whom the planets take especial interest, and who is about to have a share in the philosopher's stone, descend to lamplighting!

TOM. Perish the base idea! not by no means! I'll take in my tools though, to prevent any kind inquiries after me, at your door. (*As he shoulders the ladder the sound of violent rain is heard.*) Holloa!

MR. STARGAZER (*putting his hand on his head in amazement*). What's that?

TOM. It's coming down, rather.

MR. STARGAZER. Rain!

TOM. Ah! and a soaker, too!

MR. STARGAZER. It can't be!—it's impossible!—(*Taking a book from his pocket, and turning over the pages hurriedly.*) Look here,—here it is,—here's the weather almanack,—'Set fair,'—I knew it couldn't be! (*with great triumph*).

TOM (*turning up his collar as the rain increases*). Don't you think there's a dampness in the atmosphere?

MR. STARGAZER (*looking up*). It's singular,—it's *like* rain!

TOM. Uncommonly like.

MR. STARGAZER. It's a mistake in the elements, somehow. Here it is, 'set fair,'—and set fair it ought to be. 'Light clouds floating about.' Ah! you see, there are no light clouds;—the weather's all wrong.

TOM. Don't you think we had better get under cover?

MR. STARGAZER (*slowly retreating towards the house*). I don't acknowledge that it has any right to rain, mind! I protest against this. If Nature goes on in this way, I shall lose all respect for her,—it won't do, you know; it ought to have been two degrees colder, yesterday; and instead of that, it was warmer. This is not the way to treat scientific men. I protest against it!

[*Exeunt into house, both talking,* TOM *pushing* STARGAZER *on, and the latter continually turning back, to declaim against the weather.*]

SCENE II.—*A Room in* STARGAZER'S *house,* BETSY MARTIN, EMMA STARGAZER, FANNY BROWN, *and* GALILEO, *all murmuring together as they enter.*

BETSY. I say again, young ladies, that it's shameful! unbearable!

ALL. Oh! shameful! shameful!

BETSY. Marry Miss Emma to a great, old, ugly, doting, dreaming As-tron-o-Magician, like Mr. Mooney, who's always winking and blinking through telescopes and that, and can't see a pretty face when it's under his very nose!

GALILEO (*with a melancholy air*). There never was a pretty face under *his* nose, Betsy, leastways, since I've known him. He's very plain.

BETSY. Ah! there's poor young master, too; he hasn't even spirits enough left to laugh at his own jokes. I'm sure I pity him, from the very bottom of my heart.

FANNY *and* EMMA. Poor fellow!

GALILEO. Ain't I a legitimate subject for pity! Ain't it a dreadful thing that I, that am twenty-one come next Lady-day, should be treated like a little boy?—and all because my father is so busy with the moon's age that he don't care about mine; and so much occupied in making observations on the sun round which the earth revolves, that he takes no notice of the son that revolves round him! I wasn't taken out of nankeen frocks and trousers till I became quite unpleasant in 'em.

ALL. What a shame!

GALILEO. I wasn't, indeed. And look at me now! Here's a state of things. Is this a suit of clothes for a major,—at least, for a gentleman who is a minor now, but will be a major on the very next Lady-day that comes? Is this a fit——

ALL (*interrupting him*). Certainly not!

GALILEO (*vehemently*). I won't stand it—I won't submit to it any longer. I *will* be married.

ALL. No, no, no! don't be rash.

GALILEO. I will, I tell you. I'll marry my cousin Fanny. Give me a kiss, Fanny; and Emma and Betsy will look the other way the while. (*Kisses her.*) There!

BETSY. Sir—sir! here's your father coming!

GALILEO. Well, then, I'll have another, as an antidote to my father. One more; Fanny. (*Kisses her.*)

MR. STARGAZER (*without*). This way! this way! You shall behold her immediately.

Enter MR. STARGAZER, TOM *following bashfully.*

MR. STARGAZER. Where is my——? Oh, here she is! Fanny, my dear, come here. Do you see that gentleman? (*Aside.*)

FANNY. What gentleman, uncle? Do you mean that elastic person yonder who is bowing with so much perseverance?

MR. STARGAZER. Hush! yes; that's the interesting stranger.

FANNY. Why, he is kissing his hand, uncle. What does the creature mean?

MR. STARGAZER. Ah, the rogue! Just like me, before I married your poor aunt,—all fire and impatience. He means love, my darling, love. I've such a delightful surprise for you. I didn't tell you before, for fear there should be any mistake; but it's all right, it's all right. The stars have settled it all among 'em. He's to be your husband!

FANNY. My husband, uncle? Goodness gracious, Emma! (*Converses apart with her.*)

MR. STARGAZER (*aside*). He has made a sensation already. His noble aspect and distinguished air have produced an instantaneous impression. Mr. Grig, will you permit me? (TOM *advances awkwardly.*)—This is my niece, Mr. Grig,—my niece, Miss Fanny Brown; my daughter, Emma,—Mr. Thomas Grig, the favourite of the planets.

TOM. I hope I see Miss Hemmer in a conwivial state? (*Aside to* MR. STARGAZER.) I say, I don't know which is which.

MR. STARGAZER (*aside*). The young lady nearest here is your affianced bride. Say something appropriate.

TOM. Certainly; yes, of course. Let me see. Miss (*crosses to her*)—I—thank'ee! (*Kisses her, behind his hat. She screams.*)

GALILEO (*bursting from* BETSY, *who has been retaining him*). Outrageous insolence! (BETSY *runs off.*)

MR. STARGAZER. Halloa, sir, halloa!

TOM. Who is this juvenile salamander, sir?

MR. STARGAZER. My little boy,—only my little boy; don't mind him. Shake hands with the gentleman, sir, instantly (*to* GALILEO).

TOM. A very fine boy, indeed! and he does you great credit, sir. How d'ye do, my little man? (*They shake hands,* GALILEO *looking very wrathful, as* TOM *pats him on the head.*) There, that's very right and proper. ''Tis dogs delight to bark and bite'; not young gentlemen, you know. There, there!

MR. STARGAZER. Now let me introduce you to that *sanctum sanctorum*,—that hallowed ground,—that philosophical retreat—where I, the *genius loci*,——

TOM. Eh?

MR. STARGAZER. The *genius loci*——

TOM (*aside*). Something to drink, perhaps. Oh, ah! yes, yes!

MR. STARGAZER. Have made all my greatest and most profound discoveries! where the telescope has almost grown to my eye with constant application; and the glass retort has been shivered to pieces from the ardour with which my experiments have been pursued. There the illustrious Mooney is, even now, pursuing those researches which will enrich us with precious metal, and make us masters of the world. Come, Mr. Grig.

TOM. By all means, sir; and luck to the illustrious Mooney, say I, —not so much on Mooney's account as for our noble selves.

MR. STARGAZER. Emma!

EMMA. Yes, papa.

MR. STARGAZER. The same day that makes your cousin Mrs. Grig, will make you and that immortal man, of whom we have just now spoken, one.

EMMA. Oh! consider, dear papa,——

MR. STARGAZER. You are unworthy of him, I know; but he,—kind, generous creature,—consents to overlook your defects, and to take you, for my sake,—devoted man!—Come, Mr. Grig!—Galileo Isaac Newton Flamstead!

GALILEO. Well? (*Advancing sulkily.*)

MR. STARGAZER. In name, alas! but not in nature; knowing, even by sight, no other planets than the sun and moon,—here is your weekly pocket-money,—sixpence! Take it all!

TOM. And don't spend it all at once, my man! Now, sir!

MR. STARGAZER. Now, Mr. Grig,—go first, sir, I beg!

[*Exeunt* TOM *and* MR. STARGAZER.

GALILEO. 'Come, Mr. Grig!'—'Go first, Mr. Grig!'—'Day that makes your cousin Mrs. Grig!'—I'll secretly stick a penknife into Mr. Grig, if I live to be three hours older!

FANNY (*on one side of him*). Oh! don't talk in that desperate way, —there's a dear, dear creature!

EMMA (*on the other side*). No! pray do not;—it makes my blood run cold to hear you.

GALILEO. Oh! if I was of age!—if I was only of age!—or we could go to Gretna Green, at threepence a head, including refreshments and all incidental expenses. But that could never be! Oh! if I was only of age!

FANNY. But what if you were? What could you do, then?

GALILEO. Marry you, cousin Fanny; I could marry you then lawfully, and without anybody's consent.

FANNY. You forget that, situated as we are, we could not be

married, even if you *were* one-and-twenty;—we have no money!

EMMA. Not even enough for the fees!

GALILEO. Oh! I am sure every Christian clergyman, under such afflicting circumstances, would marry us on credit. The wedding-fees might stand over till the first christening, and then we could settle the little bill altogether. Oh! why ain't I of age!—why ain't I of age?

Enter BETSY, *in haste.*

BETSY. Well! I never could have believed it! There, Miss! I wouldn't have believed it, if I had dreamt it, even with a bit of bride-cake under my pillow! To dare to go and think of marrying a young lady, with five thousand pounds, to a common lamplighter!

ALL. A lamplighter?

BETSY. Yes, he's Tom Grig the lamplighter, and nothing more nor less, and old Mr. Stargazer goes and picks him out of the open street, and brings him in for Miss Fanny's husband, because he pretends to have read something about it in the stars. Stuff and nonsense! I don't believe he knows his letters in the stars, and that's the truth; or if he's got as far as words in one syllable, it's quite as much as he has.

FANNY. Was such an atrocity ever heard of? I, left with no power to marry without his consent, and he almost possessing the power to force my inclinations.

EMMA. It's actually worse than my being sacrificed to that odious and detestable Mr. Mooney.

BETSY. Come, Miss, it's not quite so bad as that neither; for Thomas Grig is a young man, and a proper young man enough too, but as to Mr. Mooney,—oh, dear! no husband is bad enough in my opinion, Miss; but he is worse than nothing,—a great deal worse.

FANNY. You seem to speak feelingly about this same Mr. Grig.

BETSY. Oh, dear no, Miss, not I. I don't mean to say but what Mr. Grig may be very well in his way, Miss; but Mr. Grig and I have never held any communication together, not even so much as how-d'ye-do. Oh, no indeed, I have been very careful, Miss, as I always am with strangers. I was acquainted with the last lamplighter, Miss, but he's going to be married, and has given up the calling, for the young woman's parents being very respectable, wished her to marry a literary man, and so he has set up as a bill-sticker. Mr. Grig only came upon this beat at five to-night, Miss.

FANNY. Which is a very sufficient reason why you don't know more of him.

BETSY. Well, Miss, perhaps it is; and I hope there's no crime in making friends in this world, if we can, Miss.

FANNY. Certainly not. So far from it, that I most heartily wish you could make something more than a friend of this Mr. Grig, and so lead him to falsify this prediction.

GALILEO. Oh! don't you think you could, Betsy?

EMMA. You could not manage at the same time to get any young friend of yours to make something more than a friend of Mr. Mooney, could you, Betsy?

GALILEO. But, seriously, don't you think you could manage to give us all a helping hand together, in some way, eh, Betsy?

FANNY. Yes, yes, that would be so delightful. I should be grateful to her for ever. Shouldn't you?

EMMA. Oh, to the very end of my life!

GALILEO. And so should I, you know, and lor'! we should make her so rich, when—when we got rich ourselves,—shouldn't we?

BOTH. Oh, that we should, of course.

BETSY. Let me see. I don't wish to have Mr. Grig to myself, you know. I don't want to be married.

ALL. No! no! no! Of course she don't.

BETSY. I haven't the least idea to put Mr. Grig off this match, you know, for anybody's sake, but you young people's. I am going quite *contrairy* to my own feelings, you know.

ALL. Oh, yes, yes! How kind she is!

BETSY. Well, I'll go over the matter with the young ladies in Miss Emma's room, and if we can think of anything that seems likely to help us, so much the better; and if we can't, we're none the worst. But Master Galileo mustn't come, for he is so horrid jealous of Miss Fanny that I dursn't hardly say anything before him. Why, I declare (*looking off*), there is my gentleman looking about him as if he had lost Mr. Stargazer, and now he turns this way. There.—get out of sight. Make haste!

GALILEO. I may see 'em as far as the bottom stair, mayn't I, Betsy?

BETSY. Yes, but not a step farther on any consideration. There, get away softly, so that if he passes here, he may find me alone. (*They creep gently out*, GALILEO *returns and peeps in.*)

GALILEO. Hist, Betsy!

BETSY. Go away, sir. What have you come back for?

GALILEO (*holding out a large pin*). I wish you'd take an opportunity of sticking this a little way into him for patting me on the head just now.

BETSY. Nonsense, you can't afford to indulge in such expensive amusements as retaliation yet awhile. You must wait till you come into your property, sir. There—Get you gone!

[*Exit* GALILEO.

Enter TOM GRIG.

TOM (*aside*). I never saw such a scientific file in my days. The enterprising gentleman that drowned himself *to see how it felt*, is nothing to him. There he is, just gone down to the bottom of a dry well in an uncommonly small bucket, to take an extra squint at the stars, they being seen best, I suppose, through the medium of a cold in the head. Halloa! Here is a young female of attractive proportions. I wonder now whether a man of noble aspect would be justified in tickling her. (*He advances stealthily and tickles her under the arm.*)

BETSY (*starting*). Eh! what! Lor', sir!

TOM. Don't be alarmed. My intentions are strictly honourable. In other words, I have no intentions whatever.

BETSY. Then you ought to be more careful, Mr. Grig. That was a liberty, sir.

TOM. I know it was. The cause of liberty, all over the world,—that's my sentiment! What is your name?

BETSY (*curtseying*). Betsy Martin, sir.

TOM. A name famous both in song and story. Would you have the goodness, Miss Martin, to direct me to that particular apartment wherein the illustrious Mooney is now pursuing his researches?

BETSY (*aside*). A little wholesome fear may not be amiss. (*To him, in assumed agitation.*) You are not going into *that* room, Mr. Grig?

TOM. Indeed, I am, and I ought to be there now, having promised to join that light of science, your master (a short six by the bye!), outside the door.

BETSY. That dreadful and mysterious chamber! Another victim!

TOM. Victim, Miss Martin!

BETSY. Oh! the awful oath of secrecy which binds me not to disclose the perils of that gloomy, hideous room.

TOM (*astonished*). Miss Martin!

BETSY. Such a fine young man,—so rosy and fresh-coloured, that he should fall into the clutches of that cruel and insatiable monster! I cannot continue to witness such frightful scenes; I must give warning.

TOM. If you have anything to unfold, young woman, have the goodness to give *me* warning at once.

BETSY (*affecting to recover herself*). No, no, Mr. Grig, it's nothing,—it's ha! ha! ha!—don't mind me, don't mind me, but it certainly is very shocking;—no,—no,—I don't mean that. I mean funny,—yes. Ha! ha! ha!

TOM (*aside, regarding her attentively*). I suspect a trick here,—some other lover in the case who wants to come over the stars; —but it won't do. I'll tell you what, young woman (*to her*), if this is a cloak, you had better try it on elsewhere;—in plain English, if you have any object to gain and think to gain it by frightening *me*, it's all my eye and, and—yourself, Miss Martin.

BETSY. Well, then, if you will rush upon your fate,—there (*pointing off*)—that's the door at the end of that long passage and across the gravelled yard. The room is built away from the house on purpose.

TOM. I'll make for it at once, and the first object I inspect through that same telescope, which now and then grows to your master's eye, shall be the moon—the moon, which is the emblem of your inconstant and deceitful sex, Miss Martin.

Duet.

AIR—'*The Young May-moon.*'

TOM. There comes a new moon twelve times a year.
BETSY. And when there is none, all is dark and drear.
TOM. In which I espy—
BETSY. And so, too, do I—
BOTH. A resemblance to womankind very clear.

BOTH. There comes a new moon twelve times in a year;
And when there is none, all is dark and drear.
TOM. In which I espy—
BETSY. And so do I—
BOTH. A resemblance to womankind very clear.

Second Verse.

TOM. She changes, she's fickle, she drives men mad.
BETSY. She comes to bring light, and leaves them sad.
TOM. So restless wild—
BETSY. But so sweetly wild—
BOTH. That no better companion could be had.
BOTH. There comes a new moon twelve times a year;
And when there is none, all is dark and drear.
TOM. In which I espy—
BETSY. And so do I—
BOTH. A resemblance to womankind very clear. [*Exeunt.*

SCENE III.—*A large gloomy room; a window with a telescope directed towards the sky without, a table covered with books, instruments and apparatus, which are also scattered about in other parts of the chamber, a dim lamp, a pair of globes, etc., a skeleton in a case, and various uncouth objects displayed against the walls. Two doors in flat.* MR. MOONEY *discovered, with a very dirty face, busily engaged in blowing a fire, upon which is a crucible.*

Enter MR. STARGAZER, *with a lamp, beckoning to* TOM GRIG, *who enters with some unwillingness.*

MR. STARGAZER. This, Mr. Grig, is the *sanctum sanctorum* of which I have already spoken; this is at once the laboratory and observatory.

TOM. It's not an over-lively place, is it?

MR. STARGAZER. It has an air of solemnity which well accords with the great and mysterious pursuits that are here in constant prosecution, Mr. Grig.

TOM. Ah! I should think it would suit an undertaker to the life; or perhaps I should rather say to the death. What may that cheerful object be now? (*Pointing to a large phial.*)

MR. STARGAZER. That contains a male infant with three heads, —we use it in astrology;—it is supposed to be a *charm*.

TOM. I shouldn't have supposed it myself, from his appearance. The young gentleman isn't alive, is he?

MR. STARGAZER. No, he is preserved in spirits. (MR. MOONEY *sneezes*.)

TOM (*retreating into a corner*). Halloa! What the—— (MR. MOONEY *looks vacantly round*.) That gentleman, I suppose, is out of spirits?

MR. STARGAZER (*laying his hand upon* TOM's *arm and looking toward the philosopher*). Hush! that is the gifted Mooney. Mark well his noble countenance,—intense thought beams from every lineament. That is the great astrologer.

TOM. He looks as if he had been having a touch at the black art. I say, why don't he say something?

MR. STARGAZER. He is in a state of abstraction; see he directs his bellows this way, and blows upon the empty air.

TOM. Perhaps he sees a strange spark in this direction and wonders how he came here. I wish he'd blow me out. (*Aside*.) I don't half like this.

MR. STARGAZER. You shall see me rouse him.

TOM. Don't put yourself out of the way on my account; I can make his acquaintance at any other time.

MR. STARGAZER. No time like the time present. Nothing awakens him from these fits of meditation but an electric shock. We always have a strongly charged battery on purpose. I'll give him a shock directly. (MR. STARGAZER *goes up and cautiously places the end of a wire in* MR. MOONEY'S *hand. He then stoops down beside the table as though bringing it in contact with the battery*. MR. MOONEY *immediately jumps up with a loud cry and throws away the bellows*.)

TOM (*squaring at the philosopher*). It wasn't me, you know,—none of your nonsense.

MR. STARGAZER (*comes hastily forward*). Mr. Grig,—Mr. Grig, —not that disrespectful attitude to one of the greatest men that ever lived. This, my dear friend (*to* MOONEY),—is the noble stranger.

MR. MOONEY. A ha!

MR. STARGAZER. Who arrived, punctual to his time, this afternoon.

MR. MOONEY. O ho!

MR. STARGAZER. Welcome him, my friend,—give him your hand. (MR. MOONEY *appears confused and raises his leg.*) No—no, that's your foot. So absent, Mr. Grig, in his gigantic meditations that very often he doesn't know one from the other. Yes, that's your hand, very good, my dear friend, very good (*pats* MOONEY *on the back, as he and* TOM *shake hands, the latter at arm's length*).

MR. STARGAZER. Have you made any more discoveries during my absence?

MR. MOONEY. Nothing particular.

MR. STARGAZER. Do you think—do you think, my dear friend, that we shall arrive at any great stage in our labours, anything at all approaching to their final consummation in the course of the night?

MR. MOONEY. I cannot take upon myself to say.

MR. STARGAZER. What are your opinions upon the subject?

MR. MOONEY. I haven't any opinions upon any subject whatsoever.

MR. STARGAZER. Wonderful man! Here's a mind, Mr. Grig.

TOM. Yes, his conversation's very improving indeed. But what's he staring so hard at me for?

MR. STARGAZER. Something occurs to him. Don't speak,—don't disturb the current of his reflections upon any account. (MR. MOONEY *walks solemnly up to* TOM, *who retreats before him; taking off his hat turns it over and over with a thoughtful countenance and finally puts it upon his own head.*)

MR. STARGAZER. Eccentric man!

TOM. I say, I hope he don't mean to keep that, because if he does, his eccentricity is unpleasant. Give him another shock and knock it off, will you?

MR. STARGAZER. Hush! hush! not a word. (MR. MOONEY, *keeping his eyes fixed on* TOM, *slowly returns to* MR. STARGAZER *and whispers in his ear.*)

MR. STARGAZER. Surely; by all means. I took the date of his birth, and all other information necessary for the purpose just now. (*To* TOM.) Mr. Mooney suggests that we should cast your nativity without delay, in order that we may communicate to you your future destiny.

MR. MOONEY. Let us retire for that purpose.

MR. STARGAZER. Certainly, wait here for a few moments, Mr. Grig: we are only going into the little laboratory and will return immediately. Now, my illustrious friend. (*He takes up a lamp and leads the way to one of the doors. As* MR. MOONEY *follows,* TOM *steals behind him and regains his hat.* MR. MOONEY *turns round, stares, and exit through door.*)

TOM. Well, that's the queerest genius I ever came across,—rather a singular person for a little smoking party. (*Looks into the crucible.*) This is the saucepan, I suppose, where they're boiling the philosopher's stone down to the proper consistency. I hope it's nearly done; when it's quite ready, I'll send out for six-penn'orth of sprats, and turn 'em into gold fish for a first experiment. 'Cod! it'll be a comfortable thing though to have no end to one's riches. I'll have a country house and a park, and I'll plant a bit of it with a double row of gas-lamps a mile long, and go out with a French polished mahogany ladder, and two servants in livery behind me, to light 'em with my own hands every night. What's to be seen here? (*Looks through telescope.*) Nothing particular, the stopper being on at the other end. The little boy with three heads (*looking towards the case*). What a comfort he must have been to his parents!—Halloa! (*taking up a large knife*) this is a disagreeable-looking instrument,—something too large for bread and cheese, or oysters, and not of a bad shape for sticking live persons in the ribs. A very dismal place this,—I wish they'd come back. Ah!—(*coming upon the skeleton*) here's a ghastly object,—what does the writing say?—(*reads a label upon the case*) 'Skeleton of a gentleman prepared by Mr. Mooney.' I hope Mr. Mooney may not be in the habit of inviting gentlemen here, and making 'em into such preparations without their own consent. Here's a book, now. What's all this about, I wonder? The letters look as if a steam-engine had printed 'em by accident. (*Turns over the leaves, spelling to himself.*)

GALILEO *enters softly unseen by* TOM, *who has his back towards him.*

GALILEO (*aside*). Oh, you're there, are you? If I could but suffocate him, not for life, but only till I am one-and-twenty, and then revive him, what a comfort and convenience it would be!

I overheard my cousin Fanny talking to Betsy about coming here. What can she want here? If she can be false,—false to *me*;—it seems impossible, but if she is?—well, well, we shall see. If I can reach that lumber-room unseen, Fanny Brown,—beware. (*He steals toward the door on the* L.—*opens it, and exit cautiously into the room. As he does so,* TOM *turns the other way.*)

TOM (*closing the book*). It's very pretty Greek, I think. What a time they are!

MR. STARGAZER *and* MOONEY *enter from room.*

MOONEY. Tell the noble gentleman of his irrevocable destiny.

MR. STARGAZER (*with emotion*). No,—no, prepare him first.

TOM (*aside*). Prepare him! 'prepared by Mr. Mooney.'—This is a case of kidnapping and slaughter. (*To them.*) Let him attempt to prepare me at his peril!

MR. STARGAZER. Mr. Grig, why this demonstration?

TOM. Oh, don't talk to me of demonstration;—you ain't going to demonstrate me, and so I tell you.

MR. STARGAZER. Alas! (*Crossing to him.*) The truth we have to communicate requires but little demonstration from our feeble lips. We have calculated upon your nativity.

MOONEY. Yes, we have, we have.

MR. STARGAZER. Tender-hearted man! (MOONEY *weeps.*) See there, Mr. Grig, isn't that affecting?

TOM. What is he piping his boiled gooseberry eye for, sir? How should I know whether it's affecting or not?

MR. STARGAZER. For you, for you. We find that you will expire to-morrow two months, at thirty minutes—wasn't it thirty minutes, my friend?

MOONEY. Thirty-five minutes, twenty-seven seconds, and five-sixths of a second. Oh! (*Groans.*)

MR. STARGAZER. Thirty-five minutes, twenty-seven seconds, and five-sixths of a second past nine o'clock.

MOONEY. A.M. (*They both wipe their eyes.*)

TOM (*alarmed*). Don't tell me, you've made a mistake somewhere;—I won't believe it.

MOONEY. No, it's all correct, we worked it all in the most satisfactory manner.—Oh! (*Groans again.*)

TOM. Satisfactory, sir! Your notions of the satisfactory are of an extraordinary nature.

MR. STARGAZER (*producing a pamphlet*). It is confirmed by the prophetic almanack. Here is the prediction for to-morrow two months,—'The decease of a great person may be looked for about this time.'

TOM (*dropping into his chair*). That's me! It's all up! inter me decently, my friends.

MR. STARGAZER (*shaking his hand*). Your wishes shall be attended to. We must have the marriage with my niece at once, in order that your distinguished race may be transmitted to posterity. Condole with him, my Mooney, while I compose my feelings, and settle the preliminaries of the marriage in solitude.

(*Takes up lamp and exit into room* R. MOONEY *draws up a chair in a line with* TOM, *a long way off. They both sigh heavily.* GALILEO *opens the lumber-room door. As he does so the room door opens and* BETSY *steals softly in, beckoning to* EMMA *and* FANNY *who follow. He retires again abruptly.*)

BETSY (*aside.*) Now, young ladies, if you take heart only for one minute you may frighten Mr. Mooney out of being married at once.

EMMA. But if he has serious thoughts?

BETSY. Nonsense, Miss, he hasn't any thoughts. Your papa says to him, 'Will you marry my daughter?' and he says, 'Yes, I will'; and he would and will if you ain't bold, but bless you, he never turned it over in his mind for a minute. If you, Miss (*to* EMMA), pretend to hate him and love a rival, and you, Miss (*to* FANNY), to love him to distraction, you'll frighten him so betwixt you that he'll declare off directly, I warrant. The love will frighten him quite as much as the hate. He never saw a woman in a passion, and as to one in love, I don't believe that anybody but his mother ever kissed that grumpy old face of his in all his born days. Now, do try him, ladies. Come, we're losing time.

(*She conceals herself behind the skeleton case.* EMMA *rushes up to* TOM GRIG *and embraces him, while* FANNY *clasps* MOONEY *round the neck.* GALILEO *appears at his door in an attitude of amazement, and* MR. STARGAZER *at his, after running in again with the lamp, which before he sees what is going forward he had in his hand.* TOM *and* MOONEY *in great astonishment.*)

FANNY (*to* MOONEY).
EMMA (*to* GRIG). } Hush! hush!

(TOM GRIG *and* MOONEY *get their heads sufficiently out of the embrace to exchange a look of wonder.*)

EMMA. Dear Mr. Grig, I know you must consider this strange, extraordinary, unaccountable conduct.

TOM. Why, ma'am, without explanation, it does appear singular.

EMMA. Yes, yes, I know it does, I know it will, but the urgency of the case must plead my excuse. Too fascinating Mr. Grig, I have seen you once and only once, but the impression of that maddening interview can never be effaced. I love you to distraction. (*Falls upon his shoulder.*)

TOM. You're extremely obliging ma'am, it's a flattering sort of thing,—or it would be (*aside*) if I was going to live a little longer,—but you're not the one, ma'am;—it's the other lady that the stars have——

FANNY (*to* MOONEY). Nay, wonderful being, hear me—this is not a time for false conventional delicacy. Wrapt in your sublime visions, you have not perceived the silent tokens of a woman's first and all-absorbing attachment, which have been, I fear, but too perceptible in the eyes of others; but now I must speak out. I hate this odious man. You are my first and only love. Oh! speak to me.

MOONEY. I haven't anything appropriate to say, young woman. I think I had better go. (*Attempting to get away.*)

FANNY. Oh! no, no, no (*detaining him*). Give me some encouragement. Not one kind word? not one look of love?

MOONEY. I don't know how to look a look of love.—I'm, I'm frightened.

TOM. So am I! I don't understand this. I tell you, Miss, that the other lady is my destined wife. Upon my word you mustn't hug me, you'll make her jealous.

FANNY. Jealous! of you! Hear me (*to* MOONEY). I renounce all claim or title to the hand of that or any other man and vow to be eternally and wholly yours.

MOONEY. No, don't, you can't be mine,—nobody can be mine.—I don't want anybody—I—I——

EMMA. If you will not hear her—hear *me*, detested monster.—

Hear me declare that sooner than be your bride, with this deep passion for another rooted in my heart,—I——

MOONEY. You need not make any declaration on the subject, young woman.

MR. STARGAZER (*coming forward*). She shan't,—she shan't. That's right, don't hear her. She shall marry you whether she likes it or not,—she shall marry you to-morrow morning,—and you, Miss (*to* FANNY), shall marry Mr. Grig if I trundle you to church in a wheelbarrow.

GALILEO (*coming forward*). So she shall! so she may! Let her! let her! I give her leave.

MR. STARGAZER. You give her leave, you young dog! Who the devil cares whether *you* give her leave or not? and what are you spinning about in that way for?

GALILEO. I'm fierce, I'm furious,—don't talk to me,—I shall do somebody a mischief;—I'll never marry anybody after this, never, never, it isn't safe. I'll live and die a bachelor!—there—a bachelor! a bachelor! (*He goes up and encounters* BETSY. *She talks to him apart, and his wrath seems gradually to subside.*)

MOONEY. The little boy, albeit of tender years, has spoken wisdom. I have been led to the contemplation of womankind. I find their love is too violent for my staid habits. I would rather not venture upon the troubled waters of matrimony.

MR. STARGAZER. You don't mean to marry my daughter? Not if I say she *shall* have you? (MOONEY *shakes his head solemnly.*) Mr. Grig, you have not changed your mind because of a little girlish folly?

TOM. To-morrow two months! I may as well get through as much gold as I can in the meantime. Why, sir, if the pot nearly boils (*pointing to the crucible*),—if you're pretty near the philosopher's stone,——

MR. STARGAZER. Pretty near! We're sure of it—certain; it's as good as money in the Bank. (GALILEO *and* BETSY, *who have been listening attentively, bustle about, fanning the fire, and throwing in sundry powders from the bottles on the table, then cautiously retire to a distance.*)

TOM. If that's the case, sir, I am ready to keep faith with the planets. I'll take her, sir, I'll take her.

MR. STARGAZER. Then here's her hand, Mr. Grig,—no resistance,

Miss (*drawing* FANNY *forward*). It's of no use, so you may as well do it with a good grace. Take her hand, Mr. Grig. (*The crucible blows up with a loud crash; they all start.*)

MR. STARGAZER. What!—the labour of fifteen years destroyed in an instant!

MOONEY (*stooping over the fragments*). That's the only disappointment I have experienced in this process since I was first engaged in it when I was a boy. It always blows up when it's on the point of succeeding.

TOM. Is the philosopher stone gone?

MOONEY. No.

TOM. Not gone, sir?

MOONEY. No—it never came!

MR. STARGAZER. But we'll get it, Mr. Grig. Don't be cast down, we shall discover it in less than fifteen years this time, I dare say.

TOM (*relinquishing* FANNY'S *hand.*) Ah! Were the stars very positive about this union?

MR. STARGAZER. They had not a doubt about it. They said it *was* to be, and it must be. They were peremptory.

TOM. I am sorry for that, because they have been very civil to me in the way of showing a light now and then, and I really regret disappointing 'em. But under the peculiar circumstances of the case, it can't be.

MR. STARGAZER. Can't be, Mr. Grig! What can't be?

TOM. The marriage, sir. I forbid the banns. (*Retires and sits down.*)

MR. STARGAZER. Impossible! such a prediction unfulfilled! Why, the consequences would be as fatal as those of a concussion between the comet and this globe. Can't be! it must be, shall be.

BETSY (*coming forward, followed by* GALILEO). If you please, sir, may I say a word?

MR. STARGAZER. What have you got to say?—speak, woman!

BETSY. Why, sir, I don't think Mr. Grig is the right man.

MR. STARGAZER. What!

BETSY. Don't you recollect, sir, that just as the house-clock struck the first stroke of five, you gave Mr. Galileo a thump on the head with the butt end of your telescope, and told him to get out of the way?

MR. STARGAZER. Well, if I did, what of that?

BETSY. Why, then, sir, I say, and I would say it if I was to be killed for it, that he's the young gentleman that ought to marry Miss Fanny, and that the stars never meant anything else.

MR. STARGAZER. He! Why, he's a little boy.

GALILEO. I ain't. I'm one-and-twenty next Lady-day.

MR. STARGAZER. Eh! Eighteen hundred and—why, so he is, I declare. He's quite a stranger to me, certainly. I never thought about his age since he was fourteen, and I remember that birthday, because he'd a new suit of clothes then. But the noble family——

BETSY. Lor', sir! ain't it being of noble family to be the son of such a clever man as you?

MR. STARGAZER. That's true. And my mother's father would have been Lord Mayor, only he died of turtle the year before.

BETSY. Oh, it's quite clear.

MR. STARGAZER. The only question is about the time, because the church struck afterwards. But I should think the stars, taking so much interest in my house, would most likely go by the house-clock,—eh! Mooney?

MOONEY. Decidedly,—yes.

MR. STARGAZER. Then you may have her, my son. Her father was a great astronomer; so I hope that, though you *are* a blockhead, your children may be scientific. There! (*Joins their hands.*)

EMMA. Am I free to marry who I like, papa?

MR. STARGAZER. Won't you, Mooney? Won't you?

MOONEY. If anybody asks me to again I'll run away, and never come back any more.

MR. STARGAZER. Then we must drop the subject. Yes, your choice is now unfettered.

EMMA. Thank you, dear papa. Then I'll look about for somebody who will suit me without the delay of an instant longer than is absolutely necessary.

MR. STARGAZER. How very dutiful!

FANNY. And, as my being here just now with Emma was a little trick of Betsy's, I hope you'll forgive her, uncle.

EMMA. }
GALILEO. } Oh, yes, do.

FANNY. And even reward her, uncle, for being instrumental in fulfilling the prediction.

EMMA.
GALILEO. } Oh, yes; do reward her—do.

FANNY. Perhaps you could find a husband for her, uncle, you know. Don't you understand?

BETSY. Pray don't mention it, Miss. I told you at first, Miss, that I had not the least wish or inclination to have Mr. Grig to myself. I couldn't abear that Mr. Grig should think I wanted him to marry me; oh no, Miss, not on any account.

MR. STARGAZER. Oh, that's pretty intelligible. Here, Mr. Grig. (*They fall back from his chair.*) Have you any objection to take this young woman for better, for worse?

BETSY. Lor', sir! how ondelicate!

MR. STARGAZER. I'll add a portion of ten pounds for your loss of time here to-night. What do you say, Mr. Grig?

TOM. It don't much matter. I ain't long for this world. Eight weeks of marriage might reconcile me to my fate. I should go off, I think, more resigned and peaceful. Yes, I'll take her, as a reparation. Come to my arms! (*He embraces her with a dismal face.*)

MR. STARGAZER (*taking a paper from his pocket*). Egad! that reminds me of what I came back to say, which all this bustle drove out of my head. There's a figure wrong in the nativity (*handing the paper to* MOONEY). He'll live to a green old age.

TOM (*looking up*). Eh! What?

MOONEY. So he will. Eighty-two years and twelve days will be the lowest.

TOM (*disengaging himself*). Eh! here! (*calling off*). Hallo, you, sir! bring in that ladder and lantern.

A Servant enters in great haste, and hands them to TOM.

SERVANT. There's such a row in the street,—none of the gas-lamps lit, and all the people calling for the lamplighter. *Such* a row! (*Rubbing his hands with great glee.*)

TOM. Is there, my fine fellow? Then I'll go and light 'em. And as, under existing circumstances, and with the prospect of a green old age before me, I'd rather *not* be married, Miss Martin, I beg to assure the ratepayers present that in future I shall pay the strictest attention to my professional duties, and do my best for the contractor; and that I shall be found upon my beat as long as they condescend to patronise the Lamplighter. (*Runs off*. MISS MARTIN *faints in the arms of* MOONEY.)

CURTAIN

THE END

MR. NIGHTINGALE'S DIARY

A Farce

IN ONE ACT

[1851]

BY CHARLES DICKENS AND
MARK LEMON

DRAMATIS PERSONÆ

At Devonshire House, Tuesday, *May* 27, 1851

Mr. Nightingale	Mr. Dudley Costello.
Mr. Gabblewig (*of the Middle Temple*) . .	Mr. Charles Dickens.
Tip (*his Tiger*)	Mr. Augustus Egg.
Slap (*professionally Mr. Formiville*) . .	Mr. Mark Lemon.
Lithers (*landlord of the 'Water-Lily'*) . .	Mr. Wilkie Collins.
Rosina	Miss Ellen Chaplin.
Susan	Mrs. Coe.

MR. NIGHTINGALE'S DIARY

SCENE.—*The Common Room of the Water-Lily Hotel at Malvern. Door and Window in flat. A carriage stops. Door-bell rings violently.*

TIP (*without*). Now, then! Wai-ter! Landlord! Somebody! (*Enter* TIP, *through door, with a quantity of luggage.*)

Enter LITHERS, L., *running in.*

LITHERS. Here you are, my boy.

TIP (*much offended*). My boy! Who are you boying of! Don't do it. I won't have it. The worm will turn if it's trod upon.

LITHERS. I never trod upon you.

TIP. What do you mean by calling *me* a worm?

LITHERS. You called yourself one. You ought to know what you are better than I do.

GABBLEWIG (*without*). Has anybody seen that puppy of mine—answers to the name of 'Tip'—with a gold-lace collar? (*Enters.*) O, here you are! You scoundrel, where have you been?

LITHERS. Good gracious me! Why, if it ain't Mr. Gabblewig, Junior!

GABBLEWIG. What, Lithers! Do *you* turn up at Malvern Wells, of all the places upon earth?

LITHERS. Bless you, sir, I've been landlord of this little place these two years! Ever since you did me that great kindness—ever since you paid out that execution for me when I was in the greengrocery way, and used to wait at your parties in the Temple—which is five years ago come Christmas—I've been (through a little legacy my wife dropped into) in the public line. I'm overjoyed to see you, sir. How do you do, sir? Do you find yourself pretty well, sir?

GABBLEWIG (*moodily seating himself*). Why, no, I can't say I *am* pretty well.

TIP. No more ain't I.

GABBLEWIG. Be so good as to take those boots of yours into the kitchen, sir.

TIP (*reluctantly*). Yes, sir.

GABBLEWIG. And the baggage into my bedroom.

TIP. Yes, sir. (*Aside.*) Here's a world! [*Exit*, L.

LITHERS. The Queen's Counsellor, that is to be, looks very down —uncommonly down. Something's wrong. I wonder what it is. Can't be debt. Don't look like drinking. Hope it isn't dice! Ahem! Beg your pardon, Mr. Gabblewig, but you'd wish to dine, sir. He don't hear. (*Gets round, dusting the table as he goes, and at last stoops his head so as to come face to face with him.*) What would you choose for dinner, Mr. Gabblewig?

GABBLEWIG. O, ah, yes! Give me some cold veal.

LITHERS. Cold veal! He's out of his mind.

GABBLEWIG. I'm a miserable wretch. I *was* going to be married. I am *not* going to be married. The young lady's uncle refuses to consent. It's all off—all over—all up!

LITHERS. But there are other young ladies——

GABBLEWIG. Don't talk nonsense.

LITHERS (*aside*). All the rest are cold veal, I suppose. But,—you'll excuse my taking the liberty, being so much beholden to you, —but couldn't anything be done to get over the difficulty?

GABBLEWIG. Nothing at all. How's it possible? Do you know the nature of the uncle's objection? But of course you don't. I'll tell you. He says I speak too fast, and *am* too slow,—want reality of purpose, and all that. He says I'm all words. What the devil else does he suppose I *can* be, being a lawyer! He says I happen to be counsel for his daughter just now, but after marriage might be counsel for the opposite side. He says I am wanting in earnestness,—deficient in moral go-aheadism.

LITHERS. In which?

GABBLEWIG. Just so. In consequence of which you behold before you a crushed flower. I am shut up and done for,—the peace of the valley is fled;—I have come down here to see if the cold-water cure will have any effect on a broken heart. Having had a course of wet blanket, I am going to try the wet sheet; —dare say I shall finish before long with a daisy counterpane.

LITHERS (*aside*). Everybody's bit by the cold water. It will be the ruin of our business.

GABBLEWIG. If the waters of Malvern were the waters of Lethe,

I'd take a douche forty feet high, this afternoon, and drink five-and-twenty tumblers before breakfast to-morrow morning. Anything to wash out the tormenting remembrance of Rosina Nightingale.

LITHERS. Nightingale, Mr. Gabblewig?

GABBLEWIG. Nightingale. As the Shakespeare duet went, in the happy days of our amateur plays:

> The Nightingale alone,
> She, poor bird, as all forlorn,
> Lean'd her breast uptil a thorn.

I've no doubt she's doing it at the present moment—or leaning her head against the drawing-room window, looking across the Crescent. It's all the same.

LITHERS. The Crescent, Mr. Gabblewig?

GABBLEWIG. The Crescent.

LITHERS. Not at Bath?

GABBLEWIG. At Bath.

LITHERS (*feeling in his pockets*). Good gracious! (*Gives a letter.*) Look at that, sir.

GABBLEWIG. The cramped hand of the obstinate old bird, who might, could, and should have been—and wouldn't be my father-in-law! (*Reads.*) 'Christopher Nightingale's compliments to the landlord of the Water-Lily, at Malvern Wells.'

LITHERS. The present establishment.

GABBLEWIG (*reading*). 'And hearing it is a quiet, unpretending, well-conducted house, requests to have the following rooms prepared for him on Tuesday afternoon.'

LITHERS. The present afternoon.

GABBLEWIG (*reading*). 'Namely, a private sitting-room with a'—what! a weed? He don't smoke.

LITHERS (*looking over his shoulder*). A view, sir.

GABBLEWIG. Oh! 'with a view.' Ay, ay. 'A bedroom for Christopher N. with a'—what? with a wormy pew?

LITHERS (*looking over his shoulder*). A warming-pan.

GABBLEWIG. To be sure; but it's as like one as the other. 'With a warming-pan, and two suitable chambers for Miss Rosina Nightingale.'—Support me.

LITHERS. Hold up, Mr. Gabblewig.

GABBLEWIG. You might knock me down with a feather.

LITHERS. But you needn't knock *me* down with a barrister. Hold up, sir.

GABBLEWIG (*reading*). 'And her maid. Christopher Nightingale intends to try the cold-water cure.'

LITHERS. I beg your pardon, sir. What's his complaint?

GABBLEWIG. Nothing.

LITHERS (*shaking his head*). He'll never get over it, sir. Of all the invalids that come down here, the invalids that have nothing the matter with them are the hopeless cases.

GABBLEWIG (*reading*). 'Cold-water cure, having drunk (see Diary) four hundred and sixty-seven gallons, three pints and a half of the various celebrated waters of England and Germany, and proved them all to be humbugs. He has likewise proved (see Diary) all pills to be humbugs. Miss Rosina Nightingale, being rather low, will also try the cold-water cure, which will probably rouse her.'—Never!

Perhaps she, like me, may struggle with—

(And I have no doubt of it, Lithers, for she has the tenderest heart in the world)

Some feeling of regret

(awakened by the present individual).

But if she loved as I have loved,

(And I have no doubt she did—and does)

She never can forget.

(And she won't, I feel convinced, if it's only in obstinacy.) (*Gives back letter.*)

LITHERS. Well, sir, what'll you do? I'm entirely devoted to you, and ready to serve you in any way. Will you have a ladder from the builder's, and run away with the young lady in the middle of the night; or would the key of the street-door be equally agreeable?

GABBLEWIG. Neither. Can't be done. If it could be done I should have done it at Bath. Grateful duty won't admit of union without consent of uncle,—uncle won't give consent;—stick won't beat dog,—dog won't bite pig,—pig won't get over the stile;—and so the lovers will never be married! (*Sitting down as before.*) Give me the cold veal, and the day before yesterday's paper.

[*Exit* LITHERS, L., *and immediately returns with papers.*

SLAP (*without*). Halloa, here! My name is Formiville. Is Mr. Formiville's luggage arrived? Several boxes were sent on beforehand for Mr. Formiville; are those boxes here? (*Entering at door, preceded by* LITHERS, *who bows him in.*) Do you hear me, my man? Has Mr. Formiville's luggage—I am Mr. Formiville—arrived?

LITHERS. Quite safely, sir, yesterday. Three boxes, and a pair of foils.

SLAP. *And* a pair of foils. The same. Very good. Take this cap. (LITHERS *puts it down.*) Good. Put these gloves in the cap. (LITHERS *does so.*) Good. Give me the cap again, it's cold. (*He does so.*) Very good. Are you the landlord?

LITHERS. I am Thomas Lithers, the landlord, sir.

SLAP. Very good. You write in the title-pages of all your books, no doubt:—

Thomas Lithers is my name,
And landlord is my station;
Malvern Wells my dwelling-place,
And Chalk my occupation.

What have you got to eat, my man?

LITHERS. Well, sir, we could do you a nice steak; or we could toss you up a cutlet; or——

SLAP. What have you ready dressed, my man?

LITHERS. We have a very fine York ham, and a beautiful fowl, sir——

SLAP. Produce them! Let the banquet be served. Stay; have you——

LITHERS (*rubbing his hands*). Well, sir, we have, and I can strongly recommend it.

SLAP. To what may that remark refer, my friend?

LITHERS. I thought you mentioned Rhine-wine, sir.

SLAP. O truly. Yes, I think I did. Yes, I am sure I did. Is it very fine?

LITHERS. It is uncommon fine, sir. Liebfraumilch of the most delicious quality.

SLAP. You may produce a flask. The price is no consideration (*aside*)—as I shall never pay for it.

LITHERS. Directly, sir.

SLAP. So. He bites. He will be done. If he *will* be done he *must* be done. I can't help it. Thus men rush upon their fate. A stranger? Hum! Your servant, sir. My name is Formiville——

GABBLEWIG (*who has previously observed him*). Of several provincial theatres, I believe, and formerly engaged to assist an amateur company at Bath, under the management of——

SLAP (*with a theatrical pretence of being affected*). Mr. Gabblewig! Heavens! This recognition is so sudden, so unlooked for, —it unmans me. (*Aside.*) Owe him fifteen pounds, four shirts, and a waistcoat. Hope he's forgotten the loan of those trifles.—O sir, if I drop a tear upon that hand——

GABBLEWIG. Consider it done. Suppose the tear, as we used to say at rehearsal. How are you going on? You have left the profession?

SLAP (*aside*). Or the profession left me. I either turned *it* off, or *it* turned *me* off; all one. (*Aloud.*) Yes, Mr. Gabblewig, I am now living on a little property—that is, I have expectations—(*aside*) of doing an old gentleman.

GABBLEWIG. I have my apprehensions, Mr. Formiville, otherwise I believe, Mr. Slap——

SLAP. Slap, sir, was my father's name. Do not reproach me with the misfortunes of my ancestors.

GABBLEWIG. I was about to say, Slap, otherwise Formiville, that I have a very strong belief that you have been for some time established in the begging-letter-writing business. And when a gentleman of that description drops a tear on my hand, my hand has a tendency to drop itself on his nose.

SLAP. I don't understand you, sir.

GABBLEWIG. I see you don't. Now the danger is, that I, Gabblewig, may take the profession of the law into my own hands, and eject Slap, otherwise Formiville, from the nearest casement or window, being at a height from the ground not exceeding five-and-twenty feet.

SLAP (*angrily*). Sir, I perceive how it is. A vindictive old person, of the name of Nightingale, who denounced me to the Mendicity Society, and who has pursued me in various ways, has prejudiced your mind somehow, publicly or privately, against an injured and calumniated victim. But let that Nightingale beware; for, if the Nightingale is not a bird, though an old one, that I will catch yet once again with chaff, and clip the wings of, too, I'm—(*Aside.*) Confound my temper, where's it running? (*Affects to weep in silence.*)

GABBLEWIG (*aside*). Oho. That's what brings him here, is it? A trap for the Nightingales! I may show the old fellow that I have some purpose in me, after all!—Those amateur dresses among my baggage!—Lithers's assistance—done! Mr. Formiville.

SLAP (*with injured dignity*). Sir!

GABBLEWIG (*taking up hat and stick*). As I am not ambitious of the honour of your company, I shall leave you in possession of this apartment. I believe you are rather absent, are you not?

SLAP. Sir, I *am*, rather so.

GABBLEWIG. Exactly. Then you will do me the favour to observe that the spoons and forks of this establishment are the private property of the landlord. [*Exit*, L.

SLAP. And that man wallows in eight hundred a year, and half that sum would make my wife and children (if I had any) happy!

Enter LITHERS (L.), *with tray, on which are fowl, ham, bread, and glasses.*

But arise, black vengeance! Nightingale shall suffer doubly. Nightingale found me out. When a man finds me out in imposing on him, I never forgive him,—and when he don't find me out, I never leave off imposing on him. Those are my principles. What ho! Wine here!

LITHERS (*arranging table and chair*). Wine coming, sir, directly! My young man has gone below for it. (*Bell rings without.*) More company! Mr. Nightingale, beyond a doubt! (*Showing him in at door.*) This way, sir, if you please! Your letter received, sir, and your rooms prepared.

SLAP (*looking off melodramatically before seating himself at table*). Is that the malignant whom these eyes have never yet bel-asted with a look? Caitiff, tereremble!

Sits, as NIGHTINGALE *enters with* ROSINA *and* SUSAN. NIGHTINGALE *muffled in a shawl, and carrying a great-coat.*

NIGHTINGALE (*to* LITHERS). That'll do, that'll do. Don't bother, sir. I am nervous, and can't bear to be bothered. What I want is peace. Instead of peace, I've got (*looking at* ROSINA) what rhymes to it, and is not at all like it. (*Sits, covering his legs with his great-coat.*)

ROSINA. O uncle! Is it not enough that I am never to redeem those pledges which——

NIGHTINGALE. Don't talk to me about redeeming pledges, as if I was a pawnbroker! Oh! (*Starts.*)

ROSINA. Are you ill, sir!

NIGHTINGALE. Am I ever anything else, ma'am! Here! Refer to Diary (*gives book*). Rosina, save me the trouble of my glasses. See last Tuesday.

ROSINA. I see it, sir (*turning over leaves*).

NIGHTINGALE. What's the afternoon entry?

ROSINA (*reading*). 'New symptom. Crick in back. Sensation as if self a stiff boot-jack suddenly tried to be doubled up by strong person.'

NIGHTINGALE (*starts again*). O!

ROSINA. Symptom repeated, sir?

NIGHTINGALE. Symptom repeated. I must put it down. (SUSAN *brings chair, and produces screw-inkstand and pen from her pocket.* NIGHTINGALE *takes the book on his knee, and writes.*) 'Symptom repeated.'—Oh! (*Starts again.*) 'Symptom re-repeated.' (*Writes again.*) Mr. Lithers, I believe?

LITHERS. At your service, sir.

NIGHTINGALE. Mr. Lithers, I am a nervous man, and require peace. We had better come to an understanding. I am a water patient, but I'll pay for wine. You'll be so good as to call the pump sherry at lunch, port at dinner, and brandy-and-water at night. Now, be so kind as to direct the chambermaid to show this discontented young lady her room.

LITHERS. Certainly, sir. This way, if you please, Miss. (*He whispers her. She screams.*)

NIGHTINGALE (*alarmed*). What's the matter?

ROSINA. O uncle! I felt as if—don't be frightened, uncle,—as if something had touched me here (*with her hand upon her heart*) so unexpectedly, that I—don't be frightened, uncle—that I almost dropped, uncle.

NIGHTINGALE. Lord bless me! Boot-jack and strong person contagious! Susan, a mouthful of ink. (*Dips his pen in her inkstand, and writes.*) 'Symptom shortly afterwards repeated in niece.' Susan, *you* don't feel anything particular, do you?

SUSAN. Nothing whatever, sir.

NIGHTINGALE. You never do. You are the most aggravating young woman in the world.

SUSAN. Lor', sir, you wouldn't wish a party ill, I'm sure!

NIGHTINGALE. Ill! you *are* ill, if you only knew it. If you were as intimate with your own interior as I am with mine, your hair would stand on end.

SUSAN. Then I'm very glad of my ignorance, sir, for I wish it to keep in curl. Now, Miss Rosina! (*Exit* ROSINA, *making a sign of secrecy to* LITHERS, *who goes before.*) Oho! There's something in the wind that's not the boot-jack! [*Exit* SUSAN, L.

NIGHTINGALE (*seated*). There's a man, yonder, eating his dinner, as if he enjoyed it. I should say, from his figure, that he generally *did* enjoy his dinner. I wish I did. I wonder whether there is anything that would do me good. I have tried hot water, and hot mud, and hot vapour, and have imbibed all sorts of springs, from zero to boiling, and have gone completely through the pharmacopœia; yet I don't find myself a bit better. My Diary is my only comfort. (*Putting it into his great-coat pocket, unconsciously drops it.*) When I began to book my symptoms, and to refer back of an evening, then I began to find out my true condition. O! (*starts*) what's that? That's a new symptom. Lord bless me! Sensation as if small train of gunpowder sprinkled from left hip to ankle, and exploded by successful Guy Fawkes. I must book it at once, or I shall be taken with something else before it's entered. Susan, another mouthful of ink! Most extraordinary! [*Exit*, L.

(SLAP *cautiously approaches the Diary; as he does so,* GABBLEWIG *looks in and listens.*)

SLAP. What's this—hum! A Diary,—remarkable passion for pills, and quite a furor for doctors.—Very unconjugal allusions to Mrs. Nightingale.—Poor Maria, most valuable of sisters, to me an annuity,—to your husband a tormentor. Hum! shall I bleed him, metaphorically bleed him? Why not? He never regarded the claims of kindred; why should I? He returns. (*Puts down book.*)

Re-enter NIGHTINGALE, *looking about.*

NIGHTINGALE. Bless my heart, I've left my Diary somewhere. O! here is the precious volume—no doubt where I dropped it.

(*Picks up book.*) If the stranger had opened it, what information he might have acquired! He'd have found out, by analogy, things concerning himself that he little dreams of. He has no idea how ill he is, or how thin he ought to be. [*Exit*, L.

SLAP. Now, then (*tucking up his wristbands*), for the fowl in earnest! Where is that wine! Hallo, where is that wine?

Enter (L.) GABBLEWIG, *disguised as Boots.*

GABBLEWIG. Here you are, sir! (*Starting.*) What do I behold! Mr. Formiville! the imminent tragedian?

SLAP. Who the devil are you? Keep off!

GABBLEWIG. What! Don't you remember me, sir?

SLAP. No, I don't indeed.

GABBLEWIG. Not wen I carried a banner, with a silver dragon on it; wen you played the Tartar Prince, at What's-his-name; and wen you used to bring the ouse down with that there pint about rewenge, you know?

SLAP. What! Do you mean when I struck the attitude, and said, 'Ar-recreant! The Per-rincess and r-r-revenge are both my own! She is my per-risoner—Tereremble!'

GABBLEWIG. Never! This to decide. (*They go through the motions of a broadsword combat.* SLAP, *having been run through the body, sits down and begins to eat voraciously.* GABBLEWIG, *who has kept the bottle all the while, sits opposite him at table.*) Ah! Lor' bless me, what a actor you was! (*Drinks.*) That's what I call true tragic fire—wen you strike it out of the swords. Give me showers of sparks, and then I know what you're up to! Lor' bless me, the way I've seen you perspire! I shall never see such a actor agin.

SLAP (*complacently*). I *think* you remember me.

GABBLEWIG. Think? Why, don't you remember, wen you left Taunton, without paying that there washerwoman; and wen she——

SLAP. You needn't proceed, it's quite clear you remember me.

GABBLEWIG (*drinks again*). Lor' bless my heart, yes, what a actor you was! What a Romeo you was, you know. (*Drinks again.*)

SLAP. I believe there was something in me, as Romeo.

GABBLEWIG. Ah! and something *of* you, too, you know. The Montagues was a fine family, when you was the lightest weight among 'em. And Lor' bless my soul, what a Prince Henry you was! I see you a drinking the sack now, I do! (*Drinks again.*)

SLAP. I beg your pardon, my friend, is that my wine?

GABBLEWIG (*affecting to meditate, and drinking again*). Lor' bless me, wot a actor! I seem to go into a trance like when I think of it. (*Is filling his glass again, when* SLAP *comes round and takes the bottle.*) I'll give you, Formiville and the Draymer! Hooray! (*Drinks, and then takes a leg of the fowl in his fingers.* SLAP *removes the dish.*)

SLAP (*aside*). At least he doesn't know that I was turned out of the company in disgrace. That's something. Are you the waiter here, my cool but discriminative acquaintance?

GABBLEWIG. Well, I'm a sort of a waiter and a sort of a half-boots: I was with a Travelling Circus, arter I left you. 'The riders—the riders! Be in time—be in time! Now, Mr. Merry-man, all in to begin!' All that you know. But I shall never see acting no more. It went right out with you, bless you! (*All through this dialogue, whenever* SLAP, *in a moment of confidence, replaces the fowl or wine,* GABBLEWIG *helps himself.*)

SLAP (*aside*). I'll pump him—rule in life. Whenever no other work on hand, pump! (*To him.*) I forget your name.

GABBLEWIG. Bit—Charley Bit. That's my real name. When I first went on with the banners, I was Blitheringtonfordbury. But they said it came so expensive in the printing, that I left it off.

SLAP. Much business done in this house?

GABBLEWIG. Wery flat.

SLAP. Old gentleman in nankeen trousers been here long?

GABBLEWIG. Just come. Wot do you think I've heerd? S'posed to be a bachelor, but got a wife.

SLAP. No!

GABBLEWIG. Yes.

SLAP. Got a wife, eh? Ha, ha, ha! You're as sharp as a lancet. Ha, ha, ha! Yes, yes, no doubt. Got a wife. Yes, yes.

GABBLEWIG (*aside*). Eh! A flash! The intense enjoyment of my friend suggests to me that old Nightingale hasn't got a wife,—that he's free, but don't know it. Fraud! Mum! (*To him.*) I say, you're a—but Lor' bless my soul, wot a actor you wos!

SLAP. It's really touching, his relapsing into that! But I can't indulge him, poor fellow. My time is precious. You were going to say——

GABBLEWIG. I was going to say, you are up to a thing or two, and so—but, Lor' bless my heart alive, wot a Richard the Third you wos! Wen you used to come the sliding business, you know. (*Both starting up and doing it.*)

SLAP. This child of nature positively has judgment! It *was* one of my effects. Calm yourself, good fellow. 'And so'—you were observing——

GABBLEWIG (*close to him, in a sudden whisper*). And so I'll tell you. He hasn't really got a wife. She's dead. (SLAP *starts,*— GABBLEWIG *aside.*) I am right. He knows it! Mrs. Nightingale's as dead as a door-nail. (*A pause; they stand close together, looking at each other.*)

SLAP. Indeed? (*Gabblewig nods.*) Some piece of cunning, I suppose. (GABBLEWIG *winks.*) Buried somewhere, of course? (GABBLEWIG *lays his fingers on his nose.*) Where? (GABBLEWIG *looks a little disconcerted.*) All's safe. No proof. (*Aloud.*) Take away.

GABBLEWIG (*as he goes up to table*). Too sudden on my part. Formiville wins first knock-down blow. Never mind. Gabblewig up again, and at him once more. (*Clears the table and takes the tray away.*)

SLAP. How does *he* know? He's in the market. Shall I buy him? Not yet. Necessity not yet proved. With Nightingale here, and my dramatic trunks upstairs, I'll strike at least another blow on the hot iron for myself, before I think of taking a partner into the forge. [*Exit,* L.

As GABBLEWIG *returns from clearing away, enter* SUSAN.

GABBLEWIG. Susan! Susan!

SUSAN. Susan, indeed! Well, diffidence ain't the prevailing complaint at Malvern.

GABBLEWIG. Don't you know me? Mr. Gabble——

SUSAN. —Wig! Why, la, sir, then *you're* the boot-jack! Now I understand, of course.

GABBLEWIG. More than I do. I the boot-jack! Susan, listen! Did you know that Mr. Nightingale had been married?

SUSAN. Why, I never heard it exactly.

GABBLEWIG. But you've seen it, perhaps? Had a peep into that eternal Diary—eh?

SUSAN. Well, sir, to say the pious truth, I did read one day something or another about a—a wife. You see he married a wife when he was very young.

GABBLEWIG. Yes.

SUSAN. And she was the plague of his life ever afterwards.

GABBLEWIG. O, Rosina, can such things be! Yes. Susan, I think you are a native of Malvern?

SUSAN. Yes, sir, leastways I was so, before I went to live in London.

GABBLEWIG. *You* persuaded Mr. Nightingale to come down here, in order that he might try the cold-water cure?

SUSAN. La, sir!

GABBLEWIG. And in order that you might see your relations?

SUSAN. La, sir, how did you know?

GABBLEWIG. Knowledge of human nature, Susan. Now rub up your memory and tell me—did you ever know a Mrs. Nightingale who lived down here? Think,—your eyes brighten,—you smile;—you did know Mrs. Nightingale who lived down here.

SUSAN. To be sure I did, sir; but that could never have been——

GABBLEWIG. Your master's wife,—I suspect she was. She died?

SUSAN. Yes, sir.

GABBLEWIG. And was buried?

SUSAN. You know everything.

GABBLEWIG. In——

SUSAN. Why, in Pershore churchyard; my uncle was sexton there.

GABBLEWIG. Uncle living?

SUSAN. Ninety years of age. With a trumpet.

GABBLEWIG. That he plays on?

SUSAN. Plays on? No. Hears with.

GABBLEWIG. Good. Susan, make it your business to get me a certificate of the old lady's death, and that within an hour.

SUSAN. Why, sir?

GABBLEWIG. Susan, I suspect the old lady walks, and I intend to lay her ghost. You ask how?

SUSAN. No, sir, I didn't.

GABBLEWIG. You thought it. That you shall know by and by. Here comes the old bird. Fly! (*Exit* SUSAN.) Whilst I reconnoitre the enemy. [*Exit, through door.*

Enter NIGHTINGALE *and* ROSINA.

ROSINA. My dear uncle, pray do nothing rash: you are in capital health at present, and who knows what the doctors may make you.

NIGHTINGALE. Capital health? I've not known a day's health for these twenty years. (*Refers to Diary.*) 'January 6th, 1834. Pain in right thumb: query, gout. Send for Blair's pills. Take six. Can't sleep all night. Doze about seven.' (*Turns over leaf.*) 'March 12th, 1839: Violent cough: query, damp umbrella, left by church-rates in hall? Try lozenges. Bed at six—gruel—tallow nose—dream of general illumination. March 13th: Miserable': cold always makes me miserable. 'Receive a letter from Mrs. Nightin—' hem!

ROSINA. What did you say, sir?

NIGHTINGALE. Have the nightmare, my dear. (*Aside.*) Nearly betrayed myself! (*Aloud.*) You hear this, and you talk about capital health to a sufferer like me!

Enter SLAP, *at back, dressed as a smug physician. He appears to be looking about the room.*

O! my spirits, my spirits! I wonder what water will do for them.

ROSINA. Why, reduce them, of course. Ah, my dear uncle, I often think I am the cause of your disquietude. I often think that I ought to marry.

NIGHTINGALE. Very kind of you, indeed, my dear.

Enter GABBLEWIG, *with a very large tumbler of water.*

O! all right, young man. I had better begin. So you think that you really ought, my love,—purely on my account—to marry a Magpie, don't you? (GABBLEWIG *starts and spills water over* NIGHTINGALE.) What are you about?

GABBLEWIG. I beg pardon, sir. (*Aside to* ROSINA.) Bless you!

ROSINA. Ah! Gab!—O uncle—don't be frightened—but——

NIGHTINGALE (*about to drink, spills water*). Return of boot-jack and strong person! I declare, I'm taking all this water externally, when I ought to——

SLAP (*seizing his hand*). Rash man, forbear! Drain that chalice, and your life's not worth a bodkin.

NIGHTINGALE. Dear me, sir! it's only water. I'm merely a pump patient. (GABBLEWIG *and* ROSINA *speak aside, hurriedly.*)

SLAP. Persevere, and twelve men of Malvern will sit upon you in less than a week, and, without retiring, bring in a verdict of 'Found drowned.'

GABBLEWIG (*aside to* ROSINA). I have my cue, follow me directly. I'll bring you another glass, sir, in a quarter of an hour.

[*Exit at door.* ROSINA *steals after him.*

SLAP. A most debilitated pulse—(*taking away water*)—great want of coagulum—lymphitic to an alarming degree. Stamina (*strikes him gently*) weak—decidedly weak.

NIGHTINGALE. Right! Always was, sir. In '48,—I think it was '48 —(*Refers.*)—Yes, here it is. (*Reads.*) 'Dyspeptic. Feel as if kitten at play within me. Try chalk and pea-flour.'

SLAP. And grow worse.

NIGHTINGALE. Astonishing! I did—yes. (*Reads.*)—'Fever—have head shaved.'

SLAP. And grow worse.

NIGHTINGALE. Amazing! Sir, you read me like a book. As there appears to be no dry remedy for my unfortunate case, I thought I'd try a wet one; and here I am, at the cold water.

SLAP. Water, unless in combination with alcohol, is poison to you. You want blood. In man there are two kinds of blood. One in a vessel called a vein, hence venous blood.—The other in the vessel called artery; hence arterial blood—the one dark, the other bright. Now, sir, the crassamentum of your blood is injured by too much water. How shall we thicken, sir? (*Produces bottle.*) By mustard and milk.

NIGHTINGALE. Mustard and milk!

SLAP. Mustard and milk, sir. Exhibited with a balsam known only to myself. (*Aside.*) Rum! (*Aloud.*) Single bottles, one guinea; case of twelve, ten pounds.

NIGHTINGALE. Mustard and milk! I don't think I ever tried—Eh? Yes. (*Opens Diary.*) 1836; I recollect I once took—I took —Oh, ah! 'Two quarts of mustard-seed, fasting.'

SLAP. Pish!

NIGHTINGALE. And you'd really advise me not to take water?

Enter at door GABBLEWIG *and* ROSINA, *both equipped in walking dresses, thick shoes, etc. They keep walking about during the following.*

GABBLEWIG. Who says don't take water? Who says so?

NIGHTINGALE. Why, this gentleman, who is evidently a man of science.

GABBLEWIG. Pshaw! Eh, dear. Not take water! Look at us—look at us—Mr. and Mrs. Poulter. Six months ago, I never took water, did I, dear?

ROSINA. Never!

GABBLEWIG. Hated it. Always washed in gin-and-water, and shaved with spirits of wine. Didn't I, dear?

ROSINA. Always!

GABBLEWIG. Then what was I? What were *we*, I may say, my precious?

ROSINA. You may.

GABBLEWIG. A flabby, dabby couple, like a pair of wet leather gloves;—no energy—no muscle—no go-ahead. Now you see what we are; eh, dear? Ten miles before breakfast—home—gallon of water—ten miles more—gallon of water and leg of mutton,—ten miles more,—gallon of water—in fact, we're never quiet, are we, dear?

ROSINA. Never.

GABBLEWIG. Walk in our sleep—sometimes—can't walk enough, that's a fact, eh, dear?

ROSINA. Yes, dear!

SLAP. Confound this fellow, he'll spoil all.

NIGHTINGALE. Well, sir, if you really could pull up for a few minutes, I should be extremely obliged to you.

GABBLEWIG. Here we are, then,—don't keep us long. (*Looks at watch*, ROSINA *does the same.*)—Say a minute, chronometer time.

NIGHTINGALE. You must know I'm an invalid.

GABBLEWIG. Five seconds.

NIGHTINGALE. Come down here to try the cold-water cure.

GABBLEWIG. Ten seconds.

NIGHTINGALE. Dear me, sir, I wish you wouldn't keep counting the time in that way; it increases my nervousness.

GABBLEWIG. Can't help it, sir,—twenty seconds;—go on, sir.

NIGHTINGALE. Well, sir, this gentleman tells me that my cranerany——

SLAP. Crass. Crassa-mentum must not be made too sloppy.

NIGHTINGALE. And thereby he advises, sir,——

GABBLEWIG. Forty seconds,—eh, dear? (*Show watches to each other.*)

ROSINA. Yes, dear!

NIGHTINGALE. I wish you wouldn't—and that he advises me to try mustard and milk, sir.

SLAP. In combination with a rare balsam known only to myself, one guinea a bottle,—case of twelve, ten pounds.

GABBLEWIG. Time's up. (*Walks again.*) My darling, mustard and milk? Eh, dear? Don't we know a case of mustard and milk,—Captain Blower, late sixteen stone, now ten and one half, all mustard and milk?

SLAP (*aside*). Can anybody have tried it?

GABBLEWIG (*to* NIGHTINGALE). Don't be done! If I see Blower, I'll send him to you;—can't stop longer, can we, dear?—ten miles and a gallon to do before dinner. Leg of mutton and a gallon at dinner. Five miles and a wet sheet after dinner. Come, dear! (*They walk out at door.*)

NIGHTINGALE. A very remarkable couple.—What do you think now, sir?

SLAP. Think, sir? I think, sir, that any man who professes to walk ten miles a day, is a humbug, sir; I couldn't do it.

NIGHTINGALE. But then the lady——

SLAP. I grieve to say that I think she's a humbugess. Those people, my dear sir, are sent about as cheerful examples of the effects of cold water. Regularly paid, sir, to waylay new comers.

NIGHTINGALE. La! do you think so? do you think there are people base enough to trade upon human infirmities?

SLAP. Think so?—I know it. There are men base enough to stand between you (*shows bottle*) and perfect health (*shakes bottle*) who would persuade you that perpetual juvenility was dear at one pound one a bottle, and that a green old age of a hundred and twenty was not worth ten pounds the case. That perambulating water-cart is such a man!

NIGHTINGALE. Wretch! What an escape I've had. My dear doctor. You are a doctor?

SLAP. D.D. and M.D., and corresponding member of the Mendicity Society.

NIGHTINGALE. Mendicity!

SLAP. Medical (what a slip).

NIGHTINGALE. Then I shall be happy to try a bottle to begin with. (*Gives money.*)

SLAP. Ah, one bottle. (*Gives bottle.*) I've confidence in your case,—you've none in mine. Ah! well!

NIGHTINGALE. A case be it then, and I'll pay the money at once. Permit me to try a little of the mixture. (*Drinks.*) It's not very agreeable. I think I'll make a note in my Diary of my first sensations.

Enter at door GABBLEWIG *and* ROSINA, *the former as a great invalid, the latter as an old nurse.*

GABBLEWIG (*aside, calling*). Rosina, quick, your arm. (*Aloud.*) I tell you, Mrs. Trusty, I can't walk any further.

ROSINA. Now do try, sir; we are not a quarter of a mile from home.

GABBLEWIG. A quarter of a mile!—why, that's a day's journey to a man in my condition.

ROSINA. O dear! what shall I do?

NIGHTINGALE. You seem very ill, sir?

GABBLEWIG. Very, sir. I'm a snuff, sir,—a mere snuff, flickering before I go out.

ROSINA. Oh, sir! pray don't die here; try and get home, and go out comfortably.

GABBLEWIG. Did you ever hear of such inhumanity? and yet this woman has lived on board wages, at my expense, for thirty years.

NIGHTINGALE. My dear sir, here's a very clever friend of mine who may be of service.

GABBLEWIG. I fear not,—I fear not. I've tried everything.

SLAP. Perhaps not *everything*. Pulse very debilitated; great want of coagulum; lymphitic to an alarming degree; stamina weak —decidedly weak.

GABBLEWIG. I don't want you to tell me that, sir.

SLAP. Crassamentum queer—very queer. No hope, but in mustard and milk.

GABBLEWIG (*starting up*). Mustard and milk!

ROSINA. Mustard and milk!

SLAP (*aside*). Is this Captain Blower?

GABBLEWIG (*to* NIGHTINGALE). Are you, too, a victim? Have you swallowed any of that man-slaughtering compound?

NIGHTINGALE (*alarmed*). Only a little,—a very little.

GABBLEWIG. How do you feel? Dimness of sight,—feeblesness of limbs?

NIGHTINGALE (*alarmed*). Not at present.

GABBLEWIG. But you will, sir,—you will. You'd never think I once rivalled that person, in rotundity.

NIGHTINGALE. Never.

ROSINA. But he'll never do it again; he'll never do it again.

GABBLEWIG. You'd never think that Madame Tussaud wanted to model my leg, and announce it as an *Extraordinary addition.*

NIGHTINGALE. I certainly should *not* have thought it.

GABBLEWIG. She might now put it in the Chamber of Horrors. Look at it!

ROSINA. It's nothing at all out of the flannel, sir.

GABBLEWIG. All mustard and milk, sir. I'm nothing but mustard and milk!

NIGHTINGALE (*seizes* SLAP). You scoundrel! and to this state you would have reduced me.

SLAP. O, this is some trick, sir, some cheat of the water-doctors.

NIGHTINGALE. Why, you won't tell me that he's intended as a cheerful example of the effects of cold water?

SLAP. I never said he was,—he's one of the failures; but as two of a trade can never agree, I'll go somewhere else and spend your guinea. [*Exit.*

GABBLEWIG (*in his own voice*). What a brazen knave! Second knock-down blow to Gabblewig. Betting even. Anybody's battle. Gabblewig came up smiling and at him again.

NIGHTINGALE (*goes to* GABBLEWIG). My dear sir, what do I not owe you? (*Shakes his hand.*)

GABBLEWIG. O, don't do that, sir, I shall tumble to pieces like a fantoccini figure if you do. I am only hung together by threads.

NIGHTINGALE. But let me know the name of my preserver, that I may enter it in my Diary.

GABBLEWIG. Captain Blower, R.N. (NIGHTINGALE *writes.*) I'm happy to have rescued you from that quack. I declare the excitement has done me good. Rosi—Mrs. Trusty, I think I can walk now.

ROSINA. That's right, sir. Lean upon me.

GABBLEWIG. Oh! Oh!

NIGHTINGALE. What's the matter, Captain Blower?

GABBLEWIG. That's the milk, sir. Oh!

NIGHTINGALE. Dear me, Captain Blower!

GABBLEWIG. And that's the mustard, sir.

[*Exeunt at door* GABBLEWIG *and* ROSINA.

NIGHTINGALE. Really, this will be the most eventful day in my Diary, except one,—that day which consigned me to Mrs. Nightingale and twenty years of misery. I've not seen her for nineteen; though I have periodical reminders that she is still in the land of the living, in the shape of quarterly payments of twenty-five pounds, clear of income-tax. Well! I'm used to it; and so that I never see her face again, I'm content. I'll go find Rosina, and tell her what has happened. Quite an escape, I declare. [*Exit*, L.

Enter at door SUSAN, *in bonnet, etc.*

SUSAN. What a wicked world this is, to be sure! Everybody seems trying to do the best they can for themselves, and what makes it worse, the complaint seems to be catching; for I'm sure I can't help telling Mr. Gabblewig what a traitor that Tip is. I hope Mr. G. won't come in my way, and tempt me. Ah! here he is, and I'm sure I shall fall.

Enter GABBLEWIG.

GABBLEWIG. Well, Susan, have you got the certificate?

SUSAN. No, sir, but uncle has, and he'll be here directly. Oh, sir, if you knew what I've heard!

GABBLEWIG. What!

SUSAN. I'm sure you'd give half-a-sovereign to hear; I'm sure you would.

GABBLEWIG. I'm sure I should, and there's the money.

SUSAN. Well, sir, your man Tip's a traitor, sir, a conspirator, sir. I overheard him and another planning some deception. I couldn't quite make out what, but I know it's something to deceive Mr. Nightingale.

GABBLEWIG. Find out with all speed what this scheme is about, and let me know. What's that mountain in petticoats? Slap, or I'm not Gabblewig!

SUSAN. And with him Tip, or I'm not Susan!

GABBLEWIG. Another flash! I guess it all! Susan, your mistress shall instruct you what to do. Vanish, sweet spirit!

[*Exeunt* GABBLEWIG, R., *and* SUSAN, L.

Enter at door, R., SLAP *in female attire. Looks about cautiously.*

SLAP. I hope he's not gone out. I've a presentiment that my good luck is deserting me; but before we *do* part company, I'll make a bold dash, and secure something to carry on with. Now, Calomel,—I mean Mercury,—befriend me. (*Rings.*)

Enter LITHERS, L.

LITHERS. Did you ring, ma'am?

SLAP. Yes, young man; I wish to speak with a Mr. Nightingale, an elderly gent, who arrived this morning.

LITHERS. What name, ma'am?

SLAP. Name no consequence; say I come from M'ria.

LITHERS. M'ria?

SLAP. M'ria, a mutual friend of mine and Mr. Nightingale, and one he ought not to be ashamed of.

LITHERS. Yes, ma'am. (*Aside.*) Mr. Gabblewig's right. [*Exit.*

SLAP. M'ria has been dead these twelve years, during which time my victim has paid her allowance with commendable regularity to me, her only surviving brother. Ah, I thought that name was irresistible, and here he is.

Enter NIGHTINGALE, L., *closing door at back.*

His trepidation is cheering. He'll bleed freely; what a lamb it is! (*Curtseys as* NIGHTINGALE *comes down.*) Your servant, sir.

NIGHTINGALE. Now don't lose a moment; you say you come from Maria: what Maria?

SLAP. Your Maria.

NIGHTINGALE. I am sorry to acknowledge the responsibility.

SLAP. Ah, sir; that poor creature's much changed, sir.

NIGHTINGALE. For the worse, of course?

SLAP. I'm afraid so. No gin now, sir.

NIGHTINGALE. Then it's brandy.

SLAP. Lives on it, sir, and breaks more windows than ever. She's heard that you've come down here.

NIGHTINGALE. So I suppose, by this visit.

SLAP. She lives about a mile from Malvern.

NIGHTINGALE (*starts*). What! I thought she was down in Yorkshire.

SLAP. Was and is is two different things. She wanted for to come and see you.

NIGHTINGALE. If she does, I'll stop her allowance.

SLAP. And have her call every day? M'ria's my friend,—but I know that wouldn't be pleasant. She'd a proposal to make, so, M'ria says I,—I'll see your lawful husband,—as you is, sir, and propose for you.

NIGHTINGALE. I'll listen to nothing.

SLAP. Not if it puts the sad sea-waves between you and M'ria for ever?

NIGHTINGALE (*interested*). Eh!

SLAP. You know she'd a brother, an excellent young man, who went to America ten years ago.

NIGHTINGALE (*takes out Diary*). I know. (*Reads aside.*) '16th of May 1841, sent fifty pounds to Mrs. N.'s vagabond brother, going to America—qy. to the devil?'

SLAP. He has written to M'ria to say that if you'll give her two hundred pounds, and she'll come out, he'll take care of her for ever.

NIGHTINGALE. Done!—it's a bargain.

SLAP. *He bites!*—and her son for a hundred more.

NIGHTINGALE. What son?

SLAP. Ah, sir! you don't know your blessings. Shortly after you and M'ria separated, a son was born; but M'ria, to revenge herself—which was wrong; oh, it was wrong in her, that was, —never let you know it; but sent him to the Workus, as a fondling she had received in a basket.

NIGHTINGALE. I don't believe a word of it.

SLAP. She said you wouldn't. But seeing is believing, and so I've brought the innocent along with me. I've got the Pretty here.

NIGHTINGALE. Here! in your pocket?

SLAP. No—at the door. (*They rise.*)

NIGHTINGALE. At the door!

SLAP. Come in, Christopher! Named after you, sir! for in spite of M'ria's feelings, you divided her heart with Old Tom.

Enter at door TIP *as a Charity Boy.*

NIGHTINGALE. O nonsense!

SLAP. Christopher, behold your Par. (*Boxes him.*) What do you stand there for like a eight-day clock or a idol, as if Pars were found every day?

TIP (*aside*). Don't; you make me nervous. (*Aloud.*) And is that my Par!

SLAP. Yes, child. Me, who took you from the month, can vouch for it.

TIP. O Par!

NIGHTINGALE. Keep off, you young yellow-hammer; or I'll knock you down. Hark'ee, ma'am. If you can assure me of the departure of your friend and this cub, I will give you the money! For twenty years I have been haunted by——

Enter GABBLEWIG *at door, disguised as Old Woman.*

GABBLEWIG. Which the blessed innocent has been invaygled of, and man-trapped,—leastways boy-trapped;—and never no more will I leave this 'ouse until I find a parent's 'ope—a mother's pride—and nobody's (as I'm aweer on) joy.

NIGHTINGALE *and Susan place Chair.*

SLAP (*aside*). What on earth is this! Who is a mother's pride and nobody's joy? (*To* TIP.) You don't mean to say you are?

TIP (*solemnly*). I'm a horphan. (*Goes up to* GABBLEWIG.) What are you talking about, you old Bedlam?

GABBLEWIG. Oh! (*screaming and throwing her arms about his neck*)—my 'ope—my pride—my son!

TIP (*struggling*). Your son!

GABBLEWIG (*aside to him*). If you don't own me for your mother, you villain, on the spot, I'll break every bone in your skin, and have your skin prepared afterwards by the Bermondsey tanners.

TIP (*aside*). My master!—My mother! (*They embrace.*)

SLAP. Are you mad? Am I mad? Are we all mad? (*To* TIP.) Didn't you tell me that whatever I said——

TIP. *You* said? What is your voice to the voice of Natur? (*Embraces his master again.*)

SLAP. Natur! Natur! ah-h-h! (*Screams. Chair brought.*) O you unnat'ral monster! Who see your first tooth drawn on a deceitful world? Who watched you running alone in a go-cart, and tipping over on your precious head upon the paving-stones in the confidence of childhood? Who give you medicine that reduced you when you was sick, and made you so when you wasn't?

GABBLEWIG (*rising*). Who? Me!

SLAP. You, ma'am?

GABBLEWIG. Me, ma'am, as is well beknown to all the country round, which the name of this sweetest of babbies as was giv to his own joyful self when blest in best Whitechapel mixed upon a pincusheon, and mother saved likewise was Absolom. Arter his own parential father, as never (otherwise than through being bad in liquor) lost a day's work in the wheelwright business, which it was but limited, Mr. Nightingale, being wheels of donkey shays and goats, and one was even drawed by geese for a wager, and went right into the centre aisle of the parish church on a Sunday morning on account of the obstinacy of the animals, as can be certified by Mr. Wigs the beadle afore he died of drawing on his Wellington boots, to which he was not accustomed, arter a hearty meal of beef and walnuts, to which he was too parshal, and in the marble fountain of that church this preciousest of infants was made Absolom, which never can be unmade no more, I am proud to say, to please or give offence to no one nowheres and nohows.

SLAP. Would you forswear your blessed mother, M'ria Nightingale, lawful wedded wife of this excellent old gent? Why don't the voice o' Natur claim its par?

NIGHTINGALE. O, don't make *me* a consideration on any account!

GABBLEWIG. M'ria Nightingale, which affliction sore long time she bore——

NIGHTINGALE. And so did I.

GABBLEWIG. Physicians was in vain,—which she never had none partickler as I knows, of exceptin one which she tore his hair by handfuls out in consequence of differences of opinion relative to her complaint, but it was wrote upon her tombstone ten year and more ago, and dead she is as the hosts of the Egyptian Fairies.

NIGHTINGALE. Dead! Prove it, and I'll give you fifty pounds.

SLAP. Prove it! I defies her. (*Aside.*) I'm done.

GABBLEWIG. Prove it!—which I can and will, directly minit, by my brother the sexton, as I will here produce in the twinkling of a star or human eye. (*Aside.*) From this period of the contest Gabblewig had it all his own way, and went in and won. No money was laid out, at any price, on Formiville. Fifty to one on Gabblewig freely offered, and no takers. [*Exit at door.*

SLAP (*aside*). I don't like this,—so exit Slap!

NIGHTINGALE (*seizing him*). No, ma'am, you don't leave this place till the mystery is cleared up.

SLAP. Unhand me, monster! I claims my habeas corpus. (*Breaks from him.* NIGHTINGALE *goes to the door and prepares to defend the pass with a chair.*) (*To* TIP.) As for you, traitor, though I'm not pugnacious, I'll give you a lesson in the art of self-defence you shall remember as long as you live.

TIP. You! the bottle imp as has been my ruin! Reduce yourself to my weight, and I'll fight you for a pound. (*Squares.*)

GABBLEWIG (*without*). I'll soon satisfy the gentleman.

SLAP. Then I'm done! very much done! I see nothing before me but premature incarceration, and an old age of gruel.

Enter GABBLEWIG *at door as Sexton.*

NIGHTINGALE. He's very old! My invaluable centenarian, will you allow me to inquire——

SEXTON. I don't hear you.

NIGHTINGALE. He's very deaf. (*Aloud.*) Will you allow me to inquire——

SEXTON. It's no use whispering to me, sir, I'm hard o' hearing.

NIGHTINGALE. He's very provoking. (*Louder.*) Whether you ever buried——

SEXTON. Brewed? Yes, yes, I brewed—that is, me and my wife, as has been dead and gone now this forty year, next hop-picking—(my wife was a Kentish woman)—we brewed, especially one year, the strongest beer ever you drunk. It was called in our country Sampson with his hair on—alluding to its great strength, you understand,—and my wife, she said——

NIGHTINGALE (*very loud*). Buried—not brewed!

SEXTON. Buried? O, ah! Yes, yes. Buried a many. They was strong, too,—once.

NIGHTINGALE. Did you ever bury a Mrs. Nightingale?

SEXTON. Ever bury a Nightingale? No, no, only Christians.

NIGHTINGALE (*in his ear*). Missis—Mis-sis Nightingale?

SEXTON. O yes, yes. Buried *her*—rather a fine woman,—married (as the folks told me) an uncommon ugly man. Yes, yes. Used to live here. Here (*taking out pocket-book*) is the certificate of her burial. (*Gives it.*) I got it for my sister. O yes! Buried *her*. I thought you meant a Nightingale. Ha, ha, ha!

NIGHTINGALE. My dear friend, there's a guinea, and it's cheap for the money. (*Gives it.*)

SEXTON. I thank'ee, sir. I thank'ee. (*Aside.*) Formiville heavily grassed, and a thousand to one on Gabblewig! [*Exit at door.*

NIGHTINGALE (*after reading certificate*). You—you—inexpressible swindler. If you were not a woman, I'd have you ducked in the horse-pond.

TIP (*on his knees*). O, sir, do it. He deserves it.

NIGHTINGALE. He?

TIP. Yes, sir, she's a he. He deluded me with a glass of rum-and-water; and the promise of a five-pound note.

NIGHTINGALE. You scoundrel!

SLAP. Sir, you are welcome to your own opinion. I am not the first man who has failed in a great endeavour. Napoleon had his Waterloo,—Slap has his Malvern. Henceforth, I am nobody. The eagle retires to his rock.

Enter GABBLEWIG *in his own dress.*

GABBLEWIG. You had better stop here. Be content with plain Slap,—discard counterfeit Formiville,—and we'll do something for you.

SLAP. Mr. Gabblewig! [*Exit at door.*

GABLEWIG. Charley Bit, Mr. Poulter, Captain Blower, respectable female, and deaf sexton, all equally at anybody's service.

NIGHTINGALE. What do I hear?

GABBLEWIG. Me.

NIGHTINGALE. And what do I see?

ROSINA (*entering at door*). Me! Dear uncle, you would have been imposed upon and plundered, and made even worse than you ever made yourself, but for——

GABBLEWIG. Me. My dear Mr. Nightingale, you did think I could do nothing but talk. If you now think I can act—a little—let me come out in a new character. (*Embracing* ROSINA.) Will you?

NIGHTINGALE. Will I? Take her, Mr. Gabblewig. Stop, though.

Ought I to give away what has made me so unhappy. Memorandum—Mrs. Nightingale—see Diary. (*Takes out book.*)

GABBLEWIG. Stop, sir! Don't look! Burn that book, and be happy!—(*Brings on* SLAP *at door.*)—Ask your doctor. What do *you* say, Mustard and Milk?

SLAP. I say, sir, try me; and when you find I am not worth a trial, don't try me any more. As to that gentleman's destroying his Diary, sir, my opinion is that he might perhaps refer to it once again.

GABBLEWIG (*to audience*). Shall he refer to it once more? (*To* NIGHTINGALE.) Well, I think you may.

CURTAIN

THE END

NO THOROUGHFARE

A Drama

IN FIVE ACTS AND
A PROLOGUE

[1867]

BY CHARLES DICKENS AND
WILKIE COLLINS

CAST OF CHARACTERS

At New Royal Adelphi Theatre, December 26, 1867

Veiled Lady	Mrs. Billington.
Sarah (*otherwise* Sally) Goldstraw	Mrs. Alfred Mellon.
Little Walter Wilding	Master Sidney.
First Husband	Mr. R. Romer.
Second Husband	Mr. Pritchard.
First Wife	Mrs. Stoker.
Second Wife	Mrs. D'Este.
Mr. Walter Wilding	Mr. Billington.
Mr. Bintry (*a man of law*)	Mr. G. Belmore.
Joey Ladle (*head cellarman*)	Mr. Benjamin Webster.
George Vendale	Mr. H. G. Neville.
Jules Obenreizer	Mr. Fechter.
Marguerite	Miss Carlotta Leclercq.
Madame Dor	Mrs. A. Lewis.
Jean Marie (*a guide*)	Mr. C. F. Smith.
Jean Paul (*ditto*)	Mr. Branscombe.
Father Francis	Mr. R. Phillips.
Monks	Mr. Aldridge. Mr. Tomlinson.

Time of playing.—Three hours and forty minutes.

Music.—A 'mysterious' theme always to Obenreizer's entrances. Melodrama music to Scene 1st, Act 4th, on and after Obenreizer's entrance with knife.

Remarks.—Except Vendale and Joey, all pronounce 'Obenreizer' in the English manner, that is 'Oben-righ-sir.' Joey calls him 'Open-razor,' and Vendale gives it the Swiss or German pronunciation, 'Obenright-zer.'

Stage Directions.—R. means Right of Stage, facing the Audience; L. Left; C. Centre; R. C. Right of centre; L. C. Left of centre. D. F. Door in the Flat, or Scene running across the back of the Stage; C. D. F. Centre Door in the Flat; R. D. F. Right Door in the Flat; L. D. F. Left Door in the Flat; R. D. Right Door; L. D. Left Door; 1 E. First Entrance; 2 E. Second Entrance; U. E. Upper Entrance; 1, 2, or 3 G. First, Second or Third Groove.

COSTUMES (Modern).

Obenreizer.—Act 1st: *Black hat, black neck-tie, long-skirted black frock-coat, light pants, dark vest, hair rather long behind, cane.* Act 2nd,

Scene 1st: *Black suit, coat is short-skirted;* Scene 3rd: *Same, with hat and gloves.* Act 3rd, Scene 1st: *Same, with hat and gloves;* Scene 3rd: *Travelling dress; round, black Astracan cap, russet waistcoat with some of the breast buttons left unbuttoned, showing white vest under, wallet with strap, watch.* Act 4th, Scene 1st: *Same as last, with pants tucked into top of boots;* 2nd entrance, *in waistcoat, with sleeves drawn tight, collar open;* Scene 2nd and 3rd: *Same as* 1st entrance; Scene 1st: *Well buttoned up, thick gloves.* Act 5th: *Russet waistcoat, black pants in high boots, black coat, snuff-box.*

George Vendale.—Act 1st: *Suit of grey mixture, cut-away coat, black low-crowned hard felt hat, watch and chain.* Act 2nd, Scene 1st *and* 2nd: *Grey pants, black high hat, black coat, white vest, jewels in case, to bring on with him.* Act 3rd, Scene 1st: *Black suit;* Scene 3rd: *Dark grey pants, black coat and vest, hat.* Act 4th, Scene 1st: *Same;* Scenes 2nd and 3rd: *Pants in high russet boots, tall black felt hat, black overcoat buttoned up to neck, thick gloves.* Act 5th: *Same as last, but without hat, gloves and overcoat.*

Mr. Bintry.—*Black suit, with brown overcoat in* Act 5th. *Grizzled wig and iron-grey side whiskers, white stand-up collar and cravat, black gloves.*

Walter Wilding.—*Black suit, except grey pants; light hair and fair complexion; an habitual action of putting his hand to his head when pausing for a word.*

Joey Ladle.—Act 1st and 2nd: *Black hair, bald on top of head and forehead, small black side whiskers; dark suit of velveteen; leather apron, much wrinkled and stained, from his neck to mid-leg, with collar-strap and waist-string; small skull-cap of oil-skin; slow in speech and thick in comprehension. Made up stout.* Act 3rd, Scene 1st: *Same;* Scene 3rd: *Same without apron; coat on.* Act 4th, Scene 3rd: *Muffler round neck, black overcoat and cap; black gloves, legs bandaged in the Italian brigand style.* Act 5th: *Same as last.*

Landlord.—*As a Swiss peasant; grey stockings, blue breeches, banded vest, in red and blue, embroidered; black felt hat.*

Guides.—*Felt hats, pinned up with crosses; long cloaks, sheep-skin jackets, high boots, alpenstocks (pine poles six feet long, with iron at end).*

First and Second Husband *in* Scene 2nd, Prologue: *Ordinary walking dresses. The* First *is a man of fifty; the* Second *a young man of twenty-five. Hats and gloves.*

Father Francis, a Monk.—*Russet gown, sandals; tonsure on black wig; black beard.*

A Monk.—*Like* Father Francis.

Little Walter Wilding. *In dark blue jacket and pants; fair-haired and fair complexion.*

Foundling Boys.—*A number, about twelve years old, in blue suits.*

Two Men.—*To bring in flowers,* Act 2nd, Scene 1st: *Ordinary dress, coats and caps.*

Marguerite.—Act 1st: *Straw hat, with red and blue ribbons; blue dress, with bodice cut square and low, in Swiss fashion; gilt buckle to waist-*

belt, buckles to shoes; light hair, braided; ear-rings, and cross at neck. Acts 2nd and 3rd: *House dress, dark colour, Swiss waist.* Act 4th: *Plain dress, with mantle of same, with hood; hair braided.* Act 5th: *Blue dress, with four inches deep black border at bottom hem; black jacket, with gilt buttons.*

VEILED LADY.—*Black dress, black bonnet, with long black veil; face pale.*

SALLY GOLDSTRAW.—Prologue, Scene 1st: *Black dress, shawl and bonnet;* Scene 2nd: *Same dress, white cuffs and collar; apron.* Act 1st: *White bonnet, with fancy ribbons; shawl, plain dress.* Act 2nd: *Dark dress, black apron.* Act 4th: *In black.*

FIRST WIFE.—*A woman of forty; grey hair, slightly empurpled face; shawl and bonnet trimmed gaily; coloured dress.*

SECOND WIFE.—*Walking dress, bonnet and mantle.*

MADAME DOR.—Act 1st: *Bonnet, dark dress, with black 'lace square'; she is made up stout, with her hair frizzled out on each side of face, to make it seem broader.* Act 2nd: *House dress, hair as before; she walks sidewise, keeping her face from the other performers when crossing stage or making an exit.*

TWO GIRLS (for the Hospital).—Prologue, Scene 1st: *Dark dresses, bonnets and mantles;* Scene 2nd: *Neat brown dresses, white cuffs, collars, aprons and caps.*

PROPERTIES

Prologue, Scene 1st: Small wad of paper, as of two coins in it, for VEILED LADY; *Scene 2nd:* Two large platters, with roast meat on them, for tables—L. 1 and 2 E.; carving-knives and forks to them, and spoons; knives, forks and plates for the boys; cloth, castors, cruets, etc., to set table; on L. 1 and 2 E., C. on F. and R. 1 E. set, framed placards, headed 'Patrons, 1760,' etc. *Act 1st, Scene 1st:* Wine-baskets, boxes and casks to make picture of stage; a hackney-coach, to hold two persons, to cross L. U. E. to D. C. in wall set on four grooves; eye-glasses for BINTRY; candle to burn, held in the end of a cleft stick, two feet long; a large cask and two small ones, to serve as table and chairs; bottle and two glasses; umbrella for BINTRY; an odd glove for MADAME DOR to be rubbing with cloth. *Act 2nd, Scene 1st:* Two books on table, R. C. front; stockings and ball of worsted for MADAME DOR; jewels in case for VENDALE, needlework for MARGUERITE; two large handsome gilt flower-stands with flowers, to be brought on D. in F.; jewels in case for OBENREIZER; *Scene 3rd:* A long rod; three candles to burn at end of cleft sticks; a starting-mallet, tasting-rod and tin measures laid on barrels; a small cask placed R. C.; cobweb to fall. *Act 3rd, Scene 1st:* Writing materials on desk up L.; three letters, strong box in flat, R. to E.; framed calendar over mantelpiece; straw L. side, about the painted set of open wine-box, two bottles for same; quill to be worn by VENDALE behind his ear; *Scene 2nd:* Small basket for SALLY; *Scene 3rd:* Long pipe for OBENREIZER; small travelling-trunk, pen and ink on R. table; flat writing-case. *Act 4th, Scene 1st:* Pipe as before for

OBENREIZER; box of matches, candle to burn; red fire in fireplace, bottle, and two glasses; writing-case of *Scene 3rd*, *Act 3rd;* knife for OBENREIZER; *Scene 2nd:* Two alpenstocks (pine poles six feet long, tipped with iron hook); leather case, with strap, to go over shoulders, for OBENREIZER; *Scene 3rd:* The two alpenstocks. *Act 5th*, *Scene 1st:* A large brass-clasped Bible and bag of money for FATHER FRANCIS; snuff-box for OBENREIZER; in clock-safe, two packets of papers on upper shelf, three on lower; bell to strike eight; legal paper for BINTRY; small vial for OBENREIZER; pen and ink, lighted candle on table R.

NO THOROUGHFARE

PROLOGUE

SCENE I.—*Gas down*—VEILED LADY *enters* L. *to* C., *pauses, then to* R., *by gate in* F.—*Two Girls enter by gate in* F., *draw their shawls closer around them, cross and exeunt* L.—VEILED LADY *follows them to* C., *looking at their faces, shakes her head, stops, returns to gate.*—SALLY GOLDSTRAW *enters by gate, crosses to exit* L., *but* VEILED LADY *overtakes her and stops her,* C.

SALLY. What do you want of me?

VEILED LADY. I wish to speak with you. I must speak with you.

SALLY. What is it you want?

VEILED LADY. You are called Sally Goldstraw, you are one of the nurses at the hospital, and I must speak with you.

SALLY. You seem to know all about me, ma'am. May I make so bold as to ask who you are?

VEILED LADY. Come, look at me under this lamp (*to gate, removing veil*).

SALLY (*shakes head*). No, ma'am (*replaces the* LADY's *veil*), I don't know you; I never saw you before this night.

VEILED LADY. Do I look like a happy woman?

SALLY. No! you look as if you had something on your mind.

VEILED LADY. I *have* something on my mind, Sally! I am one of those miserable mothers who have never known what happy motherhood is! My child is one of those poor children in this foundling hospital, put there when a boy, and I have never seen him!

SALLY. O dear, dear, dear! what can I say, what can I do?

VEILED LADY. Carry your memory back twelve years. The day when you entered the foundling must have been a memorable one!

SALLY. It was. But twelve years is a long time!

VEILED LADY. If it is long to you, think how long it must be to me! I have paid the penalty of my disgrace! My family forced me to live in a foreign land ever since. But now I find myself released,—free to come back. Sally Goldstraw, I have come back. It lies in your power to make me a happy woman!

SALLY. Me! and how can I do that?

VEILED LADY. Here are two guineas in this paper. (*Offers roll of paper.*) Take my poor little present, and I will tell you.

SALLY (*repulses paper*). You may know my face, but not my nature, ma'am. There is not a child in all the house that I belong to, who has not a good word for Sally. Could I be so well thought of if I was to be bought?

VEILED LADY. I did not mean to buy you; I meant only to reward you very slightly.

SALLY. I want no reward. If there is anything I can do for you, ma'am, that I will do for its own sake. You are much mistaken in me if you think that I will do it for money. What is it you want?

VEILED LADY. The day when you entered the foundling hospital must be a marked day in your life?

SALLY. It is a marked day!

VEILED LADY. You must remember what passed on that day?

SALLY. Everything!

VEILED LADY. Then you remember a child that was received in your care?

SALLY. I do remember the child.

VEILED LADY (*eagerly*). That child is still living?

SALLY. Living and hearty!

VEILED LADY (*clasps hands*). Thank heavens! You still take care of him?

SALLY. Oh, let me go. I am doing wrong to listen to you! (*Crosses to* L. C., *detained by* VEILED LADY.)

VEILED LADY. What of the child?

SALLY. He—he is still here. He was still here when I came back from our country establishment to learn the ways of the place.

VEILED LADY. I, too, have learnt the ways of the place. They have given my child a name—a Christian name and a surname? Tell me, what have they called him?

SALLY. Oh, you mustn't ask me! indeed, you must not! (*to* L.).

VEILED LADY. His Christian name! You must tell me! I am his mother! Come back, come back! (C.) You may some day be a mother! As you hope to be a happy wife, as you are a living, loving woman! tell me the name of my child (*detaining* SALLY *by shawl*).

SALLY. Don't! please don't! you are trying to make me do wrong!

VEILED LADY. The surname and the Christian name, Sally! (*clinging to* SALLY).

SALLY. Oh, don't, don't kneel to me!

VEILED LADY. His name, Sally, his name!

SALLY. You promise——

VEILED LADY. Anything!

SALLY. Put your two hands in mine (LADY *does so*) and promise that you will not ask me to tell you anything but the surname and the Christian name!

VEILED LADY. I promise!

SALLY (*putting her lips close to her face*). Walter Wilding!

VEILED LADY. Walter Wilding! (*sob*) kiss him for me! (*Exit* SALLY, *hiding her face*, L.) Oh! (*sobbing, goes along flat to* R.) Oh! [*Exit, sobbing*, R.

SCENE II.—*Gas up*—FIRST *and* SECOND HUSBANDS *and* WIVES *discovered* L. C., *the two Girls*, L., *at table carving—Boys enter*, R. U E., *and sing* 'God Save the Queen.' *They take seats*. VEILED LADY *enters*, R. U. E. *to* L. C., *down stage, earnestly regarding the Boys*.

FIRST WIFE. Mr. Jones, whatever made you bring me here?

FIRST HUSBAND. Why, my dear, you wanted to come!

FIRST WIFE. How dare you tell me that I wanted to come?

FIRST HUSBAND. You did! to see the pretty children——

FIRST WIFE. I—I—I! The man who would bring his wife to see these examples of vice is lost to the commonest sense of decency! I blush for human nature!

FIRST HUSBAND. Human nature is very much obliged to you, my dear.

FIRST WIFE. Ugh! give me your arm, Mr. Jones! you are a fool.

FIRST HUSBAND. When I married you, that left no doubt of it! (*to* R., *proscenium* E., *with* FIRST WIFE) but you had better keep that opinion to yourself. [*Exit* R., *pros.* E.

SECOND WIFE. Oh, I should like to kiss these dear boys.

SECOND HUSBAND. Kiss them! Think of your own boys at home.

SECOND WIFE. It is sad to think that none of them have ever known a mother's love, or sat on a father's knee! It is a noble charity.

SECOND HUSBAND. A noble charity indeed! I have counted more than forty boys in this room, and every one of them is as well-kept and fat as our Tom! [*Leads* WIFE *off* R., *proscenium* E.

SALLY (*to* VEILED LADY). Didn't you faithfully promise you would not ask me to say anything more? (L. C. *front.*)

VEILED LADY. I told you I would not ask you to say more, but point me him out, dear Sally, good Sally!

SALLY (*aside*). Oh! I am going to do wrong again!

VEILED LADY. My heart is breaking! to know that my boy is here, but I can't tell which he is!

SALLY. You must not speak so loud here! Be patient a moment. I am going to walk round the table. Follow me with your eyes. The boy that I stop at and speak to will *not* be the one. *But* the boy that I touch will be Walter Wilding. (VEILED LADY *nods.* SALLY *goes up to* R. U. E. *corner, around table, comes down* R. *side of table, and bends over the* SECOND BOY *to speak to him, resting her right hand on the left shoulder of* WILDING, *the* FIRST BOY *at front end. After seeming to speak, pats* WILDING'S *shoulder, looks over at* VEILED LADY, *turns and goes off* R., *proscenium* E.)

VEILED LADY. Ah! (*slowly to head of table, to* WILDING.) How old are you, my boy?

WILDING. I am twelve.

VEILED LADY. Ah! Are you well and happy?

WILDING. Yes, ma'am.

VEILED LADY. Would you like to be provided for and be your own master when you grow up?

WILDING. Yes, ma'am!

VEILED LADY (*with growing emotion*). Would you like to have a home of your own and a mother who loves you? (*Sob.*)

WILDING. Oh, yes, ma'am!

(VEILED LADY *embraces him sobbing.—All the Boys rise and sing* 'God save the Queen.')

WILDING—VEILED LADY.
C., *at head of table.*

Boys at table.	*The two Girls.*
R. *to* C.	L.

CURTAIN

ACT I

SCENE.—*Court-yard in Wine Merchant's discovering* WALTER WILDING *and* MR. BINTRY *seated at cash table*, R. C., *front —two men carry cases from* L. U. E. *off* R. 2 E.

WILDING. I don't know how it may appear to you, Mr. Bintry, but what with the emotion, and what with the heat of the weather, I feel that old singing in the head, and buzzing in my ears.

BINTRY. A little repose will refresh you, Mr. Wilding.

WILDING. How do you like the forty-five years' old port?

BINTRY. How do I like it? I a lawyer! Did you ever hear of a lawyer who did not like port? Capital wine! much too good to be given away—even to lawyers!

WILDING. And now to my affairs. I think we have got everything straight, Mr. Bintry? (BINTRY *nods.*) A partner secured?

BINTRY (*nods*). Partner secured. (*Drinks.*)

WILDING. A housekeeper advertised for?

BINTRY (*nods*). A housekeeper advertised for, to 'apply personally at Cripple Corner, Great Tower Street, from ten to twelve.'

WILDING. My late dear mother's affairs wound up—and all charges paid?

BINTRY (*chuckling and slapping his vest pockets lightly*). All charges paid, without an item being taxed! the most unprofessional thing I ever heard of in all my career. (*Looks* R. 1. E.) Dear me! you have her portrait there?

WILDING. My mother's. One I have in my own room—the other there in my counting-house in full view. Ah! it seems but yesterday when she came to the Foundling to give me a home, and ask me if I could love her. Oh, you (her lawyer) know how I loved her! And now that I can love her no more, I honour and revere her memory. The utmost love was cherished between us, and we never were separated till death took her from me six months ago. Everything I have I owe to her. I hope my love for her repaid her. She had been deeply deceived, Mr. Bintry, and had cruelly suffered. But she never spoke of that —she never betrayed her betrayer!

BINTRY (*drinking*). She had made up her mind, and she *could* hold her peace. (*Aside.*) A devilish deal more than *you* ever can!

WILDING. I am not ashamed of her! I mean, not ashamed of being a foundling. I never knew a father, but I can be a father to all in my employment. I hope my new partner will second my desire, and that the housekeeper will help me, my people living in the same house, and eating at the same table with me.

JOEY *enters from cellar door*, L. 2 E., *with candle in stick which he puts* L. *on barrel, comes down* C.

JOEY. Respecting this same boarding and lodging, (*cap in hand*) young Master Wilding?

BINTRY. Ah, ha! This is one of your new family! That boy in a leather pinafore won't cost much in washing.

WILDING. Yes, Joey? (*interrogatively*).

JOEY. If you wish to board and lodge me, take me. I can peck as well as most men. Where I pecks ain't so high a h'objeck as what I peck, nor even so high a h'objeck as how much I peck.

BINTRY. Master Joey, you ought to have been a lawyer. Where *we* peck is not so high an object as what we peck and how much we peck! Human nature is much the same in all professions. Mr. Wilding, I'll try another glass of the forty-five.

JOEY. Is it all to live in the house, young Master Wilding? The two other cellarmen, the three porters, the two 'prentices, and the odd men?

WILDING. Yes, Joey, I hope we shall be a united family.

JOEY. Ah, I hope they may be.

WILDING. They? Rather say we, Joey!

JOEY. Don't look to me to make jolly on it, young Master Wilding. It's all werry well for you gentlemen that is accustomed to take your wine into your systems by your conwivial throttles to put a lively face upon it; but I have been accustomed to take my wine in at the pores. And took that way, it acts depressing! It's one thing, gentlemen, to charge your glasses in a dining-room with a Hip Hurrah and a Jolly Companions Every One! and another thing to charge yourself by the pores in a low cellar. I've been a cellarman all my life, and what's the consequence? I'm as muddled a man as lives—you won't find a muddleder than me, or my ekal in moloncolly!

BINTRY. I don't want to stop the flow of Master Joey's philosophy, but it is past ten o'clock, and the new housekeeper is coming.

WILDING. Let her come! my friend George Vendale is to see them and recommend the one that seems best.

BINTRY (*rises*). I'll look in again presently. (JOEY *goes up* C. *with him to open* D. *in* F.) Thank you, Joey. [*Exit* D. *in* F.

JOEY (*comes down* C.). So you have taken a new partner, young Master Vendale in, sir?

WILDING. Yes, Joey.

JOEY. But don't change the name of the firm again, young Master Wilding! It was bad luck enough to make it Yourself and Co. Better by far have left it Pebbleson Nephew, that good luck always stuck to! Never change luck when it is good, sir! never change luck. (*Up* L.)

Enter from set house on stoop, L., GEORGE VENDALE.

VENDALE. Well, I have seen the new housekeeper. Her name is Sarah Goldstraw!

WILDING (*startled*, R. C.). Goldstraw! Surely I have heard that name before.

VENDALE. If she is an old acquaintance, all the better. Here she is, I'll go and inspect the rest of the establishment.

[*Exit down back of stairs*, L. U. E.

Enter from house and down front steps, SALLY.

WILDING. I *have* seen her before!

SALLY (*aside*). Wilding! Wilding! It is a common name enough! (*Recognises* WILDING.) Ah!

JOEY (*to* WILDING). Take her, young Master Wilding. You won't find a match for Sarah Goldstraw in a hurry! (*Aside.*) I feel as if I had taken something new into my system at the pores! Has that pleasant woman brought the pleasant sunshine into this moloncolly place, I wonder? I will think over it in the cellar.

[*Exit* L. 2 E. *cellar door.*

WILDING. Will you please step this way into the counting-room?

SALLY (*aside*). I must be mistaken. (*Crosses to* R. 1 E., *opens door, starts.*) Oh, my!

WILDING (R. C.). What's the matter?

SALLY. Nothing.

WILDING. Nothing?

SALLY. No! excepting—what—what is that—that portrait hanging up in the counting-house?

WILDING. The portrait of my late dear mother!

SALLY. Of your mother? (*Aside.*) It is like the lady who spoke to me twelve years ago. (*Aloud.*) I hope you will pardon my taking up your time, sir. (*Crossing to* L.) I don't think this place will suit me! (R.)

WILDING. Stop, stop! There is something wrong here! something I do not understand!—Your face puzzles me! Ah! (*Hand to forehead, bewildered.*) I have it! You were at the Foundling twelve years ago!

SALLY. What shall I say?

WILDING. You were the nurse who was kind to my mother, and pointed me out to her!

SALLY. Great heaven forgive me! I was.

WILDING. Great heaven forgive you? What do you mean? Speak out.

SALLY. Dreadful consequences have followed, I am afraid, because I forgot my duty, for that lady——

WILDING. That lady! She calls my mother the lady. When you speak of my mother why don't you say—my mother?

SALLY. Oh! sir, I was deceived and so was the lady.

WILDING. Why can't you speak plainer? You mean my mother?

SALLY. I will speak the truth, but I wish I hadn't to do it, sir! When I was away to our country institution, there came to our house a lady, a Mrs. Miller, who adopted out one of the children. Six months afterwards I came back, and knew nothing about that. That's how the child was taken away——

WILDING. You—you mean me?

SALLY. No, sir. I mean the child of that lady. (*Points off* R. 1 E.) You were not her child. You cannot regret it more than I do. A few days after I had gone away the child was adopted and taken away. But another boy had just been received, and so they gave him his place and called *him* Walter Wilding! Of course, I knew nothing of this! I thought you were still the same infant that I had cared for at the first. Indeed, I was not to blame! It was not my fault.

WILDING. Is it dark, or am I dreaming? Give me your hand! (SALLY *comes to him*, C.)

SALLY. What is the matter?

WILDING. I can't see you! The noise is in my head.

SALLY. Shall I get some water? Shall I call for help?

WILDING. No! give me your hand! How do I know your story is true?

SALLY. Would I have told you if I were mistaken.

WILDING. Oh! I loved her so dearly. I felt so fondly that I was her son!

SALLY. Let your head rest on my shoulder,—not the first time, my boy. I have rocked you to sleep in my arms when a child, many and many's the time. (*Embraces* WILDING, *who is seated on barrel*, L. *of table-barrel.*)

WILDING. Oh, Sally, why did you not speak before?

SALLY. I couldn't, sir! I did not know it till two years ago, when I went to the institution to see one of the girls, and she told me all. If I had only not come here for the housekeeper's place you would never have known to your dying day what you know now! Oh, don't blame me! You forced me to speak! don't blame me!

WILDING. You would have concealed this from me, if you could? (C.) Don't talk that way! She left me all that I possess in the persuasion that I was her son. I am not her son. Would you have me enjoy the fortune of another man? He must be found! What was the name of the lady who adopted the child?

SALLY. Mrs. Miller, sir.

WILDING. Where does she live?

SALLY. No one knows, sir. She took the child to Switzerland.

WILDING. Switzerland? What part of Switzerland?

SALLY. No one knows, sir.

BINTRY *enters* R. 1 E.

BINTRY. How are you getting on with the new housekeeper? Bless me, what is the matter?

JOEY, *with candle, enters* L. 2 E., *cellar-door, slowly, stays up* L.

WILDING. Sally, tell him in your own words,—I cannot speak. (*To* L., *leaning against banisters.*)

BINTRY (*to* SALLY). Step into the counting-house for a little time. I will be with you.

[*Exit* SALLY, R. 1 E. D., *crosses to* WILDING.

JOEY (*comes down*). I hope, young Master Wilding, that Sarah Goldstraw is not going to be sent away?

WILDING. Sarah Goldstraw is a good, kind-hearted woman, and shall stay here. Mr. Bintry, the lost Walter Wilding must be found.

BINTRY. Not easy after a lapse of twenty years. At this time of day, you will find it no thoroughfare, sir, no thoroughfare.

WILDING. It must be done. I will make my will, and leave all I have to him before I sleep this night.

Enter VENDALE, R. 1 E.

My friend, you don't know what a blow has befallen me.

VENDALE (*shaking* WILDING'S *hand*). Sarah has just told me.

WILDING. You will take my side, George! You will help me to find the lost man! If neither of you will help me, I will go to Switzerland myself.

VENDALE. Don't talk like that. I am your partner in all ways.

BINTRY. How will you find the lost man? If we advertise, we lay ourselves open to every rogue in the kingdom. (R. C.)

WILDING. You don't understand me! It is because I loved her that I feel it my duty to do justice to her son! If he is a living man, I will find him, for her sake, his and my own! (C.) I am only a miserable impostor!

VENDALE. Don't talk like that! As to your being an impostor, that is simply absurd, for no man can be that without being a consenting party to the imposition. You need not distress yourself. We will help you. Come, compose yourself. (L. C.)

JOEY, *who has been up at gate in* F., *comes down with letter and card.*

WILDING. What is it, Joey?

JOEY. A foreign gentleman give me this card and letter.

WILDING (*reads card*). Jules Obenreizer!

VENDALE (*takes letter*). Obenreizer! from Switzerland.

WILDING. Switzerland!

VENDALE. I have seen him before.

WILDING. Something tells me I am near the man!

VENDALE. Mr. Obenreizer is an old travelling companion, whose acquaintance I made in Switzerland. (*Reads letter.*) 'Mr. Obenreizer is fully accredited as our agent, and we do not doubt you will esteem his merits.' Signed 'Defresnier & Co., Neuchâtel.' (C.)

WILDING. So you met him on the mountains? (R. C.)

BINTRY (L. *aside*). Mr. Vendale seems confused. That is a bad sign to begin with.

VENDALE. Yes, he was with a young lady——

WILDING. His daughter?

VENDALE. No! he is no older than you are. His niece.

BINTRY. And you fell in love with her? Excuse my legal habit of helping out an unwilling witness!

VENDALE (*laughs*). I am not an unwilling witness, Mr. Bintry! I do love her—I loved her then, and I shall love her to the end of the calendar! Is that an unwilling answer?

BINTRY. I can't say. I am not professionally acquainted with the subject.

WILDING. George, you seem confused?

VENDALE. The fact is, I rather talked of my family, to make an impression on the young lady.

WILDING. Come, if you object you need not meet him.

VENDALE. Pshaw! Mr. Obenreizer is recommended to our house, and we would be sure to meet in the way of business, so that the sooner it is over the better for me.

JOEY *opens gate and lets in* OBENREIZER, *who comes down* C. *to shake* WILDING'S *hand.*

WILDING. I am glad to see you sir. This is my friend and legal adviser, Mr. Bintry.

OBENREIZER (*shakes* BINTRY'S *hand*). Charmed! charmed to make Mr. Bintry's acquaintance. (L.)

BINTRY (*aside*). He is too civil by half. I don't like him.

WILDING. Mr. Vendale you know!

VENDALE (*shakes* OBENREIZER'S *hand*). You are doubtless surprised to meet me here as partner with Mr. Wilding?

OBENREIZER. On the contrary, no. As I said when we were on the mountains. We call them vast, but the world is so little, one cannot keep away from some persons. (*Quickly.*) Not that any one would wish to get rid of you, Mr. Vendale! Oh, dear no! So glad to have met you! So glad! (*Half embracing* VENDALE.)

BINTRY (*aside*). Rather a tigerish way of being glad.

OBENREIZER. Though you are descended from so fine a family, you have condescended to come into trade? Stop though. Wines? Is it trade in England or profession? Not fine arts? (*Smiling.*)

VENDALE. Mr. Obenreizer, I was but a silly young fellow in the first flush of coming into the fortune my parents left me. I hope what I said when we travelled together was more youthful openness of speech than vanity!

OBENREIZER. You tax yourself too heavily! You tax yourself, my faith! as if you were your government taxing you! I liked your conversation! I like your conversion. It is the misfortune of trade that any lower people may take to it and climb by it. I for example—I a man of low origin—for what I know of it—no origin at all!

WILDING (*aside to* BINTRY, L.). Do you hear that?

BINTRY. No! I am deaf on principle to all humbugs!

VENDALE (R. C., *to* OBENREIZER). And Madame Dor?

OBENREIZER. Oh, she is well. She is with Marguerite——

BINTRY. You seem rather young to be a young lady's guardian, Mr. Obenreizer?

OBENREIZER. Young in years, Mr. Bintry, but old in discretion and in experience. Her father was my half-brother—if he was my brother?—a poor peasant, and when he was dying, leaving her a little fortune, he called me to him, and told me, 'All for Marguerite.' Ah, Mr. Wilding! I may be this, or I may be that, but one thing I know! I shall live and I shall die true to my trust! (*Pause.*) Well, we are house-hunting now, and she shall have a home replete with gratified wishes! (*Aside.*) Though where the money is to come from is another matter. (*Turns up* C. *a little.*)

WILDING (*to* BINTRY). He is not sure of his origin! he is doubtful of his parentage! Do you hear that?

BINTRY. No! Mr. Wilding, I do *not* hear that!

VENDALE (R. C., *to* OBENREIZER). And Madame Dor?

OBENREIZER. Oh, she is well. She is with Marguerite——

VENDALE. Abroad?

OBENREIZER. Here! here waiting for me without.

WILDING. What! ladies kept waiting at my door? I will go bring them in——

OBENREIZER. Not for worlds! (*Prevents* VENDALE *and* WILDING *going up* C., *goes up* C. *to gate which* JOEY *opens slowly.*)

WILDING (*to* BINTRY). I must do something in this!

BINTRY. There is one thing you can do—hold your tongue!

OBENREIZER (*leads* MARGUERITE *and* MADAME DOR *down* C.). My niece! (MARGUERITE *comes down* L. C., *to* VENDALE.) Madame Dor! (MADAME DOR *crosses sidewise to* R., *side of barrel-table, back to characters on stage, rubbing glove.*) The guardian angel of my wardrobe! you will excuse her—she is now at my gloves! to-morrow, it may be, darning my stockings or making pudding. Ah! you English, who delight in domestic matters. You like it in your pictures, you like it in your books! Ah, Madame Dor makes me my good, solid, heavy, indigestible English pudding! Only look at her back—(*points to* MADAME DOR, R. *by table*) it is as broad as her heart! (C.)

VENDALE (*to* MARGUERITE). Mr. Obenreizer was saying that the world is so small a place that people cannot escape one another. If it had been less, I might have found you sooner! It is still a curious coincidence that you come to London the day I become partner in a house to which Mr. Obenreizer's firm in Switzerland introduce him.

OBENREIZER (*coming between*). Ah! London is the place—city of luxury, if you are rich, like Mr. Vendale here! Some are lucky! While they were saying to him, 'Come here, my darling, kiss me!' I was called 'Little wretch, come taste the stick!' (*gesture with cane*) I dwelt among a sorry set in Switzerland! Would I could forget it! (WILDING *touches* BINTRY *to notice.*)

MARGUERITE. For my part, I love Switzerland.

OBENREIZER (*quickly, tenderly*). Marguerite, so do I. But speak in proud England.

MAGUERITE. I speak in proud earnest! And I am not noble, but a peasant's daughter.

VENDALE. And I honour and fully appreciate your sentiment!

OBENREIZER. Ah! (*interposing*) Marguerite, we will set about our house-hunting.

WILDING. Mr. Obenreizer! (C.)

BINTRY. Mr. Wilding, will you hold your tongue?

OBENREIZER. My dear Mr. Vendale, you must come see us often when we are settled. Mr. Wilding, the same. Mr. Bintry! (*bows*). We will transact business together, and be firm friends. Adieu! (*Bows, escorts* MARGUERITE *and* MADAME DOR *in* C.—VENDALE L. *side, with* BINTRY *and* WILDING R. C.)

VENDALE (*aside*). How he guards his niece!

WILDING. This may be the lost man!

CURTAIN

ACT II

SCENE I.—*Room in* OBENREIZER'S *house, discovering* MARGUERITE *standing at window,* L. *in* F., *and* MADAME DOR *seated at table by same*—OBENREIZER, R.

MARGUERITE (*aside*). Not come—not come yet! (*Turns sadly from looking out of window.*)

OBENREIZER (*counting money,* R. 1 E., *at press in set*). One hundred—two—four hundred—fifty—four hundred and fifty. Fifty pounds still wanted to make up the missing sum. That sum I must replace, or I am a lost man! (*To table* R. *front.*) Ah! this miserable luxury—this hollow show! Has Marguerite any idea of what this splendour costs me? Has she even noticed it? Yes, within the last few weeks she has been more animated and kinder. Something like affection is in her ways. She does not even think of that man Vendale.

MARGUERITE (*aside*). Still no signs of him!

OBENREIZER (*aside*). What! he has sent nothing as a birthday present. He has forgotten her, then! Oh, if he had sent her a present it would have been something so rich that her proud spirit would have revolted. I will put up the money. Yet (*hesitating*) I might replace it by a month. Nonsense! it is not to be thought of. Disgrace myself? Ah! it would ruin me for life! What would Marguerite say when she looked on me as a felon! I will put the money up; he will not come.

MARGUERITE (*suddenly*). Oh! he is crossing the square. Here he comes. (*Turns to* D. *in* F.)

OBENREIZER. He! Who?

MARGUERITE. Mr. Vendale.

OBENREIZER (*aside*). Then he has not forgotten her! (R. *front.*)

Enter VENDALE, D. *in* F.

VENDALE (*to* MARGUERITE). Permit me to wish you many happy returns of the day. Will you accept a little memento? (*Gives jewel case.*)

MARGUERITE. Jewels! They are too rich for me!

VENDALE. You have not opened it yet.

MARGUERITE. So simple a present (*turning to* OBENREIZER) I may keep?

OBENREIZER (*sneering*). The modesty of wealth!

MARGUERITE (*to* VENDALE). I own that you have pleased and flattered me. (*Puts on brooch.*)

OBENREIZER (*aside*). He forces me to it. (*Gets money from press,* R. 1 E.; *aloud.*) Mr. Vendale has reminded me that I have not yet made my offering; you will excuse me? (VENDALE *bows—up to* D. *in* F.; *aside.*) Ah, Mr. Vendale, come what may, you will not get the upper hand of me now! [*Exit,* D. *in* F.

VENDALE (*aside*). I will wait here with the greatest pleasure till he comes back! My opportunity has come at last. No! Madame Dor! Is there no means of getting this piece of human furniture out of the room? (MADAME DOR *leans forward, sleeping.*) She lets her work fall unheeded to the floor. Oh! best of women, yield to the voice of Nature, and fall asleep. (MADAME DOR *does so—*VENDALE *comes down* C. *to* MARGUERITE.) I have something to say to you—a secret to impart. (*Seated beside her.*)

MARGUERITE. What claim have I to any secret of yours, Mr. Vendale?

VENDALE. You have not forgotten the happy time when we first met and were travelling together. Out of all the impressions I brought back from Switzerland, there was one impression chief. Can you guess what it is?

MARGUERITE. I cannot guess. An impression of the mountains?

VENDALE. No, more precious.

MARGUERITE. Of the lakes?

VENDALE. No! the lakes have not grown dearer to me every day! Marguerite, all that makes life worth having, hangs, for me, on a word from your lips. Marguerite, I love you!

MARGUERITE. Oh, Mr. Vendale! Have you forgotten the distance between us?

VENDALE (*prevents her rising*). There can be but one distance between us, Marguerite—that of your own making. There is no higher rank in goodness and in beauty than yours!

MARGUERITE. Ah! Think of your family, and think of mine! (*Rises.*)

VENDALE. If you dwell on such an obstacle, I shall think only that I have offended you! (*Rises.*)

MARGUERITE (*forgetting herself*). Oh, no, George!

VENDALE. Say you love me!

MARGUERITE. I love you! (*Embrace, starts, goes up to* L. U. *corner.*)

OBENREIZER *enters,* D. *in* F.—MADAME DOR *is awakened by* MARGUERITE.

OBENREIZER (*as men bring in flowers in stand and place them up* C. *against* F.). Now you will see that your birthday is not forgotten. (R. *front.*)

MARGUERITE (C. *up*). I thank you.

OBENREIZER. Oh, not for them! My present is not made yet! Flowers will fade. Wear these! (*presents jewel-case*) and give them a beauty which is not their own.

MARGUERITE (*takes case*). Oh, how could you buy these for me! how can you expect me to wear these? I would have been contented with the flowers. (*Goes up to* L. U. *corner.*) Madame Dor, we will be late. We must dress for dinner.

[*Exit* L. D. *with* MADAME DOR.

OBENREIZER (*aside*). She wears *his* offering round her neck! My crime is useless! I have put my whole life in peril, and *this* is my reward! Oh, curses on her glitter and her beauty!

VENDALE. What is the matter, friend? (L. C.)

OBENREIZER (*sarcastically*). Friend! Nothing!

VENDALE. Stay! I have something to say to you. (C. *front.*)

OBENREIZER (R. C. *front*). Excuse me. I am not quite myself. You want to speak to me—oh! on business, I suppose.

VENDALE. On something much more important than mere business.

OBENREIZER. I am at your service. Go on. (*Seated* R. *side of table,* VENDALE *seated* L. *side.*)

VENDALE. Perhaps you may have noticed latterly that my admiration for your charming niece——

OBENREIZER. Noticed? Not I!

VENDALE. Has grown into a deeper feeling——

OBENREIZER (*uneasily*). Shall we say friendship, Mr. Vendale?

VENDALE (*rises*). I ask you to give me her hand in marriage!

OBENREIZER (*starts up*). You ask *me*! (*Restrains his anger.*)

VENDALE. Stay, I beg you to tell me plainly what objection you see to my suit?

OBENREIZER. The immense one that my niece is the daughter of a poor peasant and you the son of an English gentleman.

VENDALE. I ought to know my own countrymen better than you do, Mr. Obenreizer. In the estimation of everybody whose opinion is worth having, my wife would be the one sufficient justification of my marriage. We are both men of business, and you naturally expect me to satisfy you that I have the means of supporting a wife. I am in a trade which I see my way to gradually improving. As it stands at present I can state my annual income at fifteen hundred pounds. Do you object to me on pecuniary grounds?

OBENREIZER (*abruptly*). Yes!

VENDALE. Yes! It is not enough?

OBENREIZER. It is not half enough for a foreign wife who has half your social prejudices to conquer. Tell me, Mr. Vendale, on your £1500 a year, can your wife live in a fashionable quarter, have a butler to wait at her table, and a carriage and horses to drive about in? Yes or no?

VENDALE. Come to the point! You view this question as a question of terms?

OBENREIZER. Terms, as you say! terms beyond your reach!

VENDALE. Sir!

OBENREIZER. Make your income three thousand pounds and come to me then!

VENDALE. Then I will speak with her.

OBENREIZER. You surely would not speak to my niece on this subject?

VENDALE. I have opened my whole heart to her, and have reason to hope——

OBENREIZER (*passionately*). What! Mr. Vendale, as a man of honour, speaking to a man of honour, how can you justify such conduct as this?

VENDALE. The best excuse is the assurance that I have had from her own lips that she loves me——(R. *front*.)

OBENREIZER (*passionately*). She lo—Oh! (*violently*) we'll soon see about that! (*Goes over to* L. D.) Marguerite! Marguerite! (*Aside*.) How lovely she looks!

Enter, L. D., MARGUERITE.

MARGUERITE. You wish to speak to me?

OBENREIZER. Yes, my child, I wish to speak to you—to ask a question. Mr. Vendale says——(*hand to forehead, as in pain*).

MARGUERITE. How altered you are in your manner. Are you not well? What have I done? (*up* L.).

OBENREIZER (*forgetting himself*). Done! you have turned the knife in the wound! No! I don't mean that! I mean——But we are forgetting Mr. Vendale. He has *said* (*sneering*) that you said you loved him? It is not true, my child?

MARGUERITE (*comes down* L. C.). It is true!

OBENREIZER. Oh! Great God! (*in a suppressed voice*, C.)

MARGUERITE. You frighten me!

VENDALE (*triumphantly*). Are you satisfied now?

OBENREIZER. Wait! wait a little! I have my authority yet, as she is my ward. Marguerite, you know that your father entrusted you to me, you cannot marry without my consent. Whatever Mr. Vendale says—if I say wait, you will wait!

MARGUERITE. Oh! (VENDALE *glances at her imploringly*.)

VENDALE. Oh, Marguerite!

OBENREIZER (*violently*). You *will* wait, my child?

MARGUERITE. Yes! (*submissively clasps her hands and hangs her head*).

OBENREIZER. Are you answered?

VENDALE (*firmly*). I am. You have heard from her own lips that she loves me. I will make the fifteen hundred three thousand pounds.

OBENREIZER. Make it three thousand!

VENDALE. Adieu, Marguerite!

MARGUERITE. Oh! George! (VENDALE *turns.*)

OBENREIZER. Ah, Mr. Vendale! You are not her husband yet! (*going up* L. *with one hand of* MARGUERITE'S *in his*, VENDALE *at* D. *in* F.).

(*Scene closes in.*)

SCENE II.—*Room in* WILDING'S *house.*—MR. BINTRY *enters* R., *hands under his coat-tails, in thought, crosses to* L., *turns and to* D. R. *in* F.

Enter SALLY, R. D.

SALLY. Oh, Mr. Bintry, so you have come to see master!

BINTRY. Yes, I have come to see how he is getting on.

SALLY. I am afraid he is worse. The new doctor has ordered that he must not be disturbed. (C.)

BINTRY (R. C.) Another doctor called in! When I was here last, Mr. Wilding could walk and talk.

SALLY. He can walk and talk yet, but I must agree with the doctors. He is dying—growing back more and more like him I used to call my little child at the Foundling.

BINTRY. Well, Miss Goldstraw, you may be old enough to be his mother, but you certainly don't look it.

SALLY. Thank you, sir, for the compliment!

BINTRY. You are heartily welcome.

SALLY. Don't you think, sir, you could make him better by doing more as he wishes, sir?

BINTRY. Miss Goldstraw, you have your duty to perform, and I have mine. My duty as a professional man is to keep my old friend from all rogues—Mr. Obenreizer, for example. (*Crosses to* L.)

SALLY. But you go contrary to his will, sir.

BINTRY. Contrary to his will—I wish we could go contrary to his will. I drew it up and had it executed! the most absurd document ever put on paper! Vendale and I were bound by it as executors to find a lost man, no matter what he is! and give up to him a fortune. By drawing up that document I have committed professional suicide, and yet the worthy woman says I have not humoured my client!

SALLY. Excuse me, sir. I see closer than you. It is wearing his life out.

BINTRY. Come, speak out if you think I can be of any service to my old friend! What can I do?

SALLY. Find the lost man!

BINTRY. If I do, I'll be——(*stops short on* SALLY *lifting her hands*).

SALLY. Oh, sir! if you'd only promise to let him have his own way, and try to find the lost man?

BINTRY. Was there ever such perversity! Here's a man dying to find a man who will rob him of every penny he possesses and leave him a pauper. Humph! Well, I'll put an advertisement in the papers, telling the client to apply to my office, to me, mind you—it will be a devilish lucky man who will get a fortune out of me, I can tell you! (*Crosses to* L. *and returns to* C.)

SALLY (R. C.). Thank you, sir, for my master. Ah, you may have a rough outside, but I see that you are a warm-hearted man!

BINTRY (*going* R., *turns and comes close to* SALLY, *after pause*). Miss Goldstraw, don't you take away my character! Well, I will set about it, and come to-morrow. [*Exit* R.

SALLY (*to* D. *in* F., *which opens*). Oh, my dear master!

Enter WILDING, D. *in* F.

WILDING. I thought I heard Mr. Bintry? (*to* C. *assisted by* SALLY).

SALLY (R. C.). He was here only a minute. He is coming again to-morrow, sir.

WILDING. Always to-morrow! When it is now that we ought to find the man. (*Querulously.*) Nobody helps me.

SALLY. Mr. Bintry says he will try, sir.

WILDING. Mr. Bintry is too suspicious, and drives people away. (*Aside.*) The more I think of it the more I see that everything points one way. Obenreizer is the man! I think of him by day, and I dream of him by night. (*Aloud.*) Sally, I may call you Sally?

SALLY. Dear, yes, sir.

WILDING. For the sake of the old times let it be Sally.

SALLY. Of course, sir. Do you try to be the good boy that you always were at the Foundling, the good patient little boy. Try to be patient now.

WILDING. Something tells me I must lose no time. I must see Mr. Obenreizer at once.

SALLY. Yes, sir, I will send for him.

WILDING. I must and will see him.

SALLY. Yes, yes, sir.

WILDING. Where is Mr. Vendale?

SALLY. Gone to Mr. Obenreizer's.

WILDING. Ah! gone to propose to his pretty niece. Vendale's a dear good friend, and I wish him all success. He is not so suspicious as Mr. Bintry, and I think he will aid me.

SALLY. I am sure of it, sir.

WILDING. Then you will send for Mr. Obenreizer?

SALLY. I promise to send there, sir.

WILDING. You will relieve my mind.

SALLY. I will do it, sir, but be a good child, and go to bed.

WILDING. Sally, Sally! how little changed things are since we met for the first time. Mr. Obenreizer says, 'The world is so small that it is not strange how often the same people come together at various stages of life.' After all, I have come round to my foundling nurse to die!

SALLY. No! no! dear Master Wilding, not going to die! (*Leads him out* D. *in* F.) No! [*Exit* D. *in* F.

SCENE III.—*Cellar in* WILDING'S *stores*—JOEY *discovered up* R. *measuring casks and bins, etc.* VENDALE *comes down* L. *platform to front.*

VENDALE. Poor Wilding! I would tell him what took place at Obenreizer's, but he has troubles of his own to engross him. My spirits are depressed, spite of myself, as if something evil was overhanging me. Can I do what I have engaged myself to do? Can I double this business in a year's time? I have been wandering about these old cellars like a perturbed spirit. Oh, you are here, are you, Joey? (*Takes candle and comes down* L. *side listlessly, comes down around and up* C.)

JOEY. Oughtn't it rather to go, Oh, *you're* here, are you, Master George? For it's my business here, and not yours!

VENDALE. Don't grumble, Joey.

JOEY. I don't grumble! It's what I took in at the pores. Have a care that something in *you* don't begin a grumbling, Master George! Stop here long enough, and the wapors will be at work—trust 'em for it! So you've regularly come into the business, Master George?

VENDALE. Yes, Joey. I hope you don't object?

JOEY. Oh! I don't, bless you! But wapors object that you're too young. You and Master Wilding are too young. Master has not changed the luck of the firm.

VENDALE. Pooh!

JOEY. Pooh! is an easy word to speak, Master George, but I have not been a cellarman down here all my life for nothing. I know by what I notices down here when it's a-going to rain, when it's a-going to hold up, when it's a-going to blow, and when it's a-going to be calm. I know when the luck's changed quite as well.

VENDALE (*taking rod up*). Has this growth on the roof anything to do with your divination, Joey? We are famous for this growth in our vaults, aren't we?

JOEY. We are, Master George, and if you'll take advice by me, you'll let it alone.

VENDALE. Why, Joey?

JOEY. For three good reasons!

VENDALE. Let's hear the good reasons for letting the fungus alone. (*Playing with webs.*)

JOEY. Why, because it rises from the casks of wine and may leave you to judge what sort of wapors a cellarman takes into his system when he walks in the same, and because at one stage of its growth it's maggots!

VENDALE. Maggots! What other reason?

JOEY. I wouldn't keep touching of it, Master George, if I was you! Take a look at its colour!

VENDALE. I am looking. Well, Joey, the colour?

JOEY. Is it like (*mysteriously*) clotted blood, Master George?

VENDALE. It is rather like.

JOEY. Is it more than like! (*Shakes his head.*)

VENDALE. Say it is exactly like! What then? (*Playing with the cobweb as before.*)

JOEY. Well, Master George, they do say——

VENDALE (*carelessly*). Who?

JOEY. How should I know who? Them as says pretty well everything! How can I tell who they are?

VENDALE. True. Go on, Joey!

JOEY. They do say, that the man who gets by any accident a piece of that right upon his breast——

VENDALE (*playing with stick and web, mechanically*). On his breast?

JOEY. For sure and certain——

VENDALE. For sure and certain?

JOEY. Will die by murder!

VENDALE. Murder! (*Web drops on his left breast and vest, lets rod fall.*)

OBENREIZER *appears on platform,* L. *front.*

VENDALE. What do you want here?

OBENREIZER (*comes down* L. *platform to stage to* C.). Mr. Vendale, I come on a sad errand. You need a friend—a true friend. I will try to be it again. I hope you will forget how we parted, when I say that I regret my manner of receiving you. (*To* C.) Mr. Vendale, I ask your pardon.

VENDALE. I accept the apology.

OBENREIZER (*softly*). Won't you shake hands with me? (*They shake hands.*) Mr. Vendale, prepare yourself for a shock.

VENDALE. What is it?

OBENREIZER. I come to bring you sad tidings——

VENDALE. Is it of Wilding? Is my poor friend worse?

OBENREIZER. Worse!

VENDALE. Not——

OBENREIZER. He is——

VENDALE. Dead?

OBENREIZER. Dead!

JOEY (*up* C.). Dead!

VENDALE. Dead! My poor friend! Ah, Joey your superstition spoke truth. This was a warning of death.

JOEY (*comes down* R. C.) I did not say death, Master George, I said murder!

JOEY.	OBENREIZER.	VENDALE.
R.	C.	L.

CURTAIN

ACT III

SCENE I.—*Counting-room in* WILDING'S *house, discovering* VENDALE *at table* R. C. *front, and* SALLY, *beside him.*

SALLY. Have you any more questions to ask me, sir?

VENDALE. Yes—tell me again all that passed just before poor Wilding died.

SALLY. He had been asking for Mr. Obenreizer, who had been sent for—and when he came he sat up to try to speak to him, but before he could say a word, he fell back again. The doctor ordered Mr. Obenreizer to leave the room. Mr. Wilding died soon after—only spoke a word, but I am sure he breathed your name.

VENDALE. I am sure of that! (*with emotion*). So no one knows what he wanted so eagerly to say to Mr. Obenreizer. The mystery is wrapped in denser obscurity than ever. My poor dear friend! I know what his trust was, and if the missing man is to be found, I will find him. (*Knock* R. 1 E. D.) Who's there? Come in.

Enter JOEY, R. 1 E. D., *with letter.*

JOEY. A letter sir, from foreign parts.

VENDALE (*takes letter*). From Defresnier and Co., of Neuchâtel.

JOEY (*to* SALLY, L. U. E. *corner*). Do you find yourself, miss, getting over the shock of young Master Wilding's death? The answer to mine.

SALLY. Mr. Joey, we all have to submit to losses in this world. I am learning, I hope, to submit to mine. [*Exit* L. U. E.

JOEY (*aside*). Beautiful language! beautiful! The parson himself couldn't have said it better than she. I'll try to remember it before I forget it, like the catechism. 'We must all submit to learning, which is one of the losses in this world!'

VENDALE (*aside*, R. C. *front*). Just when it is most important for me to increase the value of the business, it is threatened with a loss of five hundred pounds. Ah, Marguerite!

JOEY (*comes down* R. *side*). Ah! Master George, I know what's on your mind. It's those six cases of red wine sent from the place called Noocattle, instead of the white.

VENDALE. The devil take the six cases!

JOEY. The devil sent them, sir. It's foreign to my nature to crow over the house I serve, but hasn't it come true what I said to young Master Wilding, respecting the changing the name of the firm, when I said that you might find one of these days that he'd changed the luck of the firm? Did I set myself up as a prophet? No! Has what I said to him come true? Yes! What's the consequence? You write to them at Noocattle, and they write back. You, not satisfied, write to them again; and they, not satisfied, write back again; and that's the letter you have in your hand, as chock full of bad news as a egg is full of meat. In the time of Pebbleson Nephew, young Master George, no such thing was ever known as a mistake made in a consignment to our house. I don't want to intrude my moloncolly on you, sir, so let me recommend the beautiful language of Miss Goldstraw, fitted to the case: 'We must all learn to submit to our losses, which is one of the learnings in this world!' Reflect over them, Mr. Vendale. I'm going to the wapors awaiting in the cellar for me! [*Exit* R. 1 E.

VENDALE. This is most unfortunate! (*To desk up* L.) Let me put the correspondence in order. (*Takes up letters.*) First I write to Defresnier and Co., saying the number of cases per last consignment was quite correct, but on six of them being opened they were found to contain red wine instead of champagne, a mistake probably caused by a similarity of the brand. The matter can be easily set right by your sending us six cases of champagne, or by crediting us with the value of six cases red on the five hundred pounds last remitted you, to which they reply: 'The statement of the error has led to a very unexpected discovery—a serious affair for you and us. Having no more champagne of the vintage last sent to you, we made arrangements to credit your firm with the value of the six cases, when a reference to our books resulted in the moral certainty that no such remittance as you mention ever reached our house, and a literal certainty that no such remittance has been paid to our account at the bank. We have not even a suspicion who the thief is, but we believe you will assist us towards discovery by seeing whether the receipt (forged of course) purporting to come from our house is entirely in MSS. or a numbered and printed form. Anxiously waiting your reply, we remain,' etc. etc. Ah! Next I write to the Swiss firm, and receive the answer I hold in my hand. (*Reads.*) 'Dear Sir: Your discovery that the forged receipt is executed on one of our regular forms has caused inexpressible surprise and distress to us. At the time when your remittance was stolen but three keys were in existence opening the strong box in which our receipt-forms are invariably kept. My partner had one key, I another. The third was in possession of a gentleman who, at that period, occupied a position of trust in our house. I cannot prevail on myself to inform you who the person is. Forgive my silence, the motive of it is good.' Who can this be? However, it is useless for me to inquire in my position. 'The handwriting on your receipt must be compared with certain specimens in our possession. I cannot send you them, for business reasons, and must beg you to send the receipt to Neuchâtel, and, in making this request, I must accompany it by a word of warning. If the person, at whom suspicion now points, really proves to be the person who has committed this forgery and theft, the only evidence against him is the evidence in your hands, and he is a man who will stick at nothing to obtain and destroy it. I strongly urge you not to trust the receipt to the post. Send it, without loss of time, by a private messenger accustomed to travelling, capable of speaking French; a man of courage, a man of honesty, and, above all, a man who can be trusted to let no stranger scrape acquaintance with him on the route. Tell no one—absolutely no one—but your messenger of the turn this matter has now taken. The safe transit of the receipt may depend on your interpreting *literally* the advice which I give you at the end of this letter.' Now I know the man who writes these words. He would not have written them without good reasons. Who can I send? There is no man I know of. None of the clerks speak French.

Music to OBENREIZER'S *entrance.*

OBENREIZER (*in* R. 1 E.) May I come in?

VENDALE. Certainly.

OBENREIZER, R. 1 E., *puts hat and cane on table up* R. C., *against flat, and comes down.*

JOEY (R. 1 E., *aside*). He stole in here just as he stole into the cellars to tell of Master Wilding's death. He was by when the web fell on Master George, he is by when that letter of bad news comes. I will watch. I don't like this Mr. Openrazor! [*Exit* R. 1 E.

OBENREIZER. Ah, Mr. Vendale, you look as if there was something the matter!

VENDALE. Yes, you come at a bad time. I am threatened with the loss of five hundred pounds. (R. 2 E.)

OBENREIZER. *Five* hundred pounds! (*Aside.*) Ah!

VENDALE (*at safe in wall* R. 2 E.). Your own house is one of the parties in the affair.

OBENREIZER. Indeed! (*Aside.*) The forged receipt. (*Aloud.*) Tell me how it has happened. (*Aside.*) I wonder where he has got the receipt? If he only takes it out of his safe——

VENDALE. Ah! (*Takes paper out of safe,* R. 2 E.) Here is the forged receipt.

OBENREIZER (*up* L., *aside*). He is alone. I am stronger than him. (*About to cross to* R.)

Enter JOEY, R. 1 E.

JOEY. Did you call, Master George?

VENDALE. No! Joey, don't disturb me!

JOEY. I'll keep the door open this time. [*Exit* R. 1 E.

OBENREIZER (*aside*). Force is hopeless! I must try fraud! Well?

VENDALE. Well, the latest letter wishes me to send your house the forged receipt to compare it with writing in their hands. It is wished that I must keep the whole proceedings a profound secret from everybody.

OBENREIZER. Not even excepting me! Well?

VENDALE. Not excepting. (*Surprised.*) Oh! not excepting you. They must have forgotten you.

OBENREIZER. They must have forgotten me. Then under the circumstances I can hardly advise. Yet why not take it yourself.

Nothing could happen better. I am going to Switzerland to-night.

VENDALE. And Marguerite?

OBENREIZER (*gaily*). Oh! come to the house and dine with us at seven. We can go off at once by the mail-train to-night. Is it agreed?

VENDALE. By the mail-train to-night?

OBENREIZER. Ah! well (*looking at watch*) at seven! (*up* R. *at* D. *in* F.)

VENDALE. At seven to-night.

JOEY (*enters* R. 1 E.) I will take your luggage for you to Mr. Openrazor's house.

VENDALE. You have been listening, Joey?

JOEY. Not listening, Master George, but I heard every word for all that.

JOEY.	OBENREIZER, D. *in* F.	VENDALE.
R.	R. C.	C.

SCENE II.—*Room in* WILDING'S *house—enter*, L., SALLY *and* JOEY.

SALLY (C.). Mr. Joey, why do you follow me about into my part of the house?

JOEY. Miss Goldstraw, if you was to go down into the cellars I'd follow you there with the greatest pleasure.

SALLY. But why do you follow me at all?

JOEY. For the same reason that the first man followed the first woman.

SALLY. Ay, but she led him all wrong afterwards, and I don't want to lead you wrong, Mr. Joey.

JOEY. Then there's another reason: I want to see you change your name, which if Goldstraw is good, to Ladle, which is better! That was well said, I think!

SALLY. Well, I never! Is it you of all men that would want me to change the name of the firm? What next, I wonder?

JOEY. Woman is not the *firm*. (*Putting arm round* SALLY'S *waist*.)

SALLY. Do you speak with your arm, Mr. Joey, and do you think I listen with my waist? (*Puts his arm away*.)

JOEY. Then there's another thing, Miss Goldstraw. I want you to bring back the luck of the firm!

SALLY. Me! you want me? Why, bless your innocent soul, I was the cause of all the trouble that has come into the house. If it had not been for me, none of this would have happened. If you, Joey, knew all, you would hate me.

JOEY (*shakes head*). If you brought the cross of luck, why, that's the very reason you should bring the good luck home again. (*Aside.*) That was well said, I think!

SALLY. Why, what can I do, Mr. Joey? (*Puts arm around her.*) Mr. Joey, may I ask, did you ever make love before?

JOEY. Yes; but I never got as far as this.

SALLY (*laughs*). The idea of any man making love in an apron like that!

JOEY (*aside*). She remarks my apron. Now, what follows from her being in love with my apron? Why, that she should be in love with me! (*Aloud.*) You are at liberty, Miss Goldstraw, to like any part of me, so long as you like me. Now just let my arm speak to your waist a little, while I tell you that I have something else besides wapors in my head, I have. I would go on further with the love-making but for that and my having to go to take Mr. George's luggage to Mr. Openrazor's; and in the state of mind I am in, and with the spirit of prophecy strong upon me, I don't know where I shall spend the night.

SALLY. Dear me! (*Puts aside arm.*) You'll excuse me, Master Joey, but the institution of marriage is a serious thing, and the more a man and a woman look at it in that light before marriage, the better for the parties afterwards! [*Exit* D. *in* F.

JOEY. Beautiful language! Let me turn that over in my mind before I forget it! The 'institution of a man and a woman is a serious matter, and the sooner they look at it in that light the better for all parties afterwards!' [*Exit* L. 1 E. *as he speaks.*

SCENE III.—*Same as* SCENE I., ACT II., *discovering* OBENREIZER *at table, up* L., *packing travelling-bag and putting its strap round his neck, having pipe in his hand, etc.*, MARGUERITE *and* VENDALE R. C. *front.*

VENDALE. I am all ready now, and going away.

MARGUERITE (*aside to him*). Must you go, George? Oh, do not go!

VENDALE. It is business that compels me to go. I know the parting must be hard, but I shall be back in a month.

MARGUERITE. It is not the parting, but you are going with him. Have you done anything to offend Mr. Obenreizer?

VENDALE. I?

MARGUERITE. Hush! You know the little photograph of you I have. This afternoon it happened to be on the mantelpiece, when he took it up, and I saw his face in the glass. I know you have offended him! He is merciless, he is revengeful.

VENDALE. You are letting your fancy frighten you. Obenreizer and I were never better friends than at this moment.

MARGUERITE. Don't go, George, or go alone. It is near seven. It will be too late in a few minutes. Change your mind, George, change your mind!

JOEY *enters,* D. *in* F., *and comes down* R. *to* VENDALE, *to give him letter.*

JOEY. A letter with a foreign postmark, Master George. (*Goes up to take trunk to* L. *by window, then by* D. *in* F., *waiting.*)

VENDALE. From Neuchâtel.

MARGUERITE. The journey is put off? (*Hands clasped with joy.*)

OBENREIZER (*aside, coming down* C.). The journey put off!

VENDALE (*after reading*). On the contrary. (*Reads.*) 'Dear Sir: I am called away by urgent business to Milan, where I should prevail on you to meet me.' My journey is not deferred, you see, but lengthened. (*To* OBENREIZER.) In this wintry weather I cannot expect you to accompany me on the additional route.

OBENREIZER. Why not?—Fellow-travellers, be it more or less long. To Switzerland I would have gone with you; to Milan you say now. Well, I will go with you to your journey's end!

VENDALE. Thanks, my companion.

MARGUERITE (*aside to* VENDALE). Oh, George! look at his smile now.

OBENREIZER (*looks at his watch*). Are you ready? Can I take anything for you? You have no travelling-bag. Here's mine, with the compartment for papers, open at your service. (*To* L. *after this.*)

VENDALE. Thank you. I have only one paper of importance with me, and that paper I am bound to take charge of myself. (*Touching breast-pocket of coat.*) Here it must remain till we get to Milan. (*Goes up* C.) Joey, change the address on my trunk. (JOEY *goes* L., *frustrating* OBENREIZER, *who wanted to take up trunk, brings trunk to table, up* C.) Milan, Joey. M-i-l-a-n, if you don't know how to spell it.

JOEY (*aside*). I know how to spell more than that. Miss Marguerite don't seem to like the idea of Master George going on this journey with Mr. Openrazor no more than I do. I'd give something to know her mind on the subject. (*Writes on label on trunk.*)

OBENREIZER. Marguerite, adieu. My friend, *en route*, or we'll be too late for the mail train.

MARGUERITE (C). George! (*Embraces George.*)

OBENREIZER. George, how precious you are to her! Don't be alarmed (*half embraces* VENDALE *by the shoulders*); I will take care of him. Come on (*out* D. *in* F.).

MARGUERITE. George, George, George, don't go!

VENDALE. I must.

(*Voice of* OBENREIZER *off* R. U. E.). Vendale!

VENDALE. I am coming.

(*Voice of* OBENREIZER). Vendale!

JOEY. He may come back.

VENDALE. Farewell, Marguerite. [*Exit hastily* D. *in* F.

MARGUERITE. Don't go. Ah! gone in spite of all that I could do! Oh, what is to be done?

JOEY (*comes down* R. C.). Miss Marguerite, the warning of danger's on you as it is on me?

MARGUERITE. Yes.

JOEY. Will you try to fend it off?

MARGUERITE. Yes. Joey, I am no fine lady; I am one of the people like you. I will go save him.

JOEY. And I will go with you! I will go with you!

CURTAIN

ACT IV

SCENE I.—*Interior of Swiss Inn, discovering* VENDALE R. *by fire,* OBENREIZER *over* L. *by table, pipe in hand.*

VENDALE. How still it is in the night! Is not that the rustling of the waterfall that we hear?

OBENREIZER. Yes! the waterfall on the slope of the mountain. It sounds like the old waterfall at home that my mother showed to travellers—if she was my mother!

VENDALE. If? Why do you say, if?

OBENREIZER. How do I know? I was very young and all the rest of the family were men and women, and my so-called parents were old enough to be—to be my ancestors! Anything is possible in a case like mine.

VENDALE. Did you ever doubt——

OBENREIZER. Doubt? Everything!

VENDALE. At least you are Swiss?

OBENREIZER. How do I know? I say to you, at least you are English. How do you know?

VENDALE. By what I have been told from infancy.

OBENREIZER (*sneering*). Ah! you know by what you have been told from infancy! I know of myself *that* way—it must satisfy me! While you sat on your mother's lap in your father's carriage, rolling through the rich English streets all luxury surrounding you, I was a famished, naked child among men and women with hard hand to beat me! Bah! so ends my biography. But it is getting cold here! You have let your fire go out! (*To* D. *in* F.) Halloa there! some wood! (*To* R. *by table.*)

Enter LANDLORD, *with wood.*

A drop of brandy will do neither of us any harm—we have let our flasks get empty. (*To* LANDLORD.) A bottle of brandy!

LANDLORD. Yes, gentlemen! [*Exit* D. *in* F.

VENDALE. I am afraid you will find it but bad brandy in such a place. (*To* L. *front*, *walking up and down.*)

OBENREIZER. Bad brandy is better than none.

Enter LANDLORD, *puts bottles on table.*

LANDLORD. There, gentlemen.

OBENREIZER. *Très bien*—well! You know you are to have the guide ready.

LANDLORD. Yes, sir!

VENDALE. And you're to wake us at four. (L. *front.*)

LANDLORD. Yes, sir!

OBENREIZER (*doses glass and brings to* VENDALE). Now for the laudanum!

LANDLORD. Any more orders, gentlemen?

OBENREIZER. No! you can go to bed. [*Exit* LANDLORD D. *in* F. How is it? you are a better judge than I am; bad, eh?

VENDALE. I don't like the flavour.

OBENREIZER (*carelessly*). You don't like the flavour? (*Tastes brandy.*) Pah! how is it? bad! Do you lock your door at night when you are travelling? (*Up* R. *by table.*)

VENDALE. Not I. I sleep too soundly. (*Beginning to be heavy of head.*)

OBENREIZER. You are so sound a sleeper! What a blessing!

VENDALE. Anything but a blessing to the east end of the house if I had to be knocked up from the outside of my door.

OBENREIZER. Ha! ha! I, too, leave open my door. By the bye, let me advise you, as a Swiss, you know, always when you travel in my country, put your papers—and, of course, your money—under your pillow. (*By bed, with illustrative gesture.*) Always the safest place.

VENDALE. You are not complimentary to your countrymen.

OBENREIZER (*shrugging shoulders*). Ah! my countrymen are like most men: they will take what they can get.

VENDALE. I have only one paper of importance, and I have no fear of that.

OBENREIZER. But we have to be up early in the morning. Your candle is burning low. I wish you good-night. (*Exit* D. *in* F.) Under the pillow, you know.

VENDALE. Good-night. (*Candle put out—crosses to* L. *window.*) It's a strange fellow-traveller I have. Pshaw! he is my companion of his own proposal, and can have no motive in sharing this undesirable journey. How cold it is! (*Turns from window, beginning to be unsteady of foot.*) I wonder what Wilding could have had to say to him? Can Obenreizer be the—missing man! He speaks English as if it had been the first language of his infancy. How would I like this man to be rich? to be Marguerite's guardian, and yet standing in no relationship to her? (*Abruptly.*) But what are these considerations to come between me and fidelity to the dead? (*Crosses to* R., *reeling.*) No! I am bent on the discharge of my solemn duty, and that duty must and shall be performed. (*Leans on table.*) I will speak to Obenreizer in the morning. (*Seated in chair, back to audience,* R. *side of table.*) In the morning. (*Goes to sleep.*)

Music to OBENREIZER'S *entrance.*

OBENREIZER *opens* D. *in* F., *slowly, a little way, his hand appears, then his face—pause—he enters—pause—he closes door quickly, but so as not to make noise—pause—he listens, goes cautiously to bed, knife in hand, puts hand under pillow—pause—shakes his head, goes to table,* L., *opens writing-case by springing the lock with his knife. While opening case, puts knife in mouth to overhaul papers, then lays knife on table; starts at movement of* VENDALE, *snatches up knife, lays it down. Finishes search, crosses to bed.*

VENDALE. Who is it? (*Springs up.*)

OBENREIZER. Eh! (*Intense surprise.*) Oh! (*Forced voice of anxiety*) you are not in bed—are you ill? (*Up* R. C.)

VENDALE. What do you mean? (*Hand to forehead.*)

OBENREIZER. There *is* something wrong! You are not ill?

VENDALE. Ill? No!

OBENREIZER. I have had a bad dream about you. I tried to rest after it, but it was impossible. Ha! ha! I know you will laugh at me. I was a long while waiting outside your door before I came in. Ha! ha! ha! It is so easy to laugh at a dream that you have not dreamed! (*Lights candle, and then stands by table to light his pipe.*) You have a good fire here now. My candle has burnt out. May I stop with you? You want to sleep, eh?

VENDALE (*drowsily, to* C. *up*). You can stop here, if you like, till morning comes.

OBENREIZER. Yes—ha! ha! It was a bad dream. See! I was stripped for a struggle!

VENDALE. And armed, too.

OBENREIZER (*carelessly*). This? Oh, a traveller's knife that I always carry about me. (*Plays with knife-handle.*) Do you carry no such thing?

VENDALE. No such thing. (R.)

OBENREIZER. No pistols?

VENDALE. No weapons of any kind. (*Seated* R. *as before.*)

OBENREIZER. You Englishmen are so confident. (*To bed, searching.*)

VENDALE. Where are you?

OBENREIZER. You see where I am, dear boy. My candle has burnt out. There's such a little time yet, may I sit here and keep you company?

VENDALE. If you like. Besides, I had something very important to say to you—about—(*sleeping, wakes*) I—I—meant to put it off till the morning.

OBENREIZER. Now, it will relieve your mind. Something about me?

VENDALE (*sleepily*). About you, yes—ah!—to-morrow!—to-morrow! (*Sleeps in chair.*)

OBENREIZER. The laudanum has done its work at last. (*To bed, searches.*) Not there! (*Knife in hand, to table,* L.) Not here! (*At writing-case.*) He must have it on him. (*Crosses to* R.) If I could take it without waking him—without crime! There he lies at my mercy! Marguerite's lover—my rival—who carries more than my life in the pocket of his coat. If that man goes free, I am ruined! (*Bends over* VENDALE, *knife in right hand, searching him with left.*) It is here. Could I but unbutton his coat! (*Loud knock* D. *in* F. OBENREIZER *leaps back, and conceals knife; lights his pipe.*)

VENDALE (*jumps up*). Come in. (*Bewildered.*)

OBENREIZER (*aside*). Another moment, and I——(*Sheathes knife.*)

LANDLORD *enters* D. *in* F. *Lights up.*

LANDLORD. Four o'clock, gentlemen, and the guides are waiting. (*Helps* VENDALE, *sleepy, on with overcoat,* L.)

OBENREIZER (*dresses himself with his clothes brought in by servant—aside*). It is my fate. I must kill him on the road! (*All go up to* D. *in* F.)

(*Scene closes in.*)

SCENE II.—*Exterior of Inn on* 1 G.

Enter, D. *in* F., JEAN PAUL *and* JEAN MARIE *and* LANDLORD.

LANDLORD (L.). Well, my friends, what do you think of the weather now?

JEAN MARIE (C.) I say the weather will do.

JEAN PAUL (R.). I say that it is bad.

LANDLORD. Come, you must make up your mind. The two gentlemen are coming.

Enter, D. *in* F., VENDALE *and* OBENREIZER.

VENDALE (*to* L. C.). Well, I suppose you have explained to the men? Are you ready to cross the mountain?

JEAN MARIE. I don't care, for one.

LANDLORD. You may depend upon these guides, sirs.

OBENREIZER (*aside*). That won't do.

JEAN PAUL. I say no. There's something in the air that looks like snow.

OBENREIZER (*aside*). That's better.

JEAN MARIE. I won't go unless Jean Paul goes.

JEAN PAUL. And I'll not go at all.

OBENREIZER (*to* VENDALE). I suppose you know what all this means?

VENDALE. Indeed, I do not.

OBENREIZER. Part of the trade of the poor devils:—it's to double their pay.

JEAN PAUL. You heard the rushing of the waterfall last night? Snow! You heard an unseen hand try to open the doors? Snow. You heard the far-off thunder? Snow. Yes, you'll have snow enough to bury a man upright, and wind enough to blow the hair off his head! And that won't be long from this;—it will all be before to-night.

OBENREIZER. Part of the profession. Two napoleons will change you.

JEAN PAUL. No! not two thousand would do it.

OBENREIZER (*aside*). He will not go!

JEAN PAUL (*to* VENDALE *leading him to* R. 1 E.). You do not laugh at the guide. Mark! How many peaks do you see?

VENDALE. Two!

JEAN PAUL. There are three!

VENDALE. Why can't I see the other?

JEAN PAUL. Because the storm cloud has already come down upon it. It will bring down tons and tons of snow, which will not only strike you dead but bury you at a blow. Do as you will now. I have done my duty of warning you, and I wash my hands of it.

JEAN MARIE. I'll not go unless the old man will.

LANDLORD. We'll do our best to make you comfortable in the inn, gentlemen.

OBENREIZER. Well, what do you propose? As Shakespeare says,

'Discretion is the better part of valour!' Or will you take my advice? I am mountain-born, and we would only have had to guide those poor devils of guides. If you dare to make the attempt, I will go with you——

VENDALE. The occasion is pressing! I must cross——

OBENREIZER. Yes. It is well to understand one another—friends all. This gentleman——

VENDALE. Must cross.

OBENREIZER. It is settled. We go!

VENDALE. We go! (*They take sticks from guides.*)

JEAN PAUL. Do not rush upon destruction!

OBENREIZER. Never fear! [*Exit* R. *with* VENDALE.

JEAN MARIE. Stop! here! stop, stop!

LANDLORD (*to* R.) Hi, hi! mind you keep the track! Don't leave the track!

JEAN PAUL. You need not waste your breath. You have seen the last of them.

LANDLORD. Pooh! they are two stout walkers, and one knows the mountains.

JEAN PAUL. That may be, but they are both dead men! (*To* L.)

LANDLORD. We shall see! [*Exit* D. *in* F.

JEAN PAUL. Come, brother, we must be on our way.
[*Exit* L., *with* JEAN MARIE.

Thunder distant.—Scene changes.

SCENE III.—*Mountain pass—thunder—*VENDALE *discovered* C. *front*, OBENREIZER *up* R. *on stairs, staves in hand.*

VENDALE. Is it here that we strike the path again?

OBENREIZER. Yes, the track is here again.

VENDALE. The snow seems to have passed over.

OBENREIZER. The storm will come again!

VENDALE. Let us on.

OBENREIZER. No.

VENDALE. No? why linger here?

OBENREIZER. Because we are at the journey's end.

VENDALE. Here! how here?

OBENREIZER. I promised to guide you to your journey's end! The journey of your life ends here!

VENDALE. You are a villain!

OBENREIZER. You are a fool! I have drugged you! Doubly a fool, for I am the thief and forger, and in a few moments shall take the proof from your dead body!

VENDALE. What have I done to you? (C.)

OBENREIZER (R. C.). Done! You would have destroyed me, but that you have come to your journey's end. You have made me what I am! I took that money—I stole it, to give luxury to Marguerite! You made me buy the jewels that should outshine your gift! You made me lose her love—you would have made me lose my liberty and life! Therefore you die!

VENDALE. Stand back, murderer!

OBENREIZER (*laughs*). Murderer! why, I don't touch you! I need not, to make you die! Any sleep in the snow is death. You are sleeping as you stand!

VENDALE (*violently*). Stand back, base murderer! (*Lifts up his staff,* OBENREIZER *standing on guard with his staff.*) Stand back! (*Lets staff fall, when* OBENREIZER *rakes it over to him and throws it off,* R.) God bless my Marguerite! May she never know how I died! Stand off from me—yet let me look at your murderous face. Let it remind me—of something—left to me to say—the secret must not die with me—no, no, no! Obenreizer, I must say one thing—before I sink in death. Oh! (*Reeling.*)

OBENREIZER (*aside*). My courage fails me! (*Advances, knife in hand.*) Give me the paper, or——

VENDALE. Never! (*Rushes up set bank to trap, leaps.*) Never!

OBENREIZER (*pauses on bank.*) Lost! (*Staggers down to stage.*) Lost! the—the paper. (*Falling.*) Ah! (*Falls in dead swoon,* C. *front.*)

Music kept up—pause—enter R. U. E. *by set stage,* MARGUERITE, JOEY, *and the two Guides.*

MARGUERITE. Ah, George! (*Comes to* C., *then throws herself on bank, looking over. Music.*)

All form picture.

Two Guides.	JOEY.	MARGUERITE.	OBENREIZER.
R.		R. C.	C.

CURTAIN

ACT V.

SCENE.—*Interior in Monastery, discovering* JOEY C., *a little up, and* BINTRY *beside him.*

BINTRY. What next, I wonder? Here's an adventure for a professional man. I've been rattled across the country in the railway, dragged up the mountains on mule-back, and popped into a monastery by a monk! This all comes of you, Master Joey!

JOEY. How do you make that out, sir?

BINTRY. Why, could Miss Marguerite have sent for me if you had not brought her out here, and would she have come out if you had not brought her? It's all her fault and yours.

JOEY. If it comes to that, Mr. Bintry, would Master George be living at this moment if we had not been in time to save him on the mountains?

BINTRY. Is Mr. Obenreizer mixed up in any way in this affair?

JOEY. We found him lying in the snow by the edge of the precipice, if that's what you call being mixed up with it!

BINTRY. Dead?

JOEY. In a dead swoon!

BINTRY. Did you remark anything?

JOEY. I remarked nothing. At first, I thought Master George was dead. When I felt of his heart, there was no beat; but my fingers were so numbed with the cold that perhaps I felt on the wrong side!

BINTRY. You don't comprehend what I am driving at. When will Mr. Vendale be able to travel?

JOEY. He is able to travel now.

BINTRY. And when will Miss Marguerite be able to travel?

JOEY. Just as soon as Mr. Vendale is ready to travel, and not before. (*Exchanges glances with* BINTRY, *and both laugh.*)

BINTRY. I see, I see. You mean when they do go out, their first walk will be to the nearest church?

JOEY. That is about the figure of it, sir.

BINTRY. So far, all is clear. But the rest is not so plain. Now, where is Mr. Vendale?

JOEY. Here! in this convent, where the monks brought us after they had picked us up.

BINTRY. Here with Mr. Obenreizer?

JOEY. But they have not seen one another yet.

BINTRY. What does Mr. Obenreizer say about his ward coming out?

JOEY. They have not met either. They keep the men and women apart here, sir.

BINTRY. Has Mr. Vendale said nothing out of the common?

JOEY. No.

BINTRY. Not in any way?

JOEY. He will not speak. He has something on his mind.

BINTRY. Ah! then it is he who sent for me by Miss Marguerite?

JOEY. Then Mr. Vendale will see you at once.

BINTRY. I will go at once.

JOEY (*stops him*). If you'll excuse me, sir, may I ask you one question first?

BINTRY. Certainly, as you please!

JOEY. When you left London, how did you leave that precious woman, Miss Goldstraw?

BINTRY. Leave her? I didn't leave her! Mr. Joey, prepare yourself for a great surprise. When Miss Goldstraw heard that Miss Marguerite had come out here after Mr. Vendale, she said she must go into foreign parts as well. And it's my firm belief, Master Joey, that you are at the bottom of it all!

JOEY (*chuckling.*) Not a doubt on it, sir, not a doubt on it!

BINTRY. Why, he don't seem surprised at all!

JOEY. Why, I knew all along that if I didn't go back to her, she'd come all the way out to me.

BINTRY. Is that your experience of woman, Master Joey?

JOEY. That's my experience of Sarah Goldstraw, sir. Now, what was the beautiful language that she used the last time I saw her? It went this way: 'The separation of a man and a woman is a serious institution, and the sooner they come together again after it, the better for all parties.' There's language! Now, what follows? Why, if Miss Goldstraw has come out to see me, it's all right—all right.

Enter SALLY, R. 1 E. D. *to* C., *up*.

SALLY. If you think I have come here on account of you, I will go back to London again directly!

BINTRY. For that purpose, allow me to offer you my arm, ma'am. (SALLY *takes his arm.*)

JOEY. Just allow me one moment before you walk her off!

BINTRY. Certainly, certainly.

JOEY. There's going to be two marriages. Now, if Mr. Vendale marries Miss Marguerite, who is to marry Miss Goldstraw?

SALLY. Don't you distress yourself on my account.

JOEY (*firmly*). Who is to marry Miss Goldstraw?

BINTRY. Well, you are, I am afraid.

JOEY. Then why are you walking off with her, instead of me?

SALLY. You wait a little and you will be walking off along with me all the rest of your future existence.

BINTRY. Isn't it enough to monopolise your wife after marriage, and not to want to monopolise her before she is your wife?

SALLY. Mr. Joey, I'd like you to remember this: A man had better not give a woman the chance, or it may end in her leaving him at the church door! [*Exit* D. *in* F.

JOEY (*aside*). Beautiful language!

Enter D. *in* F., FATHER FRANCIS, *with book, and* OBENREIZER *with bag of money, to table* R., *where they put them down.* FATHER FRANCIS *crosses to* L. *to shake* BINTRY'S *hand,* BINTRY *looking at him through eye-glass.*

BINTRY (*aside*). Mr. Obenreizer turned treasurer of the establishment!

OBENREIZER (*to* BINTRY, *who receives him suspiciously*). You have arrived safely—so glad! (*Shakes hands.*) Come to see Mr. Vendale? Make your mind perfectly easy; our old friend is as good a man as ever. (*Subdued tone.*) You have come on business, I suppose?

BINTRY. Humph! that's impossible to say until I shall have seen Mr. Vendale.

OBENREIZER. I shared his perils as his fellow-traveller, and yet I have not seen him yet.

FATHER FRANCIS. You shared his perils, and your sight will remind him of his perils. This gentleman will remind him of home, and can see him at once.

JOEY. I'll show you the way, sir. (*At* L. D.)

BINTRY. All right, Joey; I'll follow you at once.

[*Exit* JOEY L. D., BINTRY *to* R., *to* OBENREIZER, *snuff-box business. Exit quickly*, L. D.

OBENREIZER (*aside*). Why has he come here? What can Vendale have to say to him?

FATHER FRANCIS. Patience, my son; before the night you shall take the hand of your friend. (*At table.*) Till then you must endure, for a little longer, my poor company.

OBENREIZER. There is none I could desire better, father. Ah! pardon me! where does that door (L. D. *in* F.) lead to?

FATHER FRANCIS. Why do you ask?

OBENREIZER. That door puzzles me the more I look at it. No bolt, no bar, no lock. When I go nearer and listen, I hear something going 'tick, tick,' like the ticking of a clock.

FATHER FRANCIS. It is a clock in the room.

OBENREIZER. A room there? (*Examines thickness of wall by* R. D. *in* F.)

FATHER FRANCIS (*nods*). The door opens by clockwork. One of our brothers made it after long laborious years. It is the strongest strong-room in the world. Nothing can move the door till the time comes, and it opens of itself.

OBENREIZER. A strong-room here! Now, if you were bankers or jewellers, I could understand the need.

FRANCIS. Are we not bankers of the poor, my son?

OBENREIZER. Oh!

FRANCIS. Then we have to keep our valuables safe.

OBENREIZER. Oh! rare old manuscripts and relics. (*Laughing.*)

FRANCIS. Hush, my son, I speak seriously. The property of the travellers who have perished on the mountains is preserved by us until claimed.

OBENREIZER (*laughs*). What a quantity of waste paper you must have.

FRANCIS. Not so; sooner or later all is claimed.

OBENREIZER. Both by foreigners and natives?

FRANCIS. At the present time we have but one foreign: the Vendale papers (OBENREIZER *starts*) found on an Englishman in the snow.

OBENREIZER (*aside*). The Vendale——(*Checks himself.*) Ah!

Enter, D. *in* F., *staying there, Monk.*

MONK. The young English lady desires to speak to you, father.

FRANCIS. Presently, brother, presently. (*Exit Monk* D. *in* F.) I must put away the money and wait to set the clock. The English travellers will be on the road early. I will make it to open at one o'clock. (*To* OBENREIZER.) We keep regular hours here, and do not often have occasion to alter the hour of the safe's opening.

OBENREIZER (*looks at watch*). It is now a minute to eight. (R. C. *up*.)

FRANCIS. Then in one minute you will see that door open. (R.) (*Music, piano, long-drawn strains on violin—clock strikes eight,* L. *door in* F. *opens,* FRANCIS *pushes it back so as not to close, then to table.*)

OBENREIZER. Wonderful!

FRANCIS. So simple, too, in its action. Now, to change the hour. (*Alters the hand.*) At any hour, or part of an hour, that the regulator is fixed, the safe will open. (*To* R.)

OBENREIZER (*to* R.). I see. Don't trouble yourself, father. May I assist you? (*Takes bag of money, puts it in* L. *room, turns dial hand around, closes door with snap, stands back to it.*) Oh! (*Pretends to snatch at door.*)

FRANCIS. What have you done?

OBENREIZER. My stupidity is inexcusable! I—I leaned against the door and—and——

FRANCIS. You have closed it! (*With vexation of a man who has learnt to suppress emotion pretty well.*) Now it will not open till six to-morrow morning.

OBENREIZER (*aside*). It will open in five minutes!

FRANCIS. And my book is left out! Oh, you have caused me excessive trouble!

OBENREIZER. I am so sorry, father.

FRANCIS. The book makes no matter, but the——well, I must go see the young lady. [*Exit* R. D. *in* F.

OBENREIZER. Ah! the old idiot. How fortunate it was put in his keeping. (*Watch in hand.*) There's not a minute to be lost. Ah! the door opens! (*Music,* L. D. *in* F. *opens as before, overhauls papers.*) This is not it. Not here, not here! I know the receipt well! What is this? Vendale papers! (*To table, runs over packet.*) It is not among them. Bah! Eighteen hundred—twenty-nine years ago! (*Interested.*) What does all this mean? Certificate of death! a mother—and not a wife! Ah! ah! I have him! (*Rises, puts paper in breast.*) Ah, Mr. Vendale, I am prepared to meet you now! (*Closes* L. D. *in* F., *to* L.)

Enter MARGUERITE, R. D., VENDALE D. *in* F., *they embrace.*

OBENREIZER. Marguerite (*to* R. C.), have you no word for *me*?

VENDALE (*keeping* MARGUERITE L. C. *front*). Pardon me, Mr. Obenreizer, you will understand that you can have no further interest in this lady.

OBENREIZER. Marguerite, what does this mean? Mr. Vendale speaks in such a tone that I cannot tell whether he is in jest or earnest.

VENDALE. Do not answer. (*To* OBENREIZER.) There can be no question between us. My object in so far meeting you is to bring all further proceedings on your part to an end. Mr. Bintry will tell you how.

OBENREIZER. Marguerite, I hardly need to repeat in what position I stand towards you. That man has no claim on you—when I leave the house, you come with me.

BINTRY (*at* R. *table*, R. *side of it*). Mr. Obenreizer, when you are ready, I am. Will you sign the paper by which you relinquish all authority over your niece and leave her free to wed Mr. Vendale?

OBENREIZER (C.). Mr. Bintry, your professional enthusiasm leads you too far, clever as you are. Mr. Vendale and I made an agreement under which he was bound to double his income. (*To* VENDALE.) Have you doubled it?

VENDALE. No.

OBENREIZER. Then, more talk is useless. Mr. Bintry, you can put your paper in the fire.

BINTRY. My paper will get the better of you yet!

VENDALE. I will force you to sign it.

OBENREIZER. Force me! force is a very big word, Mr. Vendale. I beg you to withdraw it. Mr. Bintry, you are fond of curious documents; will you be so good as to look at these?

BINTRY. What? (*Takes papers.*) Impossible!

OBENREIZER. I told you so. Three years ago an English gentleman perished on the mountains, and the papers found on his body were brought here.

VENDALE. How did you come by them?

BINTRY. That it is needless to inquire. (*Examining papers eagerly.*)

OBENREIZER. Twenty-five years ago, a lady living in Switzerland, childless for years, decided on adopting a child, and her sister in England took one out of the Foundling Hospital!

VENDALE. Out of the Foundling!

MARGUERITE. Oh, George, what is this?

OBENREIZER. You shall have information enough! Here are the written proofs of what I advance. Mr. Bintry, what do you want else?

BINTRY. Proof that the father and mother are living?

OBENREIZER (*gives papers*). They are both dead.

BINTRY. List of the witnesses and their residences who can speak to the facts of the case?

OBENREIZER (*gives papers*). Are they right?

BINTRY. Complete!

OBENREIZER. Ha! ha!

BINTRY (*to* VENDALE). Mr. Vendale, allow me to congratulate you!

VENDALE (*bewildered*). What was the name of the woman in England?

OBENREIZER. Mrs. Miller.

VENDALE. Miller! then we have found the missing man!

MARGUERITE. What *does* all this mean?

VENDALE. Our poor dead friend's last wish on earth is accomplished. All is explained now. (*To* OBENREIZER.) You are the lost Walter Wilding!

OBENREIZER. I—I have not that honour. You are the man! Marguerite, do you know to whom you would have given your hand? To an impostor—a bastard! brought up by public charity!

MARGUERITE. Oh, I never loved you, George, as I love you now!

VENDALE. I the man!

BINTRY. Yes! Ah, ah, Mr. Obenreizer, he is the man who inherits all the fortune of Mr. Wilding. In one breath he has doubled his income, thanks entirely to your exertions. By your own agreement he is free to marry her now. Will you sign the paper? (R. *at table.*)

OBENREIZER (*fiercely*). Never! never!

VENDALE. Then I must force you.

OBENREIZER. Force me!

VENDALE (*shows paper*). What becomes of your authority over her now?

BINTRY. Will you sign?

OBENREIZER (*to* VENDALE *softly*). Does she know?

VENDALE (*same, aside*). She does not.

OBENREIZER (*aside to* VENDALE). Will she ever know, if I sign?

VENDALE (*to table*, R., *to burn receipt in candle*). Never!

BINTRY. I told you my paper would get the better of you at last. (*Points out place to sign.*)

OBENREIZER (*signs while* VENDALE *burns receipt—aside*). So ends the dream of my life! (*Swallows poison from vial.*)

MARGUERITE. What does all this mean?

OBENREIZER. It means that you are free—free to marry him!

MARGUERITE. Free! (*To* VENDALE, L. C.) I don't know what feeling prompts me to do this. (*Approaches* OBENREIZER, C. *front.*) I am going to begin a new and happy life. If I have ever done you wrong, forgive me! If you have ever done me wrong, for George's sake, I forgive you. Ah! you are ill!

OBENREIZER (*sadly taking* MARGUERITE'S *hand*). Marguerite, you said once I frightened you. Do I frighten you now?

MARGUERITE. What is the matter? You are looking ill.

OBENREIZER. I am looking at you for the last time, Marguerite! (*Staggers up* C., *when* VENDALE *tries to catch him—fiercely.*) Don't touch me! (*Drops his voice, mildly.*) No, I——Thanks! Farewell! (*Dies.*)

MARGUERITE (*to* VENDALE). George!

JOEY *and* SALLY *enter* D. *in* F., *look down at* OBENREIZER.

CURTAIN

THE END

Poems

SONGS FROM 'THE PICKWICK PAPERS'

[1837]

I.—THE IVY GREEN

OH, a dainty plant is the Ivy green,
That creepeth o'er ruins old!
Of right choice food are his meals, I ween,
In his cell so lone and cold.
The wall must be crumbled, the stone decayed,
To pleasure his dainty whim:
And the mouldering dust that years have made
Is a merry meal for him.
    Creeping where no life is seen,
    A rare old plant is the Ivy green.

Fast he stealeth on, though he wears no wings,
And a staunch old heart has he.
How closely he twineth, how tight he clings,
To his friend the huge Oak Tree!
And slily he traileth along the ground,
And his leaves he gently waves,
As he joyously hugs and crawleth round
The rich mould of dead men's graves.
    Creeping where grim death hath been,
    A rare old plant is the Ivy green.

Whole ages have fled and their works decayed,
And nations have scattered been;
But the stout old Ivy shall never fade,
From its hale and hearty green.
The brave old plant, in its lonely days,
Shall fatten upon the past:
For the stateliest building man can raise
Is the Ivy's food at last.

Creeping on, where time has been,
A rare old plant is the Ivy green.

II.—A CHRISTMAS CAROL

I CARE not for Spring; on his fickle wing
Let the blossoms and buds be borne:
He woos them amain with his treacherous rain,
And he scatters them ere the morn.
An inconstant elf, he knows not himself
Nor his own changing mind an hour,
He'll smile in your face, and, with wry grimace,
He'll wither your youngest flower.

Let the Summer sun to his bright home run,
He shall never be sought by me;
When he's dimmed by a cloud I can laugh aloud,
And care not how sulky he be!
For his darling child is the madness wild
That sports in fierce fever's train;
And when love is too strong, it don't last long,
As many have found to their pain.

A mild harvest night, by the tranquil light
Of the modest and gentle moon,
Has a far sweeter sheen, for me, I ween,
Than the broad and unblushing noon.
But every leaf awakens my grief,
As it lieth beneath the tree;
So let Autumn air be never so fair,
It by no means agrees with me.

But my song I troll out, for CHRISTMAS stout,
The hearty, the true, and the bold;
A bumper I drain, and with might and main
Give three cheers for this Christmas old!
We'll usher him in with a merry din
That shall gladden his joyous heart,

And we'll keep him up, while there's bite or sup,
And in fellowship good, we'll part.

In his fine honest pride, he scorns to hide
One jot of his hard-weather scars;
They're no disgrace, for there's much the same trace
On the cheeks of our bravest tars.
Then again I sing 'till the roof doth ring,
And it echoes from wall to wall—
To the stout old wight, fair welcome to-night,
As the King of the Seasons all!

III.—GABRIEL GRUB'S SONG

BRAVE lodgings for one, brave lodgings for one,
A few feet of cold earth, when life is done;
A stone at the head, a stone at the feet,
A rich, juicy meal for the worms to eat;
Rank grass over head, and damp clay around,
Brave lodgings for one, these, in holy ground!

IV.—ROMANCE

I

BOLD Turpin vunce, on Hounslow Heath,
His bold mare Bess bestrode—er;
Ven there he see'd the Bishop's coach
A-comin' along the road—er.
So he gallops close to the 'orse's legs,
And he claps his head vithin;
And the Bishop says, 'Sure as eggs is eggs,
This here's the bold Turpin!'
Chorus—And the Bishop says, 'Sure as eggs is eggs,
This here's the bold Turpin!'

II

Says Turpin, 'You shall eat your words
With a sarse of leaden bul-let';
So he puts a pistol to his mouth,
And he fires it down his gul-let.
The coachman, he not likin' the job,
Set off at a full gal-lop,
But Dick put a couple of balls in his nob,
And perwailed on him to stop.
Chorus (*sarcastically*)—But Dick put a couple of balls in his nob,
And perwailed on him to stop.

POLITICAL SQUIBS FROM 'THE EXAMINER'

[1841]

I.—THE FINE OLD ENGLISH GENTLEMAN

NEW VERSION

(*To be said or sung at all Conservative Dinners*)

I'LL sing you a new ballad, and I'll warrant it first rate,
Of the days of that old gentleman who had that old estate;
When they spent the public money at a bountiful old rate
On ev'ry mistress, pimp, and scamp, at ev'ry noble gate,
In the fine old English Tory times;
Soon may they come again!

The good old laws were garnished well with gibbets, whips, and chains,
With fine old English penalties, and fine old English pains,
With rebel heads, and seas of blood once hot in rebel veins;
For all these things were requisite to guard the rich old gains
Of the fine old English Tory times;
Soon may they come again!

This brave old code, like Argus, had a hundred watchful eyes,
And ev'ry English peasant had his good old English spies,
To tempt his starving discontent with fine old English lies,
Then call the good old Yeomanry to stop his peevish cries,
In the fine old English Tory times;
Soon may they come again!

The good old times for cutting throats that cried out in their need,
The good old times for hunting men who held their fathers' creed,
The good old times when William Pitt, as all good men agreed,
Came down direct from Paradise at more than railroad speed....
Oh, the fine old English Tory times;
When will they come again!

In those rare days, the press was seldom known to snarl or bark,
But sweetly sang of men in pow'r, like any tuneful lark;
Grave judges, too, to all their evil deeds were in the dark;
And not a man in twenty score knew how to make his mark.
Oh the fine old English Tory times;
Soon may they come again!

Those were the days for taxes, and for war's infernal din;
For scarcity of bread, that fine old dowagers might win;
For shutting men of letters up, through iron bars to grin,
Because they didn't think the Prince was altogether thin,
In the fine old English Tory times;
Soon may they come again!

But Tolerance, though slow in flight, is strong-wing'd in the main;
That night must come on these fine days, in course of time was plain;
The pure old spirit struggled, but its struggles were in vain;
A nation's grip was on it, and it died in choking pain,
With the fine old English Tory days,
All of the olden time.

The bright old day now dawns again; the cry runs through the land,
In England there shall be dear bread—in Ireland, sword and brand;

And poverty, and ignorance, shall swell the rich and grand,
So, rally round the rulers with the gentle iron hand,
Of the fine old English Tory days;
Hail to the coming time!

II.—THE QUACK DOCTOR'S PROCLAMATION

TUNE—'A COBBLER THERE WAS'

AN astonishing doctor has just come to town,
Who will do all the faculty perfectly brown:
He knows all diseases, their causes, and ends;
And he begs to appeal to his medical friends.
Tol de rol:
Diddle doll:
Tol de rol, de dol,
Diddle doll
Tol de rol doll.

He's a magnetic doctor, and knows how to keep
The whole of a Government snoring asleep
To popular clamours; till popular pins
Are stuck in their midriffs—and then he begins
Tol de rol.

He's a *clairvoyant* subject, and readily reads
His countrymen's wishes, condition, and needs,
With many more fine things I can't tell in rhyme,
—And he keeps both his eyes shut the whole of the time.
Tol de rol.

You mustn't expect him to talk; but you'll take
Most particular notice the doctor's awake,
Though for aught from his words or his looks that you reap, he
Might just as well be most confoundedly sleepy.
Tol de rol.

Homœopathy, too, he has practised for ages
(You'll find his prescriptions in Luke Hansard's pages),

Just giving his patient when maddened by pain,—
Of Reform the ten thousandth part of a grain.
Tol de rol.

He's a med'cine for Ireland, in portable papers;
The infallible cure for political vapours;
A neat label round it his 'prentices tie—
'Put your trust in the Lord, and keep this powder dry!'
Tol de rol.

He's a corn doctor also, of wonderful skill,
—No cutting, no rooting-up, purging, or pill—
You're merely to take, 'stead of walking or riding,
The sweet schoolboy exercise—innocent sliding.
Tol de rol.

There's no advice gratis. If high ladies send
His legitimate fee, he's their soft-spoken friend.
At the great public counter with one hand behind him,
And one in his waistcoat, they're certain to find him.
Tol de rol.

He has only to add he's the real Doctor Flam,
All others being purely fictitious and sham;
The house is a large one, tall, slated, and white,
With a lobby; and lights in the passage at night.
Tol de rol:
Diddle doll:
Tol de rol, de dol,
Diddle doll
Tol de rol doll.

III.—SUBJECTS FOR PAINTERS
(After Peter Pindar)

To you, Sir Martin,[1] and your co. R.A.'s,
I dedicate in meek, suggestive lays,

[1] Sir Martin Archer Shee, P.R.A.

Some subjects for your academic palettes;
  Hoping by dint of these my scanty jobs,
  To fill with novel thoughts your teeming nobs,
As though I beat them in with wooden mallets.

  To you, MACLISE, who Eve's fair daughters paint
  With Nature's hand, and want the maudlin taint
Of the sweet Chalon school of silk and ermine:
  To you, E. LANDSEER, who from year to year
  Delight in beasts and birds, and dogs and deer,
And seldom give us any human vermin:

  —To all who practise art, or make believe,
  I offer subjects they may take or leave.

  Great Sibthorp and his butler, in debate
  (*Arcades ambo*) on affairs of state,
Not altogether 'gone,' but rather funny;
  Cursing the Whigs for leaving in the lurch
  Our d——d good, pleasant, gentlemanly Church,
Would make a picture—cheap at any money.

  Or Sibthorp as the Tory Sec.—at-War,
  Encouraging his mates with loud 'Yhor! Yhor!'
From Treas'ry benches' most conspicuous end;
  Or Sib.'s mustachios curling with a smile,
  As an expectant Premier without guile
Calls him his honourable and gallant friend.

  Or Sibthorp travelling in foreign parts,
  Through that rich portion of our Eastern charts
Where lies the land of popular tradition;
  And fairly worshipp'd by the true devout
  In all his comings-in and goings-out,
Because of the old Turkish superstition.

  Fame with her trumpet, blowing very hard,
  And making earth rich with celestial lard,
In puffing deeds done through Lord Chamberlain Howe;
  While some few thousand persons of small gains,

Who give their charities without such pains,
Look up, much wondering what may be the row.

Behind them Joseph Hume, who turns his pate
To where great Marlbro' House in princely state
Shelters a host of lacqueys, lords and pages,
And says he knows of dowagers a crowd,
Who, without trumpeting so very loud,
Would do so much, and more, for half the wages.

Limn, sirs, the highest lady in the land,
When Joseph Surface, fawning cap in hand,
Delivers in his list of patriot mortals;
Those gentlemen of honour, faith, and truth,
Who, foul-mouthed, spat upon her maiden youth,
And dog-like did defile her palace portals.

Paint me the Tories, full of grief and woe,
Weeping (to voters) over Frost and Co.,
Their suff'ring, erring, much-enduring brothers.
And in the background don't forget to pack,
Each grinning ghastly from its bloody sack,
The heads of Thistlewood, Despard, and others.

Paint, squandering the club's election gold,
Fierce lovers of our Constitution old,
Lords who're that sacred lady's greatest debtors;
And let the law, forbidding any voice
Or act of Peer to influence the choice
Of English people, flourish in bright letters.

Paint that same dear old lady, ill at ease,
Weak in her second childhood, hard to please,
Unknowing what she ails or what she wishes;
With all her Carlton nephews at the door,
Deaf'ning both aunt and nurses with their roar,
Fighting already, for the loaves and fishes.

Leaving these hints for you to dwell upon,
I shall presume to offer more anon.

PROLOGUE TO WESTLAND MARSTON'S PLAY 'THE PATRICIAN'S DAUGHTER'

[1842]

THE PROLOGUE

(Spoken by Mr. Macready)

No tale of streaming plumes and harness bright
Dwells on the poet's maiden harp to-night;
No trumpet's clamour and no battle's fire
Breathes in the trembling accents of his lyre;
Enough for him, if in his lowly strain
He wakes one household echo not in vain;
Enough for him, if in his boldest word
The beating heart of MAN be dimly heard.

Its solemn music which, like strains that sigh
Through charmed gardens, all who hearing die;
Its solemn music he does not pursue
To distant ages out of human view;
Nor listen to its wild and mournful chime
In the dead caverns on the shore of Time;
But musing with a calm and steady gaze
Before the crackling flames of living days,
He hears it whisper through the busy roar
Of what shall be and what has been before.
Awake the Present! Shall no scene display
The tragic passion of the passing day?
Is it with Man, as with some meaner things,
That out of death his single purpose springs?
Can his eventful life no moral teach
Until he be, for aye, beyond its reach?
Obscurely shall he suffer, act, and fade,
Dubb'd noble only by the sexton's spade?
Awake the Present! Though the steel-clad age
Find life alone within its storied page,

Iron is worn, at heart, by many still—
The tyrant Custom binds the serf-like will;
If the sharp rack, and screw, and chain be gone,
These later days have tortures of their own;
The guiltless writhe, while Guilt is stretch'd in sleep,
And Virtue lies, too often, dungeon deep.
Awake the Present! what the Past has sown
Be in its harvest garner'd, reap'd, and grown!
How pride breeds pride, and wrong engenders wrong,
Read in the volume Truth has held so long,
Assured that where life's flowers freshest blow,
The sharpest thorns and keenest briars grow,
How social usage has the pow'r to change
Good thoughts to evil; in its highest range
To cramp the noble soul, and turn to ruth
The kindling impulse of our glorious youth,
Crushing the spirit in its house of clay,
Learn from the lessons of the present day.
Not light its import and not poor its mien;
Yourselves the actors, and your homes the scene.

FROM 'THE KEEPSAKE'
[1844]

A WORD IN SEASON

They have a superstition in the East,
  That Allah, written on a piece of paper,
Is better unction than can come of priest,
  Of rolling incense, and of lighted taper:
Holding, that any scrap which bears that name,
  In any characters, its front imprest on,
Shall help the finder through the purging flame,
  And give his toasted feet a place to rest on.

Accordingly, they make a mighty fuss
  With ev'ry wretched tract and fierce oration,
And hoard the leaves—for they are not, like us,
  A highly civilised and thinking nation:

And, always stooping in the miry ways,
To look for matter of this earthy leaven,
They seldom, in their dust-exploring days,
Have any leisure to look up to Heaven.

So have I known a country on the earth,
Where darkness sat upon the living waters,
And brutal ignorance, and toil, and dearth
Were the hard portion of its sons and daughters:
And yet, where they who should have ope'd the door
Of charity and light, for all men's finding,
Squabbled for words upon the altar-floor,
And rent the Book, in struggles for the binding.

The gentlest man among these pious Turks,
God's living image ruthlessly defaces;
Their best high-churchman, with no faith in works,
Bowstrings the Virtues in the market-places:
The Christian Pariah, whom both sects curse
(They curse all other men, and curse each other),
Walks thro' the world, not very much the worse—
Does all the good he can, and loves his brother.

VERSES FROM THE 'DAILY NEWS'

[1846]

I.—THE BRITISH LION

A NEW SONG, BUT AN OLD STORY

TUNE—'THE GREAT SEA-SNAKE'

OH, p'r'aps you may have heard, and if not, I'll sing
Of the British Lion free,
That was constantly a-going for to make a spring
Upon his en-e-me;
But who, being rather groggy at the knees,
Broke down, always, before;
And generally gave a feeble wheeze
Instead of a loud roar.

Right toor rol, loor rol, fee faw fum,
The British Lion bold!
That was always a-going for to do great things,
And was always being 'sold!'

He was carried about, in a carawan,
And was show'd in country parts,
And they said, 'Walk up! Be in time! He can
Eat Corn-Law Leagues like tarts!'
And his showmen, shouting there and then,
To puff him didn't fail,
And they said, as they peep'd into his den,
'Oh, don't he wag his tail!'

Now, the principal keeper of this poor old beast,
WAN HUMBUG was his name,
Would once ev'ry day stir him up—at least—
And wasn't that a Game!
For he hadn't a tooth, and he hadn't a claw,
In that 'Struggle' so 'Sublime';
And, however sharp they touch'd him on the raw,
He couldn't come up to time.

And this, you will observe, was the reason why
WAN HUMBUG, on weak grounds,
Was forced to make believe that he heard his cry
In all unlikely sounds.
So, there wasn't a bleat from an Essex Calf,
Or a Duke or a Lordling slim;
But he said, with a wery triumphant laugh,
'I'm blest if that ain't him.'

At length, wery bald in his mane and tail,
The British Lion growed:
He pined, and declined, and he satisfied
The last debt which he owed.
And when they came to examine the skin,
It was a wonder sore,
To find that the an-i-mal within
Was nothing but a Boar!

Right toor rol, loor rol, fee faw fum,
  The British Lion bold!
That was always a-going for to do great things,
  And was always being 'sold!'

II.—THE HYMN OF THE WILTSHIRE LABOURERS

Oh God, who by Thy Prophet's hand
  Didst smite the rocky brake,
Whence water came, at Thy command,
  Thy people's thirst to slake;
Strike, now, upon this granite wall,
  Stern, obdurate, and high;
And let some drops of pity fall
  For us who starve and die!

The God, who took a little child,
  And set him in the midst,
And promised him His mercy mild,
  As, by Thy Son, Thou didst:
Look down upon our children dear,
  So gaunt, so cold, so spare,
And let their images appear
  Where Lords and Gentry are!

Oh God, teach them to feel how we,
  When our poor infants droop,
Are weakened in our trust in Thee,
  And how our spirits stoop;
For, in Thy rest, so bright and fair,
  All tears and sorrows sleep:
And their young looks, so full of care,
  Would make Thine Angels weep!

The God, who with His finger drew
  The Judgment coming on,
Write, for these men, what must ensue,
  Ere many years be gone!

Oh God, whose bow is in the sky,
 Let them not brave and dare,
Until they look (too late) on high,
 And see an Arrow there!

Oh God, remind them! In the bread
 They break upon the knee,
These sacred words may yet be read,
 'In memory of Me!'
Oh God, remind them of His sweet
 Compassion for the poor,
And how He gave them Bread to eat,
 And went from door to door!

POEMS FROM 'HOUSEHOLD WORDS'

[1850-1851]

I.—HIRAM POWER'S GREEK SLAVE

They say Ideal Beauty cannot enter
The house of anguish. On the threshold stands
This alien Image with the shackled hands,
Called the Greek Slave: as if the artist meant her
(The passionless perfection which he lent her,
Shadowed, not darkened, where the sill expands)
To, so, confront man's crimes in different lands,
With man's ideal sense. Pierce to the centre
Art's fiery finger! and break up ere long
The serfdom of this world. Appeal, fair stone,
From God's pure heights of beauty, against man's wrong!
Catch up, in thy divine face, not alone
East griefs, but west, and strike and shame the strong,
By thunders of white silence, overthrown.

II.—ASPIRE!

Aspire! whatever fate befall,
Be it praise or blame—
Aspire! even when deprived of all—
It is thy nature's aim.
The seed beneath the frozen earth,
When winter checks the fresh green birth,
Still yearningly aspires,
With ripening desires,
And, in its season, it will shoot
Up into the perfect fruit;
But had it not lain low,
It ne'er had learn'd to grow.

Aspire! for in thyself alone
That power belongs of right;
Within thyself that seed is sown,
Which strives to reach the light;
All pride of rank, all pomp of place,
All pinnacles that point in space,
But show thee, to the spheres,
No greater than thy peers;
But if thy spirit doth aspire,
Thou risest ever higher—higher—
Towards that consummate end,
When Heavenward we tend.

PROLOGUE AND SONG FROM WILKIE COLLINS'S PLAY 'THE LIGHTHOUSE'

[1855]

I.—THE PROLOGUE

(*Slow music all the time; unseen speaker; curtain down.*)

A story of those rocks where doom'd ships come
To cast them wreck'd upon the steps of home,
Where solitary men, the long year through—

The wind their music and the brine their view—
Warn mariners to shun the beacon-light;
A story of those rocks is here to-night.
Eddystone Lighthouse!

(*Exterior view discovered.*)

In its ancient form,
Ere he who built it wish'd for the great storm
That shiver'd it to nothing, once again
Behold outgleaming on the angry main!
Within it are three men; to these repair
In our frail bark of Fancy, swift as air!
They are but shadows, as the rower grim
Took none but shadows in his boat with him.

So be *ye* shades, and, for a little space,
The real world a dream without a trace.
Return is easy. It will have ye back
Too soon to the old beaten dusty track;
For but one hour forget it. Billows, rise;
Blow winds, fall rain, be black, ye midnight skies;
And you who watch the light, arise! arise!

(*Exterior view rises and discovers the scene.*)

II.—THE SONG OF THE WRECK

I

The wind blew high, the waters raved,
A ship drove on the land,
A hundred human creatures saved
Kneel'd down upon the sand.
Three-score were drown'd, three-score were thrown
Upon the black rocks wild,
And thus among them, left alone,
They found one helpless child.

II

A seaman rough, to shipwreck bred,
Stood out from all the rest,

And gently laid the lonely head
    Upon his honest breast.
And travelling o'er the desert wide
    It was a solemn joy,
To see them, ever side by side,
    The sailor and the boy.

III

In famine, sickness, hunger, thirst,
    The two were still but one,
Until the strong man droop'd the first
    And felt his labours done.
Then to a trusty friend he spake,
    'Across the desert wide,
O take this poor boy for my sake!'
    And kiss'd the child and died.

IV

Toiling along in weary plight
    Through heavy jungle mire,
These two came later every night
    To warm them at the fire.
Until the captain said one day,
    'O seaman good and kind,
To save thyself now come away,
    And leave the boy behind!'

V

The child was slumbering near the blaze:
    'O captain, let him rest
Until it sinks, when God's own ways
    Shall teach us what is best!'
They watch'd the whiten'd ashy heap,
    They touch'd the child in vain;
They did not leave him there asleep,
    He never woke again.

PROLOGUE TO WILKIE COLLINS'S PLAY 'THE FROZEN DEEP'

[1856]

THE PROLOGUE

(*Curtain rises; mists and darkness; soft music throughout.*)

One savage footprint on the lonely shore
Where one man listen'd to the surge's roar,
Not all the winds that stir the mighty sea
Can ever ruffle in the memory.
If such its interest and thrall, O then
Pause on the footprints of heroic men,
Making a garden of the desert wide
Where Parry conquer'd death and Franklin died.

To that white region where the Lost lie low,
Wrapt in their mantles of eternal snow,—
Unvisited by change, nothing to mock
Those statues sculptured in the icy rock,
We pray your company; that hearts as true
(Though nothings of the air) may live for you;
Nor only yet that on our little glass
A faint reflection of those wilds may pass,
But that the secrets of the vast Profound
Within us, an exploring hand may sound,
Testing the region of the ice-bound soul,
Seeking the passage at its northern pole,
Softening the horrors of its wintry sleep,
Melting the surface of that 'Frozen Deep.'

Vanish, ye mists! But ere this gloom departs,
And to the union of three sister arts
We give a winter evening, good to know
That in the charms of such another show,
That in the fiction of a friendly play,

The Arctic sailors, too, put gloom away,
Forgot their long night, saw no starry dome,
Hail'd the warm sun, and were again at Home.

Vanish, ye mists! Not yet do we repair
To the still country of the piercing air;
But seek, before we cross the troubled seas,
An English hearth and Devon's waving trees.

A CHILD'S HYMN

FROM 'THE WRECK OF THE GOLDEN MARY' [1856]

HEAR my prayer, O! Heavenly Father,
Ere I lay me down to sleep;
Bid Thy Angels, pure and holy,
Round my bed their vigil keep.

My sins are heavy, but Thy mercy
Far outweighs them every one;
Down before Thy Cross I cast them,
Trusting in Thy help alone.

Keep me through this night of peril
Underneath its boundless shade;
Take me to Thy rest, I pray thee,
When my pilgrimage is made.

None shall measure out Thy patience
By the span of human thought;
None shall bound the tender mercies
Which Thy Holy Son has bought.

Pardon all my past transgressions,
Give me strength for days to come;
Guide and guard me with Thy blessing
Till Thy Angels bid me home.

THE BLACKSMITH

FROM 'ALL THE YEAR ROUND'

[April 20, 1859]

Old England, she has great warriors,
Great princes, and poets great;
But the Blacksmith is not to be quite forgot,
In the history of the State.

He is rich in the best of all metals,
Yet silver he lacks and gold;
And he payeth his due, and his heart is true,
Though he bloweth both hot and cold.

The boldest is he of incendiaries
That ever the wide world saw,
And a forger as rank as e'er robbed the Bank,
Though he never doth break the law.

He hath shoes that are worn by strangers,
Yet he laugheth and maketh more;
And a share (concealed) in the poor man's field,
Yet it adds to the poor man's store.

Then, hurrah for the iron Blacksmith!
And hurrah for his iron crew!
And whenever we go where his forges glow,
We'll sing what A MAN can do.